Democracy, Freedom and Coercion

NEW HORIZONS IN LAW AND ECONOMICS

Series editors: Gerrit De Geest, *University of Ghent and University of Antwerp, Belgium and University of Utrecht, The Netherlands*; Roger Van den Bergh, *University of Rotterdam and University of Utrecht, The Netherlands*; and Thomas S. Ulen, *University of Illinois at Urbana-Champaign, USA.*

The application of economic ideas and theories to the law and the explanation of markets and public economics from a legal point of view is recognised as one of the most exciting developments in both economics and the law. This important series is designed to make a significant contribution to the development of law and economics.

The main emphasis is on the development and application of new ideas. The series provides a forum for original research in areas such as criminal law, civil law, labour law, corporate law, family law, regulation and privatization, tax, risk and insurance and competition law. International in its approach it includes some of the best theoretical and empirical work from both well-established researchers and the new generation of scholars.

Titles in the series include:

The Economics of Harmonizing European Law
Edited by Alain Marciano and Jean-Michel Josselin

Post-Chicago Developments in Antitrust Law
Edited by Antonio Cucinotta, Robert Pardolesi and Roger Van den Bergh

From Economic to Legal Competition
New Perspectives on Law and Institutions in Europe
Edited by Alain Marciano and Jean-Michel Josselin

New Perspectives on Economic Crime
Edited by Hans Sjögren and Göran Skogh

Law, Economics and Cyberspace
The Effects of Cyberspace on the Economic Analysis of Law
Niva Elkin-Koren and Eli M. Salzberger

Games and Public Administration
The Law and Economics of Regulation and Licensing
George von Wangenheim

Law and the State
A Political Economy Approach
Edited by Alain Marciano and Jean-Michel Josselin

Democracy, Freedom and Coercion
A Law and Economics Approach
Edited by Alain Marciano and Jean-Michel Josselin

Democracy, Freedom and Coercion

A Law and Economics Approach

Edited by

Alain Marciano

Professor, University of Reims Champagne Ardenne (OMI-EDJ), ECONOMIX-CNRS and Institut d'Economie Publique (IDEP), France

Jean-Michel Josselin

Professor, University of Rennes 1 and CREM-CNRS, France

NEW HORIZONS IN LAW AND ECONOMICS

Edward Elgar

Cheltenham, UK • Northampton, MA, USA

Published by
Edward Elgar Publishing Limited
Glensanda House
Montpellier Parade
Cheltenham
Glos GL50 1UA
UK

Edward Elgar Publishing, Inc.
William Pratt House
9 Dewey Court
Northampton
Massachusetts 01060
USA

A catalogue record for this book
is available from the British Library

Library of Congress Cataloging in Publication Data
Democracy, freedom and coercion: a law and economics approach / edited by Alain Marciano, Jean-Michel Josselin.
p. cm.—(New horizons in law and economics series)
Includes bibliographical references and index.
1. Democracy—Economic aspects. 2. Political corruption—Economic aspects. 3. Power (Social sciences). I. Marciano, Alain. II. Josselin, Jean-Michel.
JC423.D43986 2007
321.8—dc22

2006034673

ISBN 978 1 84720 126 3

Printed and bound in Great Britain by MPG Books Ltd, Bodmin, Cornwall

Contents

Contributors

Christian Barrère, University of Reims Champagne Ardenne

Giorgio Brosio, University of Torino

Alessandra Cepparulo, Sapienza University of Rome

Enrico Colombatto, University of Torino, ICER (Director), Collegio Carlo Alberto (Torino)

Antoaneta Dimitrova, Leiden University

Leonard Dudley, University of Montreal

Giuseppe Eusepi, Sapienza University of Rome

Lars P. Feld, Ruprecht-Karls-University Heidelburg

Manfred J. Holler, University of Hamburg

Louis M. Imbeau, Laval University, Quebec

Jean-Michel Josselin, University of Rennes 1

Alain Marciano, University of Reims Champagne Ardenne

Martin Paldam, University of Aarhus

Jan Schnellenbach, Ruprecht-Karls-University Heidelburg

Bernard Steunenberg, Leiden University

Donald Wittman, University of California, Santa Cruz

Roberto Zanola, University Eastern Piedmont

Introduction

Jean-Michel Josselin and Alain Marciano

The purpose of this book is to analyse the balance that exists in a democracy between freedom and coercion, and how and how far a democratic regime can cope with coercion. The question can be viewed from the perspective of a comparison between alternative institutional devices – or from the perspective of one regime only. This is the angle adopted in this book: to analyse the extent to which democracy can legitimize violence in order to enhance liberties. We concentrate here on democracies and investigate the institutional and legal conditions under which coercion or violence are admitted, permitted and thus have to be organized in order to preserve as much freedom as possible. The problem is analysed from the perspective of constitutional law and economics, of constitutional political economy, and more broadly, of public choice.

One crucial element of the problem – and the point of departure of our reasoning – lies in the conflict between the capacity to protect individual freedom while organizing the necessary coercion associated with any form of government, either autocratic or democratic. Whether violence is normal or abnormal, it seems that any kind of political regime, even democratic societies, although designed to protect individual freedom, nonetheless implies coercion and a certain amount of violence. In other words, the essence of a democratic power is the protection of freedom through coercion. There is no such thing as a free lunch and costs always have to be taken into account, even when the question is that of institutions. Certainly, democracies are preferable to autocratic regimes. There is no doubt about that. However, democracies have to reach a subtle balance between freedom and coercion in order to both develop and contain the state. The present book studies this balance along three directions: the necessary coercion implied by institutions; the legitimacy of democratic coercion; and the ways that can be used to tame democratic Leviathans.

DOES POWER NECESSARILY MEAN COERCION?

The choice of a set of institutions to order a society can be presented as a dilemma, what has been referred to as a 'constitutional dilemma' (Nozick,

1974) or the 'Hobbesian dilemma' as Donald Wittman names it in the concluding chapter of this book. The direct reference to the famous eighteenth-century political philosopher interestingly designates the origin of the problem: individuals have to choose between the anarchical violence and coercion of the state of nature or the institutionalized violence and coercion of a civil society. In other words, the ambiguity of constitutional choices rests on one crucial assumption: the existence of a violent state of nature. More precisely, institutions are needed, and institutionalized violence is unavoidable, because egoist and rational individuals fight each other in the state of nature.

Now, although imaginary and designed as explanatory devices, the state of nature and the social contract have real implications in that they justify specific forms of institutions: to assume that nasty, brutish and violent individuals populate the state of nature necessarily implies that a social contract is required. The social contract gives birth to a society that displaces or transforms violence into coercion. As argued by Giuseppe Eusepi and Alessandra Cepparulo in Chapter 1, Hobbes's theory is problematic because his conception of the social contract implies that power lies in the hand of the Leviathan and therefore, to put it in the terms of this volume is hardly compatible with a democracy. Is it possible to escape the problem, and to use a social contract as a foundation of a democratic regime?

The analysis developed by Eusepi and Cepparulo suggests that there are two (apparently) alternative answers to the question. The first refers to what James Buchanan named a constitutional democracy. The perspective of the 1986 Nobel Prize laureate consists in using the same assumptions about human nature as Hobbes to ground democracy on a social contract different from Hobbes's. Buchanan's social contract thus could be depicted as 'a tool through which morally equal individuals are equally free' (Eusepi and Ceparullo, this volume). In effect, from Buchanan's perspective, the social contract is designed under a veil of ignorance and during a procedure that allows individuals to choose themselves the limits of their choice set. It nonetheless remains that, argue Eusepi and Cepparulo, the individuals who have not signed the social contract are obliged to choose elements within a set of choice delineated by others. Power seems transferred into the hands of the elected officials, bureaucrats and policy makers. Coercion thus reappears during the post-constitutional stage. Constitutional democracy can then be considered as coercive because it is a regime which assumes that individual behaviours are restricted to choosing within given opportunity sets.

Another set of literature, the economic theory of freedom of choice, proceeds to the same reduction and analyses freedom by comparing 'decision situations as given by opportunity sets', as stressed by Manfred Holler (this volume) at the outset of Chapter 2. Now, freedom also depends on the capacity to control opportunity sets. Freedom cannot be restricted to the capacity of choosing in a set of given alternatives. As demonstrated by Fabienne Peter (2004), this capacity may be referred to as consumer's sovereignty but can hardly be considered as freedom. Then, it is not only important to understand how individuals are capable of selecting their most preferred element. Obviously, it becomes critical to know who holds power, or 'who controls the opportunity sets?' (Holler, this volume). Thus, a discussion on freedom of choice implies a reference to power.[1] Furthermore, and this is a particularly interesting element in Holler's contribution, power and freedom of choice necessarily relate to responsibility and guilt. Not only in the sense that decision makers, because they are granted with the capacity to influence citizens' choice sets, have also to carry the burden of their charge. Also, any individual may be held responsible because of the influence he or she may exert on social opportunity sets. Violence and coercion is not only that of policy makers. It becomes that of the society as a whole.

Alternatively, there exists a second and drastic solution for avoiding the trap of coercion in a society based on a social contract. It consists in rejecting the social contract itself. This perspective requires that strong assumptions about human nature be made. Human beings are no longer viewed as 'bad' economic men, who once lived in a war against all in the state of nature. To the contrary, they are either altruists, 'intrinsically motivated', or they feel sympathy towards the others. As a consequence of these assumptions, the state of nature can be modelled as a peaceful situation in which repeated interactions are made possible because of altruism or sympathy. In their chapter, Eusepi and Cepparulo explore the institutional settings which emerge from it. In particular, what can be noted is that no social contract is required: individuals have always lived, even if on various scales, in civil societies; violence is not the only feature of social interactions and, then, rules and institutions spontaneously emerge as the result – and even as the by-product – of interactions. Thus, from the perspective of a democratic regime that is not founded on a social contract, coercion is far less central than when a social contract is required.

Undoubtedly, when individuals are altruist or sympathetic, cooperation and order would seem to be less problematic. This argument is fundamental to spontaneous order theories, and also grounds what is labelled 'monist' democratic regimes. However, the absence of a social contract and the belief that societies are spontaneously ordered does not necessarily mean that institutions and coercion disappear. David Hume, for instance, pleaded against a social contract but nonetheless argued that coercive governments are necessary (Marciano, 2005). One explanation could be that a social contract even seems to be necessary to overcome the limits of spontaneous order because as Hume stressed, sympathy is mostly restricted to friends and acquaintances. Therefore, spontaneous order applies to small groups and small societies. Beyond such instances, for inter-group interactions, or when the size of groups increases, then institutions are required. Another explanation refers to the role of public decision makers. In theory, the latter should not interfere in the bottom-up process through which rules and institutions emerge. In practice, however, they do more than just say what rules are. By interpreting and implementing them, they often go beyond what spontaneous order requires and they tend to impose their own preferences on society. This is exactly Friedrich Hayek's problem, as is argued by Enrico Colombatto in Chapter 3. Hayek is undoubtedly known for having contributed to putting 'liberty' and 'freedom' high on the research agenda of economists and political scientists. However, Colombatto argues that Hayek's work can be viewed as a 'manifesto against freedom' because policy makers are capable of imposing their views on society. In other words, policy makers are not the impartial spectators they should be and they are not even enlightened social philosophers. They tend to influence the choice of individuals and, as said above, restrict individual freedom. The same conclusion applies as in social contract theories.

Interestingly, the limits of Hayek's theories as they are stressed by Colombatto, reinforce the idea that Holler develops about power as something necessarily coercive. The argument implies that the violence exerted by the state, through institutions and power, in civil or social contract societies cannot only be the consequence of assumptions about human nature and about the state of nature. Power *per se* implies coercion and is necessarily paradoxical when it claims such coercion in order to enhance liberties.

IS LEGITIMATE COERCION REALLY LEGITIMATE? DEMOCRACY WHAT FOR WHAT KIND OF LIBERTIES?

The first step of the book has taken the definitions of 'democracy' and 'coercion' as granted. However, even if the *demos* part of a democracy is necessary, it is not a sufficient condition. One has to take coercion into account to understand what a democratic regime means. Furthermore, the first part of the book demonstrates that a democratic regime – based or not on a social contract – cannot escape coercion. Therefore, the next step consists in asking what delineates legitimate coercion, and if or how it is possible to distinguish between legitimate coercion and abuse of power. The second part of the book is thus dedicated to understand why and when coercion can be defined as acceptable or, to the contrary, illegitimate in a democratic regime. This question touches upon the problem of the types of liberties democracy has to protect.

Basically, it is admitted that a democracy is a political regime; that is, a regime based on the protection of political liberties. Thus, most of the measures that are made to evaluate whether or not a regime is a democracy rest on variables such as elections, the existence of political parties and unions, the reality of a free press, and so on. This definition does not only consider that political freedom is more important than economic liberties; it also assumes or implies that a distinction is possible between political and economic regimes. The former define and primarily protect political liberties and the latter are meant to do the same with economic liberties. If we consider the theories presented in the first part of the book, the separation between the economic and the political sides of society is far from obvious. Thus, even in Hayek's liberal regime or in Buchanan's constitutional (and liberal) democracy, policy makers interfere with the economic choices made by individuals. Policy makers are not only in charge of political issues, but they also take decisions that have economic impact.

Chapter 4 by Christian Barrère develops a reflection upstream of the economic consequences of political actions. An economic regime is based on economic liberties such as the right to work. Political liberties become subordinated to economic rights. In a way, the definition of freedom goes beyond the choice set of individuals to reach their budget constraint. Democracy thus has both political and economic dimensions. As to the economic side, it can be limited to the consequences of political actions, democracy is then mostly political and political liberties prevail. If the economic side is prevalent, then economic liberties should be the dominant feature of democracy; political liberties would then derive as a consequence.

At the theoretical level, the debate whether the economic or the political side should prevail is mostly a matter of personal philosophical inclinations. In practice however, there are some urgent questions. To move from an undemocratic towards a democratic regime, has one to favour political or economic reforms? Should economic liberties be promoted to ensure that a transition to more political freedom will be guaranteed? Or, by contrast, are political liberties the cause for more democracy? The next two chapters are dedicated to those questions.

In Chapter 5, Martin Paldam uses the Gastil Index, which measures the degree of democracy for 171 countries between 1972 and 2003, and finds a confirmation and of the law Seymour Lipset established in 1954. Thus, with the exception of the 'rather undemocratic' Muslim countries that 'show no tendency to become more democratic when income grows' (Paldam, this volume), one observes that a democratic transition occurs as a consequence of economic development and when income increases. This would support the view that political liberties do have some relationship with economic progress, though causality is hard to unambiguously establish. When political liberties concede to economic liberties, evidence suggests poor economic performances, such as in socialist countries.

From the perspective of Paldam's chapter and in the view of the Gastil Index, not only good economic performances tend to favour democracy, but also they may be considered as a necessary condition for the existence and survival of a democratic regime. This argument can be used to explain why, in some countries, democracy survives in spite of particularly intense violence, such as in Colombia. As stated by Giorgio Brosio and Roberto Zanola in Chapter 6, Colombia is one of the most violent countries in the world. The figures they display are extraordinarily striking, as it appears in the following quotation:

> A former minister of Defence, Rafael Pardo, reported in 2000 that since the mid-1980s '4 presidential candidates, 200 judges and investigators, half of the Supreme Court's Justices, 1200 police officers, 151 journalists and more than 300,000 Colombians have been murdered'. (p. 139, this volume)

However, Colombia remains a democratic, partial or semi-democratic regime. Brosio and Zanola devote their chapter to the analysis of the impact of democracy on violence. Inspired by Becker's model of rational addiction, they show that no rational addiction to violence can be detected. On the contrary, there exists, as they note, 'a natural way of reducing violence consisting only in the passing of time'. Then, active political strategies involving incentives towards more political participation and less poverty and inequality (possibly including the affirmation of basic economic rights) can be used to accelerate the decrease in violence in Colombia. Therefore, one may say that economic factors indeed, as suggested in Paldam's chapter, play an important role in the existence of democratic regimes. Furthermore, the analysis of the evolution of violence in Colombia also indicates how important is the combination of economic circumstances and political liberties in the functioning of democracies. Finally, one may also interpret the demonstration made in this chapter as a confirmation that spontaneous processes and constructivist reforms simultaneously can help countries or societies escape from what is an obvious instance of a Hobbesian state of nature. In other words, when violence increases to levels similar to those that frightened Hobbes in seventeenth-century England, a new social contract – under the form of economic and political reforms – may improve the situation because and when society displays a natural and spontaneous tendency towards improvement.

Thus, we are told how violence – among individuals – can be decreased. However, the post-constitutional stage, the functioning of democracy and the question of the possible transformation of coercion into violence on the part of government to the detriment of citizens still remains to be dealt with.

DEMOCRATIC SAFEGUARDS AGAINST COERCION

After having stressed that coercion is unavoidable and having discussed how to define democracy in terms of coercion another problem has to be discussed: what does legitimate coercion mean? Another problem relates to the means and incentive mechanisms that can be designed and used to tame democratic Leviathans. The third step of the book is thus to study the instruments that can provide effective safeguards against illegitimate coercion.

From this perspective, to allocate power among different parties – that is to introduce competition between various institutional levels – is certainly the most frequently envisaged solution. But are there ways of splitting power between different parties (or institutional levels) that allow a better control of the functioning of democratic states? The question is discussed in this volume by Louis Imbeau in Chapter 8. He proposes a typology of power abuses and of the mechanisms that can be devised to deal with them. The chapter insists on the role of concentration and monopolization as a major source of power abuse. Thus, the problem of (both political and economic) power comes from the concentration of authority, force, wealth and knowledge in the hands of a few individuals. When one individual is able to 'use all three types of resource to pursue his objectives, then the potential for power abuse is at its apex. Recent history provides us with several examples of such concentration' (Imbeau, this volume). Accordingly, the 'best protection against power abuse is the playing of the power of one against the power of another: division and competition within each type of power relationship and between them'.

This protection can be envisaged in two forms, depending on whether it is viewed in horizontal or vertical terms. From the perspective of horizontal competition between institutional levels, division of power literally corresponds to the separation of power between different branches, the celebrated mechanism of 'checks and balances'. In Chapter 9, Lars Feld and Jan Schnellenbach analyse how the mechanism functions in different types of political regimes and in particular how it affects reforms and political innovations. Reform then appears more probable when checks and balances are 'high' (in presidential systems) than when they are 'low' (that is in parliamentary systems). In addition, they show that centralization decreases the probability of reform. Thus, checks and balances and decentralization make reform easier; control is thus easier and, one may reasonably assume, coercion decreases. However, Feld and Schnellenbach also stress the frequent reliance on political leaders to manage reforms. The role of leaders tends to decrease the importance of checks and balances as means to control the behaviours of governments.

Interestingly, this line of reasoning draws us back to both Holler's and Colombatto's chapters. Although leaders such as Ronald Reagan or Margaret Thatcher may have been inspired by liberal mentors – Thatcher being directly inspired by Hayek – they nonetheless were decision makers who benefited from power. Their action thus affected the opportunity sets of agents and certainly had a coercive dimension. Thus, the link between decision, power and coercion seems to be confirmed: decision making implies power and power implies coercion.

The picture is somewhat different when one moves to vertical competition. It is then assumed that multi-level governance is a means to control state coercion. From this perspective, no institution is in the position of a monopolist holder of power. Rather, tasks are assigned to different institutional levels, both in unitary states (through administrative decentralization) or in federations (through devolution). Furthermore, in the latter case, no responsibility is assigned once and for all but is allocated through ongoing and competitive procedures. Individual mobility reinforces the control that citizens exert on the actions and behaviours of the different governmental institutions. Furthermore, decentralization implies that tasks are delegated to the smallest institutional levels, as close as possible to the citizens. Therefore, a democracy in which tasks are decentralized (either in unitary or federal contexts) is supposedly less coercive than a unitary and centralized political regime.

However, one must not forget that the provision of some collective goods is more efficient when realized at the highest institutional level – in particular when there are economies of scale. This is a point on which Nozick (1974) particularly insists in his analysis of the production of defence and security. Thus, and although decentralization may lead to a decrease in coercion, centralization and monopolization of power are in certain circumstances unavoidable. And it is not a surprise that democracies in practice are indeed hybrid, since the economic theory of federalism predicts that a balance has to be found between a necessary (and necessarily coercive) centralization and decentralization, between monopolization and division of power.

In Chapter 7, Leonard Dudley extends this standard explanation by using network theory. His reasoning rests on the distinction between 'a standardized language or culture used by a network of citizens' and the programs proposed by governments 'whose availability increases the value of the linguistic platform to those who share it' (Dudley, this volume). It then appears that the degree of monopolization or division of power depends on the extent of economies of scale. The provision of public goods by different levels of governments is thus linked to the capacity of such goods to reach individuals. Language may be an obstacle to the spreading of a policy. If it works as a large network, it enhances social cohesion and reinforces the efficiency of large scale collective services. Concurrently, a standardized language or culture is usually obtained through coercion (at least partly), which brings us back to the difficult balance between individual freedom and coercive authority.

If there are different ways to explain that political regimes are hybrid, trying to combine the features of centralization and decentralization, one cannot be sure that the situation really results from a deliberate choice to follow the requirements of economic theory. And indeed, most of the time centralization seems to result from strategic behaviours. It certainly was the case in the USA in the nineteenth century and also probably has been in Europe since the 1950s. The European Union seems to be an instance of a democratic Leviathan, as witnessed by the number and influence of pressure groups in policy making. Furthermore, the increase in the size of the Union while its constitutional status remains vague and unsettled may generate more centralization while allowing at the same time each country to substitute private interests for common objectives. The many safeguards that were envisaged – the separation and division of power, the increase in the role of parliament and the role attributed to the European Court of Justice – do not really appear to be efficient. Another incentive mechanism – conditionality – may prove to be more efficient. In Chapter 10, Bernard Steunenberg and Antoaneta Dimitrova analyse the use of this instrument by the European Union, in particular in relation with enlargement. Conditionality can be considered as an incentive mechanism since it means that the distribution of resources depends on the capacity of the beneficiaries to fulfil certain objectives or conditions. However, Steunenberg and Dimitrova demonstrate that EU conditionality is not equally effective throughout the period of preparation of a candidate for accession.

The chapters by Dudley, Steunenberg and Dimitrova point to a dimension of our problem that has up to now been slightly overlooked. Coercion by the state is not simply of individuals. It is also of groups. These are identified as such by language, religion, historical cleavages, and so on. They can also be states in a multinational context. States' rights can often be threatened by centralizing trends or conversely can compromise the efficient provision of 'central' public goods, which brings a further dimension to the balance between liberty and coercion. Indeed, whereas individuals usually have little strategic capacity, groups or states do have some, hence the importance of a well-designed incentive mechanism, as is illustrated in the EU case by Steunenberg and Dimitrova.

CONCLUSION

Throughout the book, it should appear that the use and abuse of power is problematic even in democratic contexts – and not only in autocratic regimes. The different chapters presented above analyse various aspects of the balance between freedom and coercion in democracies. However difficult this balance may be, it nevertheless appears that, although sometimes endangered, democracies do not (always) disappear. Not all governments become repressive military dictatorships even though they all could use their power to promote their own goals. Thus, 'even when certain segments of the society . . . have the power to coerce' (Wittman), democracies function and do not systematically turn into autocratic regimes. The fact is reassuring but, as argued by Donald Wittman in the concluding chapter of this volume, puzzling for public choice scholars. Why, in contradiction with the predictions of public choice theory, do democracies function? Why are Leviathans often only paper tigers? Wittman investigates 'the more than occasional absence of extreme exploitation by those who ostensibly have the power to coerce'. Though coercive, democracy can remain 'dictator-proof' whenever well-designed democratic coercion enhances freedom. However, and despite all the efforts exerted in this book, there remains a flavour of mystery in it.

ACKNOWLEDGEMENTS

We heartily thank the contributors to this book. During our working sessions in Marseille and in Reims and throughout the editorial preparation, they have demonstrated a friendly efficiency which was a great help to us. Special thanks go to Donald Wittman who made us the honour of writing the concluding chapter of this book.

NOTE

1. In his chapter, presented in the third part of this introduction, Louis Imbeau considers that power is problematic when it is concentrated in the hands of a limited number of

individuals. In Holler's view, power is problematic as long and as soon as it exists, in itself because whatever its concentration it restricts the choice set of others.

REFERENCES

Marciano, A. (2005), 'Non-benevolence, sympathy and the proper role of government. From new political economy back to old political economy', *The Economic Theory of Government: History of Political Economy Annual Supplement*, **37**, pp. 43–70.

Nozick, R. (1974), *Anarchy, State and Utopia*, New York: Basic Books.

Peter, F. (2004), 'Choice, consent, and the legitimacy of market transactions', *Economics and Philosophy*, **20**(1), 1–18.

PART 1

Does power (and the democratic use of power in particular) necessarily mean coercion?

1. Variations on the *Lupus et Agnus* story: in search of the *homo sapiens*

Giuseppe Eusepi and Alessandra Cepparulo

Ad rivum eundem Lupus et Agnus venerant siti compulsi: superior stabat Lupus, longeque inferior Agnus . . . Cur, inquit, turbulentam fecisti mihi istam bibenti? . . . Respondit Agnus: equidem natus non eram. Pater hercle tuus, inquit, maledixit mihi. (Phaedrus)

INTRODUCTION

The quotation in the epigraph gives this work the classical flavour of ancient time fables, where animals were used as a way to criticize human vices. Unusual to the modern reader as this fashion is, we follow this mode. Not as a literary exercise, but in Hobbes's footsteps who grounds his construction on the idea that humans are wolves. Hobbes is, in fact, the mainstay of our analysis as well as that of the authors we scrutinize.

No doubt Hobbes was central to Buchanan's analysis in the *Limits of Liberty*. This is not the least true of *The Calculus of Consent* where the influence of Spinoza stands out in his pages[1] with intense strength. Yet, Buchanan labels himself as a Hobbesian, not a Spinozian, so there is no reason for us to speculate on this.

The present chapter sets out thus to propose a variation on the theme of the state of nature and the relationships among the individuals therein. In the next three sections, it addresses the impact of the *homo lupus* construction on institution-making from the original Hobbes's paradigm in the second section to Buchanan's nuanced version in the third section and finally, in the fourth section, to Frey's formulation of it, which is only seemingly antithetic. If the chapter had ended here its title should have been 'Variations on the *Lupus et Agnus* story' since Hobbes's, Buchanan's and Frey's reasoning has homogeneous individuals as a reference point. Our intent is instead that of introducing a fourth variation based on Smith who, by considering morally equal individuals heterogeneous, makes it possible that the *Lupus et Agnus* coexist. The evaluation of our *homo sapiens*, however, does not simply depend on the distance that separates the evaluator from the person to be evaluated.

HOMO HOMINI LUPUS: THE PURE ECONOMIC MAN

To start with, let us imagine a mind experiment that brings us back to pre-institutional arrangements such as the Hobbesian state of nature. The term 'chaos' best describes this kind of context whereby there are neither property rights, nor a criterion to evaluate whether an action is good or bad, just or unjust. In Hobbes's words 'setting aside the arts grounded upon words, and especially that skill of proceeding upon general and infallible rules, called science, which very few have and but in few things, as being not a native faculty born with us, nor attained, as prudence, while we look after somewhat else I find yet a greater equality amongst men than that of strength'.[2] Equality should be extended to attitudes if as Hobbes underlines 'such is the nature of men that howsoever they may acknowledge many others to be more witty, or more eloquent or more learned, yet they will hardly believe there be many so wise as themselves; for they see their own wit at hand, and other men's at a distance'.[3] Equality in potentialities derives directly from the assumption that individuals are homogeneous and so are their objectives. Since individuals' desires are also homogeneous, each individual is perceived as an enemy by other individuals. For when the object of contention cannot be enjoyed jointly, given the nature of the human condition in which resources are scarce, either one of the contenders has to be subdued, or killed for the other to satisfy his desire or need. This is the reason why each individual distrusts his own fellow-men and why he is as well in search of dominion over all other individuals in order to ensure for himself a condition characterized by peace and security for the goods he has succeeded in possessing. There can be no doubt that such a crude environment nurtures the war of each individual against everybody else.

> In such condition there is no place for industry, because the fruit thereof is uncertain: and consequently no culture of the earth; no navigation, nor use of the commodities that may be imported by sea; no commodious building; no instruments of moving and removing such things as require much force; no knowledge of the face of the earth; no account of time; no arts; no letters; no society; and which is worst of all, continual fear, and danger of violent death; and the life of man, solitary, poor, nasty, brutish, and short.[4]

Since each individual has the natural right as his sole right, he is free 'to use his own power as he will himself for the preservation of his own nature

. . . his own life and consequently, of doing anything which, in his own judgement and reason, he shall conceive to be the aptest means thereunto'.[5] The result will be a scenario of 'all against all', whereby everybody has a right over everything: 'even to one another's body',[6] if the assurance of survival will require it.

To Hobbes, the only way reason dictates to avoid the natural course of life being broken off in an untimely way is to follow the two main natural laws:[7]

- 'to seek peace and follow it';
- 'to lay down this right to all things; and be contented with so much liberty against other men as he would allow other men against himself'.

The willingness and acceptance of such laws gives rise to a trust contract that would be impossible in a conflicting environment such as the one depicted above. For there isn't anything, except for promises, that could bind an individual 'to bridle men's ambition, avarice, anger, and other passions',[8] 'for he which performeth first does but betray himself to his enemy, contrary to the right he can never abandon of defending his life and means of living'.[9]

Certainly there is no basis for holding that rights are to be relinquished to insure the maintenance of a peaceful condition. It is required, instead, that all individuals should reciprocally alienate their rights to a third party: the Leviathan.[10] Simply stated, it is as if each individual declared 'I authorise and give up my right of governing myself to this man, or to this assembly of men, on this condition; that thou give up thy right to him, and authorise all his actions in like manner'.[11]

According to Hobbes, once individuals have voluntarily relinquished their natural rights they cannot have any claim on them because the Leviathan is supposed to do what every man could have done for keeping

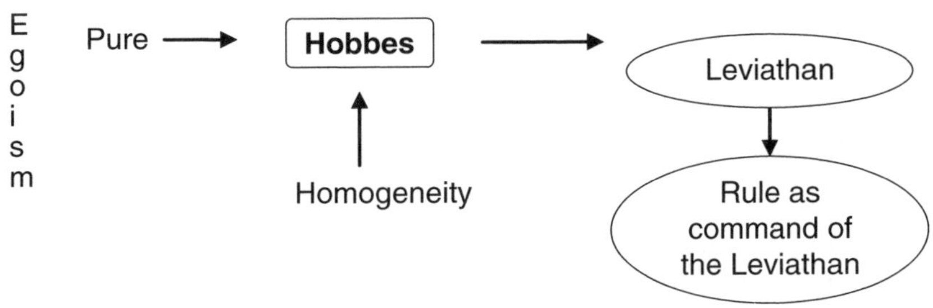

Figure 1.1 The pure economic man

order and peace. This carries with it the implication that subjects cannot rebel against the Leviathan. It might be said, then, that the Leviathan could never intentionally act against anyone because it would equal, according to Hobbes, charging someone with actions made by someone else. The Leviathan's task is that of keeping order and peace, so he enacts whatever decision he deems appropriate to the pursuit of his design. Little wonder, then, that he has the power to judge, to set rules and property rights, to lead an army, to declare war, to collect taxes, to choose his own advisers and so on. Caught up in such a predicament, subjects haven't any possibility, not even conceptual, to impose any limits whatsoever on the Leviathan, including a term limit,[12] because the latter would involve that the subjects be one of the contracting parties – surely this is something that subjects are incapable of being.

Concluding in the same vein, one might wonder what the characteristic feature of the rule that governs this setting is. One might reply to this that the mere fact of its duplex nature – natural law and civil law – the rule is unavoidably 'a command' consisting 'in declaration or manifestation of the will of him that commandeth, by voice, writing, or some other sufficient argument of the same'. The natural law, in fact, becomes law and loses 'qualities that dispose men to peace and to obedience' in the condition of mere nature, only when 'a Commonwealth is settled', because the 'sovereign power . . . obliges men to obey them',[13] thus becoming part of the civil law.

Despite this impressive array of shortcomings and limits, the whole of modern academic learning has been beguiled by the Hobbesian theory. Yet no one would conclude that they have succeeded in overcoming the obscurities inborn in its prescriptions. That these considerations hit their mark seems to us indicated by the attempts scholars have made to provide variations on the Hobbesian account. In order to ease the identification of the improvements effected by the authors analysed in the remaining part of the chapter, we think it useful to list them. The most wildly ill-considered hypothesis of the Hobbesian theory is certainly that of assuming a context inhabited by individuals unreservedly prone to egoism. In fact, how can one reconcile this unreserved egoism with the emergence of institutions whose role is that of limiting egoism? Those who let themselves be led by their own ego will live in loneliness and are incapable of social interaction. Hence if it can be assumed that in a setting characterized by a multitude of subjects it is possible to distinguish individuals more egoistic than average, it would have been more desirable for Hobbes to analyse individuals mostly endowed with other passions. Hobbes then leads himself into the examination of absolutism-building. To him, due to his conception of man as a wolf, resorting to absolutism is the way out from chaos and the indeterminacy of anarchy.

This exceedingly subversive construction carries with it that the Leviathan is a creature incapable of unrighteous actions for the very fact that he represents the society as a whole and hence his will is the will of all people. Without doubt this omnicompetent architect of the salvation of his subjects is *ipso facto* an individual different from all others.

In fact, the Leviathan is the only 'wolf' endowed with the characteristics of the state of nature that all others have given up. One major implication of such an exclusive status is that he becomes an artificial 'wolf' whose natural egoism becomes exponentially strengthened because of the very fact that subjects are no longer self-interested, and hence are coercively turned into *agni*.

THE RECIPROCITY PRINCIPLE: THE IMPURE ECONOMIC MAN

Though accepting *prima facie* Hobbesian-type homogeneous individuals[14] and a primordial anarchic state, Buchanan supplies a different institutional solution to put an end to such a nasty existence. Differently from Hobbes, to whom the contract was just an excuse to justify absolutism, Buchanan suggests that the contract is a necessary instrument to get out of disorder and to restore order. Here[15] the contract emerges in its appropriate shape: it is no longer an agreement of all on a general spoliation of rights in favour of a third party, beneficiary and exclusive withholder of rights producing a state of perennial slavery, but an instrument to assert and create new rights. Whoever is a party in a contract confers and recognizes the other party equal rights (reciprocity principle) and through this contractual compromise the right to live peacefully and safely through the creation of the State, called to watch and settle latent conflicts and towards which each party 'holds rights or claims . . . as much as against other persons'.[16] The Buchanan paradigm features a double contract: one among the individuals aims to quit chaos and build a structure based on the certainty of rules. The other creates a situation in which the keeper of those rules defines his duties and powers, which cannot be but limited. The rule is the result of a negotiation between parties. Indeed Buchanan is aware of the intrinsic incoherence of the Hobbesian idea that makes possible the cohabitation of selfish individuals with an unconstrained Leviathan. In fact, we are insistent that Buchanan regards the Leviathan as an 'artificial individual' who must possess the peculiarities proper to real individuals (symmetry principle). It would be a mistake to interpret our contrasts between Hobbes and Buchanan as implying that Buchanan tries to accommodate himself somewhat surreptitiously to a genuine contractualism. Nor has he to be interpreted as the spiritual descendant of Hobbes. In fact, he is more than aware that Hobbes's leonine convention is a wicked one. To Buchanan, who recalls more Spinoza than Hobbes,[17] the contract is a tool through which morally equal individuals are equally free. A freedom that, as Buchanan underlines, has to be made secure through time. With the introduction of the State, present generations who undersigned the Hobbesian contract have, in a sense, been freed. Conversely, future generations are constrained within that order since they couldn't play any role in the original contract. They, hence, become morally unequal. The moral equality–inequality we are referring to is of the procedural, not substantial kind. Hence, if moral equality is the prerequisite of the contract, as is in Buchanan, how can it be possible to figure out a contractual solution between the master and his slave as Buchanan asserts?[18]

The solution requires that we resort to another 'variation' on the Hobbesian paradigm. This is the introduction of the time dimension that allows one to escape the immobility of a permanent constitution. The very idea of a genuine contract presupposes the possibility of constitutional renegotiation as being relevant to any determination of intergenerational moral equality. This will revitalize the gluer that is necessary to the maintenance of a steady order without which there is the risk of a falling back into anarchy.

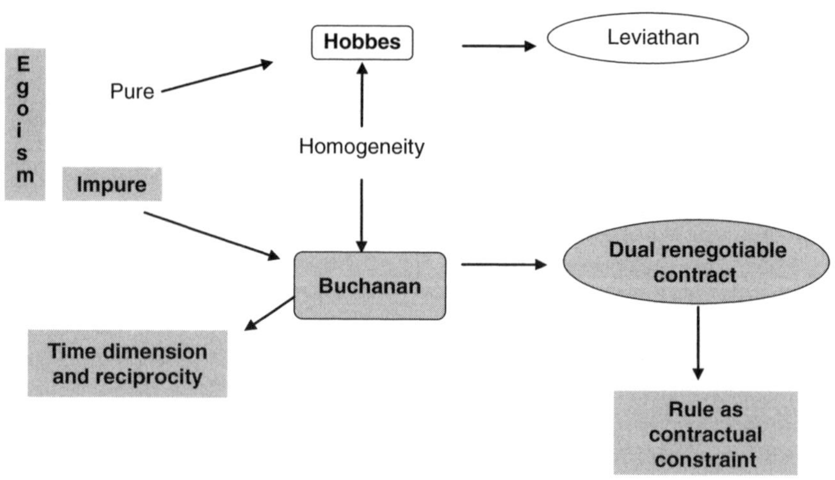

Figure 1.2 First variation: the pure economic man becomes the impure economic man

INTRINSIC VERSUS EXTRINSIC MOTIVATIONS: THE *HOMO ECONOMICUS MATURUS*

Frey could not escape Hobbes, even if, like Buchanan, he has written consciously in reaction against him. Frey strikes Hobbes's paradigm in the heart with the replacement of the homogeneous perfectly egoistic individual with the *homo economicus maturus,* or as we rather prefer to call him *homo agnus*. Frey wonders how to reconcile the idea followed by most economists that 'citizens if given the opportunity, act as knaves or crooks' [19] with that of voluntary work, blood donation, charities, fund raising for humanitarian purposes that are so widespread nowadays. The orthodox explanation based on extrinsic motivations (rewards, rents and so on) is no longer acceptable. This leads Frey to resort to intrinsic motivations to explain a non-negligible part of individual behaviours.[20]

Intrinsic motivations are those impulses such as emotions, passions, love, sympathy, compassion that induce an individual set in a context where individuals are many to consider his fellow-men not as enemies, but as friends whom one can mutually count on. It is not difficult to discern the core of Frey's argumentation: Frey is fiercely critical of the Hobbesian state of nature. His individual is a man hostile to all forms of loneliness, which produces only selves that operate in isolation. This view implies a confidence in one's neighbours as the optimum path to co-operation through

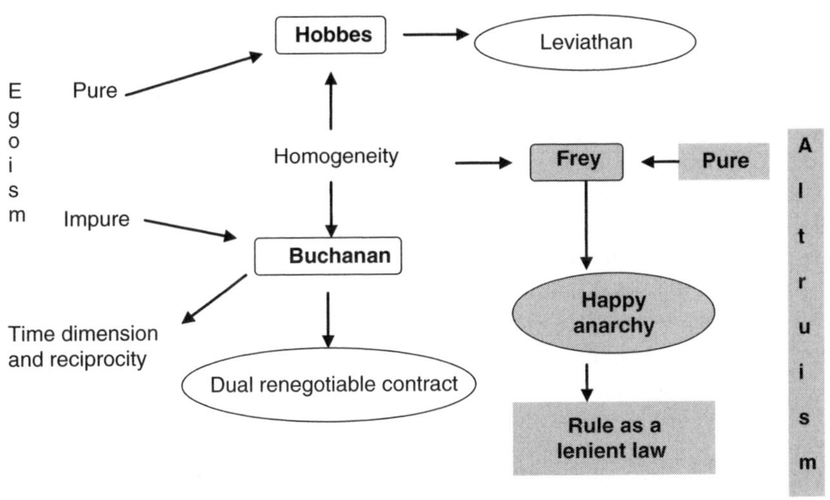

Figure 1.3 Second variation: the impure economic man becomes the homo economicus maturus

the reciprocity principle. To figure out a stable equilibrium it is required that nobody should be led by price incentives since they explain only the behaviour of the *homo economicus* and not that of the *homo economicus maturus*.

Yet attractive and stimulating as the theory of intrinsic motivations is, there are nevertheless some weaknesses. In fact, though the *homo economicus maturus*, to use Frey's expression, is goaded by a sort of inner dictum, he has a pronounced tendency to safeguard his own interest, and his fellowmen's welfare is only a secondary effect. A sort of egocentric altruism *à la* Khalil.[21] What Khalil demonstrates most clearly is that this feeling is based on the pleasure that the donor enjoys in sympathizing with people mired in catastrophes. It is from such a concept that he fashions the so-called 'vicarious pleasure', which would produce the maximization of Frey's intrinsic motivations. So interpreted, the altruistic behaviour turns out to be a cover-up for a highly egoistic attitude.

Another flaw in Frey's paradigm is linked to the attempt in his thought to depict an individual as close to reality as possible. Perhaps he has done this under the push of his enthusiasm for redeeming man from the distrust he has been the object of and around which institutions have been built.[22] However, he does not supply any uncontroversial information on intrinsic motivations. This factor becomes essential when moving on to the impact that this novel man has on institution building. While, in fact, the man as *lupus* required the introduction of rules to constrain, tame and guide him, the man as *agnus*, led by intrinsic motivations, does not seem to call for such stringent rules any longer. It is now his inner voice, and not the external rule that matters. The internalization process is critically related to the ratio between the weight assigned to intrinsic and extrinsic motivations. Frey emphasizes that for each action 'what matters after all is the intrinsic satisfaction one derives',[23] a satisfaction that, as mentioned above, involves considering anyone other than oneself a constraint to the original field of action whereby actions that imply conflicts are excluded. Yet, the more the other individual is internalized, the fewer rules to limit potential conflicts are necessary. If instead Buchanan-like rules were to be introduced in such a scenario, Frey would alert us that civic virtues would be crowded out,[24] and the *homo economicus maturus* would be driven again into a Hobbesian position. In a nutshell, even though individuals were not born as knaves, they become so because rules were designed as if individuals were such. 'The general spirit of the law . . . should acknowledge the citizens' basic good will and should support public spiritedness while still preventing exploitation by free riders.'[25] This point makes explicit that despite Frey's attempts at overcoming the Hobbesian paradigm, his intrinsic motivations solution, characterized by the absence of external limitations, seems still influenced greatly by the Hobbesian spirit, at least for what concerns the looseness of rules. To admit this does not entirely rule out the possibility that showing little trust towards ordinary citizens can turn them into knaves. Furthermore, the adverse selection process is more severe when it is related to politicians. In Frey's words 'persons with particularly low civic virtue are especially attracted to a political career because they are not burdened by mistrusting constitutional rules'[26] due to the impossibility of drawing up complete contracts. It is more convenient, according to Frey, to assume that individuals have average or high civic virtues so that contracts will produce a weak constitution able to crowd in civic virtues. Specifically, a low degree of civic virtues triggers the selection process among individuals thus following Gresham's law. Frey's paradigm is valid provided that citizens are homogeneous and intrinsically motivated to a high degree. The result will be either a state with a weak constitution or, pushed to the extreme, a sort of happy anarchy, as we like to call it, to be contrasted with Hobbes's anarchy. The *homo economicus maturus* evaluates his fellow-men's position as if it were his own, which is why in Frey there is no room for a Hobbesian-like contract. By allowing people to live in a conflict-free state of nature order is already guaranteed.

PSYCHOLOGICAL VERSUS MECHANISTIC HETEROGENEITY: FROM SYMPATHETIC MAN TO *HOMO SAPIENS*

In the preceding sections we have built an intellectual framework to explain the central role that different and homogeneous individuals play in rule making. Bringing Hobbes into the analysis of modern investigators has highlighted the flaws associated with his hypotheses. In particular, two factors stand out: the difficulty in explaining motivations of human behaviours characterized by egoism, altruism (understood as camouflaged egoism), and the assumption that individuals are homogeneous. We are led to believe that a more convincing definition of altruism in a society with heterogeneous individuals would and should be found. We begin our task with the hypothesis that man is pushed into action by two different impulses: selfishness and sympathy. The concept was keenly advocated by moral doctrine from Shaftesbury to Smith and offers a vision of how these two contrasting impulses act within each individual. As early as 1600, Shaftesbury, in opposition to the purely egoistic vision of Hobbes, maintained that man was endowed with moral and social principles, based on a psychoanthropologic-like sentiment called sympathy, an innate benevolence towards one's own fellow-men encapsulated by Hutcheson in the concept of 'moral sense', which emerges again in

Hume[27] as sympathy: 'there is no human, and indeed no sensible, creature, whose happiness or misery does not, in some measure, affect us when brought near to us, and represented in lively colours: But this proceeds merely from sympathy',[28] and as he explains better further on

> The minds of all men are similar in their feelings and operations; nor can any one be actuated by any affection, of which all others are not, in some degree, susceptible. As in strings equally wound up, the motion of one communicates itself to the rest; so all the affections readily pass from one person to another, and beget correspondent movements in every human creature. When I see the effects of passion in the voice and gesture of any person, my mind immediately passes from these effects to their causes, and forms such a lively idea of the passion, as is presently converted into the passion itself . . . No passion of another discovers itself immediately to the mind. We are only sensible of its causes or effects. From these we infer the passion: And consequently these give rise to our sympathy.[29]

A more accurate expression of such a sentiment can be found in Smith's *Theory of Moral Sentiments*[30] where he writes: 'How selfish soever man may be supposed, there are evidently some principles in his nature, which interest him in the fortune of others, and render their happiness necessary to him, though he derives nothing from it except the pleasure of seeing it.'[31]

As economists, we wonder if the pleasure coming from the observation of someone else's pleasure is one of the many variables from which individuals may derive pleasure. It happens in Becker (1962), who incorporates someone else's utility in the utility function of an individual, in Margolis (1984), who incorporates goods at someone else's disposal in the utility function of the individual, in Frey's intrinsic motivations and finally in Frank's (1989) traits or genes.

Smith himself clarifies the point when he asserts that 'Sympathy, however cannot in any sense, be regarded as a selfish principle.'[32] The egoistic side seems to be only apparent if it is true that

> my emotion . . . arises from bringing your case home to myself, from putting myself in your situation, and thence conceiving what I should feel in the like circumstances. But though sympathy is very properly said to arise from an imaginary change of situations with the person principally concerned, yet this imaginary change is not supposed to happen to me in my own person and characters but in that person with whom I sympathize. When I condole with you for the loss of your only son . . . I consider what I should suffer if I was really you, and I not only change circumstances with you, but I change persons and characters.[33]

The observer will have a function[34] similar to that of the observed: the closer to the original, the greater the information on the observed disposition and on the conditions that might affect his feelings. In this way Smith was able partially to solve what in Frey remains problematic: by varying the distance from the observed, the degree of sympathy varies as well, and so does the strength that drives men's actions *vis-à-vis* egoism.

The Smithian individual is a natural evolution of those represented so far. And, in fact, at the varying of the distance where the individual is positioned in the face of others it is possible to cover the spectrum going from the *homo economicus maturus*, where distance is zero, to the pure economic man where distance is infinite.

It is exactly the distance effect that makes individuals heterogeneous. An individual, when observed by two observers living at different distances originates two different degrees of sympathy.[35]

In order to eliminate the mechanistic component embodied in the Smithian heterogeneous individual and turn him into a *homo sapiens*, an additional factor of heterogeneity has to be added. To this end let us

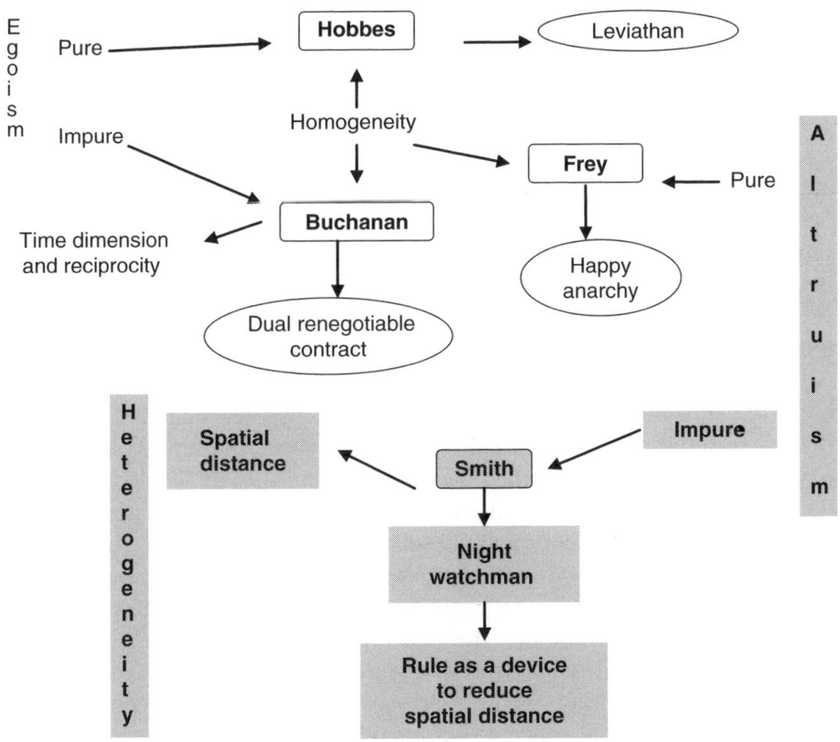

Figure 1.4 *Third variation: the* homo economicus maturus *becomes the sympathetic man*

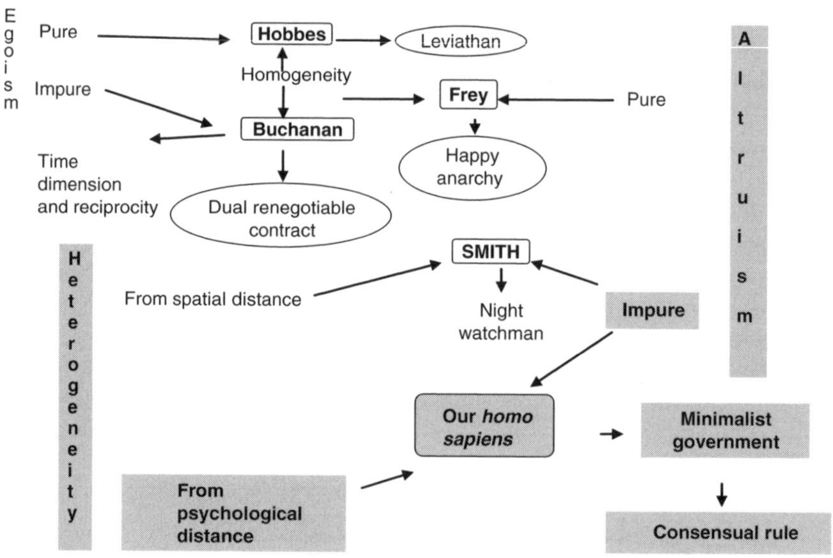

Figure 1.5 Fourth variation: the sympathetic man becomes the homo sapiens

consider two individuals located at the same spatial distance from a third one. Since individuals are endowed with different degrees of sensibility, sympathy will vary according to the personal attitude to sympathy. Hence, despite the equal spatial distance, in the case of *homo sapiens* the two individuals will evaluate the observed individual in a genuine heterogeneous manner.

According to Smith, the sympathy process is enacted if the observer is an impartial spectator, not only towards the other fellow-men, but even towards himself. Each individual has a 'man within the breast', that is his conscience, emerging from the internalization process of the other spectators' reaction. Clearly this process is hardly compatible with the pre-contractual context mentioned hitherto, it being typical of an already ordered society. Does sympathizing simply mean to feel compassionate, pitiful and benevolent? Does it mean to experiencing those benevolent and social sentiments that the literature on altruism has used to explain good actions that an individual performs in human society and that could not be explained on the grounds of pure egoism? The answer is in the negative. Sympathizing is a wide concept that includes both benevolent and positive impulses and less social, or even egoistic, passions. That Smith's analysis has strong modern denotations, is shown by his revival in recent years[36] after the Benthamite[37] obscuration.

Let us try to figure out, hopefully on a more solid ground, the relationship between the impartial spectator and the observed individual. 'The principal source of admiration' of the impartial spectator when observing the rich and the great is not linked to the fact that 'they are happier than other people but he imagines that they possess more mean of happiness'. If so, the spectator, identifying with the observed individual, includes in the utility function the goods consumed by the observed as they are perceived. The spectator, by virtue of the causation process, can capture the utility function of the observed individual from the quantity of goods that the latter consumes and the degree of sympathy is determined accordingly.

One should not forget that our man, defined as *homo sapiens*, still enshrines in himself an egoistic element that is not negative at all, but as Smith would put it, it is the expression of a virtue: prudence.[38]

INTRA-GOVERNMENTAL RELATIONSHIPS THROUGH THE LENS OF 'VARIATIONS'

So far we have dealt with abstract models, let us now use the human archetypes presented above to observe their impact on the existing institutions, especially on governance and see how the models that paid tribute to the evolution of human nature are amenable to governance paradigms like for example master–slave, principal–agent and trust relationships.

Founded on the alienation of rights to the Leviathan, permeated with the philosophy of absolutism, which by design leaves all powers to the Leviathan, the Hobbesian paradigm is only too obviously a master–slave paradigm.

Only by overcoming the double morals and embracing the behavioural symmetry of standard Public Choice, originated and developed in the extreme context of the pure *homo economicus*, the conflation of agency relationships and the separation of powers becomes a pivotal instrument in regulating social relationships. The agency relationship may take many forms: that of the voter–politician; that of the politician–bureaucrat; and currently that between national and international or supranational institutions.

If the agent, as suggested by Buchanan, is a rational egoist, an opportunistic individual enjoying a position that enables better access to information and whose interests could be in contrast with those of the principal, the individual will certainly act in a way that would favour himself rather than the principal. To avoid such a situation, the principal has a wide range of instruments such as sanctions, incentives, direct or indirect controls. There is not the slightest question that the assumption of behavioural homogeneity is the very reason that has taken to the separation of State powers of the Montesquieu kind with which we are familiar – to ensure that everyone watches over everyone else's egoistic drives. We have to turn to Frey's[39] altruistic behavioural homogeneity to learn that order is guaranteed by the sense of 'moral community'.[40] Interpreted as a result of intrinsic motivations, Buchanan's moral community is turned into happy anarchy not 'moral anarchy'. It is as if Frey's *homines economici maturi* identified themselves in a sort of enlarged 'moral unity' having characteristics similar to those of a family whereby members are felt to be reciprocally responsible and fatherly. Little wonder that under these circumstances the only conceivable relationships are thus diffused, reciprocal, of the fatherly–filial kind, and represent an extreme form of trustworthiness. Surely this sort of happy anarchy stems from the capitalization of such trust. But interestingly enough, no sooner does one member of the community cease to believe in moral unity by breaking the trust relation, than he will run the risk for inexorably falling back into the anarchy paradigm. This is an occurrence that cannot be found in Frey's elaboration because individuals are homogeneous, strenuous altruists.

Let us now transplant the above scenarios into Smith's heterogeneous compound individual. Individuals' heterogeneity, resulting from the combination of the two acting forces of altruism and egoism and the spatial distance, used as a meter to measure other individuals' welfare, not only allows us to understand the previous relationships, but also widens the spectrum of possible relationships. At this juncture, it might be interesting to contrast the Smithian individual, who subsumes all possible relationships, with the Schlicht formulation of trust.

> Factors relate to the way a situation is perceived and categorized, and thus interpreted. Individuals make distinction between the situations of command and obedience, independent agency and fiduciary obligation, and base their action on these perceptions and interpretations . . . The same objective situation will engender quite different kinds of behaviour if the situation is interpreted as an authority relationship, a principal agent relationship or a fiduciary relationship.[41]

The reason why an individual's behaviour may change according to whether he perceives himself as a slave, an agent or a trustee, can be explained by invoking not only the utilitarian approach, but also the approach of intrinsic motivations.[42] It is in this framework that it is possible to envision a less stringent form of trust relationship that nowadays is widespread at a national government level and at a supranational[43] level as well.

How is it possible to reconcile the impure individuals *à la* Buchanan with institutions such as the Constitutional Courts or the Independent Regulatory Agencies that by statutes can be controlled very little or not at all?

The answer is not a straightforward statement. The enterprise of controlling those who should control has proved to be difficult, not to say impossible, as shown recently by Brennan in his 'Trust, adjudication and the *Quis Custodiet* problem'.[44] Yet no one would conclude from this presupposition that there is no basis for solving the problem. Let us thus consider what would be the possible consequences of a heterogeneous community made up of *homines sapientes*, who by definition tend to establish trust relationships. It is not hard to imagine that such a context would favour the reconciliation of ministerial responsibility with the principle of independence. *Homo sapiens* is, in fact, by its very nature the unquestioned protagonist in a trust relationship if viewed according to the sociological meaning of trust. Conversely, the pure legal vision of trust diverts from the foundations and conditions that characterize trustworthiness, that is an unavoidable state of uncertainty that cannot be cancelled through trust relationships. According to Majone,[45] 'A trustee is an agent and something more . . . is an independent, responsible party' to whom the owner of a property, the settlor, with the agreement that he will not treat it as if it were his own property, but will run it in the interest of the beneficiary, who not necessarily is the settlor himself.

This statement seems to identify in such a transfer of powers the change in the subject's behaviour who from agent pursuing his own interests becomes a trustee agent on behalf of the principal. The idea that the assignment of a task and the transfer of a right determine an individual's behaviour is exceedingly optimistic and rooted in the Neoclassical vision, which is against motivational symmetry. According to that vision, for instance, an individual interested in the common life might turn into a benevolent despot whom one can entirely rely on – an idea that reveals a patent illogicalness as has been highlighted by Public Choice scholars.

Shapiro, by listing the numerous corruption scandals, emphasizes that a trust relationship does not imply the relinquishment of the trustee's interested behaviour. In the same vein Molm *et al.* observe that the 'Acts of trust, and attributions of trustworthiness, can be made only in situations in which the partner has both the incentive and the opportunity to exploit the actor'.[46] By this definition, trustworthiness is conceived 'as a behavioural manifestation', a 'behavior that reflects a reliance on a partner and involves a vulnerability . . . on the part of the trustor'.[47] Such a vulnerability critically depends on the heterogeneity of individuals and on the spatial distance that separates individuals. In a context of uncertainty, distance becomes the pivotal element in the calculation of the subjective probability p that each individual evaluates when considering being part of a trust relationship according to Coleman's equation.[48]

NOTES

1. J. M. Buchanan (1999), pp. 315–25.
2. T. Hobbes (1651), The first part: Of man, Chapter XIII: Of the natural condition of mankind as concerning their felicity and misery.
3. Ibid.
4. Ibid.
5. Cf. T. Hobbes (1651), The first part: Of man, Chapter XIV: Of the first and second natural laws, and of contracts.
6. Ibid.
7. 'A law of nature, lex naturalis, is a precept, or general rule, found out by reason, by which a man is forbidden to do that which is destructive of his life, or taketh away the means of preserving the same, and to omit that by which he thinketh it may be best preserved', ibid.
8. Ibid.
9. Ibid.
10. 'one person, of whose acts a great multitude, by mutual covenants one with another, have made themselves every one the author, to the end he may use the strength and means of them all as he shall think expedient for their peace and common defence'. Cf. T. Hobbes (1651), The Second Part: Of Commonwealth, Chapter XVII: Of the causes, generation, and definition of a commonwealth.
11. Ibid.
12. For Hobbes 'The sovereign of a Commonwealth, be it an assembly or one man, is not subject to the civil laws. For having power to make and repeal laws, he may, when he pleaseth, free himself from that subjection by repealing those laws that trouble him, and making of new; and consequently he was free before. For he is free that can be free when he will: nor is it possible for any person to be bound to himself, because he that can bind can release; and therefore he that is bound to himself only is not bound'. Cf. T. Hobbes (1651), The Second Part: Of Commonwealth, Chapter XXV: Of Counsel.
13. Ibid.
14. 'We live in a society of individuals, not a society of equals' . . . 'We need not follow Hobbes . . . We could assume, equally well, that even in some state of nature men behave in accordance with self interest tempered by regard for their fellows . . . individuals adopt precepts for behaviour that reflect the interest of the human species'. J. M. Buchanan (1975), pp. 11 and 26.
15. Cf. J. M. Buchanan and G. Tullock (1999).
16. Cf. J. M. Buchanan (1975), p. 83.
17. Cf. J. M. Buchanan (1999), Appendix.
18. Ibid.
19. B. S. Frey (1997), p. 43.
20. '[O]ne is said to be intrinsically motivated to perform an activity when one receives no apparent reward except the activity itself', Bruno S. Frey (1997) p. 13.
21. E. L. Khalil (2004).
22. Cf. B. S. Frey (1997), especially Chapters 6 and 7.
23. Cf. B. S. Frey (1997), p. 14.
24. An idea that Buchanan himself had in mind when he wrote: 'Institutions may have been allowed to develop and to persevere that exacerbate rather than mitigate man's ever present temptation to act as if he is an island, with others treated as part of his natural environment.' This is so because 'the sizes of community within which an individual finds himself, impose *external* bounds on possible behavior'. In fact, until Robinson Crusoe was alone he 'could be motivated by nothing other than self-interest . . . Once he acknowledges the existence of Friday, a tension develops and Crusoe finds that his behavior is modified'. J. M. Buchanan (1978), p. 364–8.
25. Cf. B. S. Frey (1997), p. 44.
26. Ibid. p. 46.

27. Hume is often recalled and quoted in the literature for the following statement: 'in contriving any system of government, and fixing the several checks and controuls of the constitution, every man ought to be supposed a knave, and to have no other end, in all his actions, than private interest'. D. Hume (1742), Part I, Essay VI: Of The Independency Of Parliament,
28. D. Hume (1739), BOOK III: Of Morals, PART II: Of justice and injustice, SECT. I: Justice, whether a natural or artificial virtue?
29. Ibid, Book III: Of Morals, PART III: Of the other virtues and vices, SECT. I: Of the origin of the natural virtues and vices.
30. A. Smith (1759), Part I, Section I: Of the Sense of Propriety, Chap. I: Of Sympathy.
31. Ibid.
32. A. Smith (1759), Part VII, Section III: Of the different Systems which have been formed concerning the Principle of Approbation, Chap. I: Of those Systems which deduce the Principle of Approbation from Self-love.
33. Ibid.
34. 'As we have no immediate experience of what other men feel, we can form no idea of the manner in which they are affected, but by conceiving what we ourselves should feel in the like situation . . . it is by the imagination only that we can form any conception or what are his sensations . . . by representing to us what would be our own, if we were in his case. It is the impressions of our own senses only, not those of his, which our imagination copy'. 'we enter as it were into his body, and become in some measure the same person with him, and thence form some idea of his sensations, and even feel something which, though weaker in degree, is not altogether unlike them'. A. Smith (1759), Part I, Section I: Of the Sense of Propriety, Chap. I: Of Sympathy.
35. Marciano in analysing Hume underlines 'sympathy decreases when the distance that separates individuals increases: "sympathy, we shall allow, is much fainter than our concern for ourselves, and sympathy with persons remote from us, much fainter that with persons near or contiguous" (Hume, *Treatise of Human Nature*, p. 116)', A. Marciano (2004), p. 18.
36. Emotions are again fundamental factors in the decision-making process. See for instance G. Loewenstein (2000), p. 426, G. Ben-Shakhar *et al.* (2004), J. Elster (1998).
37. As evidenced by Loewenstein 'when Bentham first proposed the construct of utility, emotions figured prominently in his theory. Because Bentham viewed the utility as the net sum of positive over negative emotions', p. 426.
38. Prudent to Smith is, in fact, the one who in 'the steadiness of his industry and frugality, in his steadily sacrificing the ease and enjoyment of the present moment for the probable expectation of the still greater ease and enjoyment of a more distant but of a more lasting of time', favours the wealth of nations (saving-accumulation of capital) 'always both supported and rewarded by the entire approbation of the impartial spectator and of the representative of the impartial spectator, the man within the breast'. A. Smith (1759), Part VI, Section I: Of the Character of the Individual, so far as it affects his own Happiness; or of Prudence.
39. A particular vision proper to Switzerland whose social setting is modelled on a deep sense of cohesion and homogeneity.
40. 'A *moral community* exists among a set of persons to the extent that individual members of the group identify with a collective unity, a community, rather than conceive themselves to be independent, isolated individuals', J. M. Buchanan (1986), p. 109.
41. E. Schlicht (2001), p. 81.
42. 'One is said to be intrinsically motivated to perform an activity when one receives no apparent reward except the activity itself', B. S. Frey (1997), p. 13.
43. 'EU's member governments have created and allocated increasing powers and discretion to a number of supranational organizations, including the executive Commission, the European Court of Justice (ECJ), the European Central Bank (ECB), the European Parliament (EP), and a growing number of independent agencies which are delegated regulatory and/or informational functions in specific issue-areas', M.A. Pollack (2003), p. 1.
44. G. Brennan (2000).

45. G. Majone (2001).
46. D. L. Molm *et al.* (2000), p. 1403.
47. J. A Sniezek and L. M. Van Swol (2001), pp. 289–90.
48. *G* and *L* are the payoffs of the individual's correct behaviour and incorrect behaviour respectively required in a trust relationship. $pG > (1 - p)L$
   Precisely as in Smith's case, closeness of individuals allows better reciprocal information, so reducing information costs. But it is the different attitude to sympathy that guarantees the emergence of a trust relationship whose actors are our *homines sapientes*.

REFERENCES

Becker, G. S. (1962), 'Irrational behavior and economic theory', *Journal of Political Economy*, (70), 1–13.
Ben-Shakhar G., G. Bornstein, A. Hopfensitz and F. van Winden (2004), 'Reciprocity and emotions: arousal, selfreports, and expectations', CESifo working paper, no. 1298, Category 2: Public Choice, pp. 1–22.
Brennan, G. (2000), 'Trust adjudication and the *Quis Custodiet* problem', unpublished typescript.
Buchanan, J. M. (1975), *The Limits of Liberty: Between Anarchy and Leviathan*, Chicago, IL: The University of Chicago Press.
Buchanan, J. M. (1978), 'Market, states, and the extent of morals', *The American Economic Review*, **68** (2), 364–8.
Buchanan, J. M. (1986), *Liberty, Market and State. Political Economy in the 1980s*, Brighton, UK: Wheatsheaf Books Ltd.
Buchanan, J. M. (1999), appendix, 'Marginal notes on reading political philosophy', in J. M. Buchanan and G. Tullock, *The Calculus of Consent: Logical Foundations of Constitutional Democracy*, Indianapolis, IN: Liberty Fund, pp. 315–25.
Buchanan, J. M. and G. Tullock (1999), *The Calculus of Consent: Logical Foundations of Constitutional Democracy*, Indianapolis, IN: Liberty Fund.
Elster, J. (1988), 'Emotions and economic theory', *Journal of Economic Literature*, **XXXVI**, 47–74.
Frank, R. H. (1989), *Passions within Reason*, New York: W. W. Norton & Company.
Frey, B. S. (1997), *Not Just for the Money. An Economic Theory of Personal Motivation*, Cheltenham UK, Brookfield, VT: Edward Elgar.
Hobbes, T. (1651), *Leviathan*, University of Oregon ERIS Project (1999), accessed at http://darkwing.uoregon.edu/~rbear/hobbes/leviathan.html.
Hume, D. (1739), *Treatise of Human Nature*, published by J. Carl Mickelsen, University of Idaho, accessed at http://www.class.uidaho.edu/mickelsen/ToC/hume%20treatise%20ToC.htm.
Hume, D. (1742), *Essays Moral, Political and Literary*, E. F. Miller (ed.) (1987), Liberty Fund, Inc., accessed at www.econlib.org/library/LFBooks/Hume/hmMPL6.html.
Khalil, E. L. (2004), 'What is altruism?', *Journal of Economic Psychology*, **25**, 97–123.
Loewenstein, G. (2000), 'Emotions in economic theory and economic behavior', *The American Economic Review*, **90** (2), 426–32.
Majone, G. (2001), 'Nonmajoritarian institution and the limits of democratic governance: a political transaction-cost approach', *Journal of Institutional and Theoretical Economics*, **157** (1), 57–78.

Marciano, A. (2005), 'Benevolence, Sympathy, and Hume's model of government: how different is new political economy from classical political economy?' in S. G. Medema and P. Boettke (eds), *The Role of Government in the History of Economic Thought*, annual supplement to vol. 37, History of Political Economy, Durham, NC and London: Duke University Press, pp. 43–70.
Margolis, H. (1984), *Selfishness, Altruism, and Rationality: A Theory of Social Choice*, Chicago, IL: Chicago University Press.
Molm, D. L., N. Takahashi and G. Peterson (2000), 'Risk and trust in social exchange: an experimental test of a classical proposition', *The American Journal of Sociology*, **105** (5), 1396–427.
Pollack, M. A. (2003), 'The delegation of powers to the European Commission', paper prepared for presentation at the workshop on Delegation to International Organizations, University of California, San Diego, 19–20 September.
Schlicht, E. (2001), 'Fiduciaries, servants, agents, and situational effects', *Journal of Institutional and Theoretical Economics*, **157** (1), 79–82.
Smith, A. (1759), *The Theory of Moral Sentiments*, published by A. Millar (1790 – 6th edn), accessed at www.econlib.org/library/Smith/smMS6.html.
Smith, A. (1776), *An Inquiry into the Nature And Causes of the Wealth of Nations*, reprinted 1900, London: G. Routledge.
Sniezek, J. A. and L. M. Van Swol (2001), 'Trust, confidence, and expertise in a judge–advisor system', *Organizational Behavior and Human Decision Processes*, **84** (2), 288–307.

2. Freedom of choice, power, and the responsibility of decision makers

Manfred J. Holler

INTRODUCTION

The theory of freedom of choice concerns the comparison of decision situations as given by opportunity sets. That is, when we compare freedom of choice we rank opportunity sets: does an opportunity set A imply more freedom of choice than opportunity set B? It is notable that these rankings ignore the role of decision makers. However, one might argue that decision maker i has more freedom of choice if i controls an opportunity set A instead of opportunity set B and A has more freedom of choice than set B. Moreover, we could then say that i has more freedom of choice than j if i controls A and j controls B and A offers more freedom of choice than B.

Implicit to the standard theory of freedom of choice is the assumption that the goods are not marketable and there are no prices and income such that the opportunity sets can be described by budget sets. This, of course, is the case with goods of substantial externalities, public goods, club goods, and goods which are controlled through moral or hierarchical constraints. In general, the demand and supply of these goods is not defined by purchasing power, but by social or political power. This is not to say that purchasing power has no impact, it does, as a source of power; but it is not the power itself from which the production and consumption of these non-market goods derive.

The important distinction between power and freedom of choice is that power refers to decisions and decision makers. If we consider agents, we have to distinguish between rankings of opportunity sets and preferences over elements of opportunity sets. In principle, we should expect that the rankings of opportunity sets derives from the preferences over the elements if both have their sources in the decision maker. However, this is not necessarily the case: there are intra-personal aggregation problems. Moreover, typically outsiders evaluate the freedom of choice which characterizes alternative decision situations, in general, without considering the specific preferences of the decision makers.

In any case, a straightforward adding up of utilities could be misleading as the decision maker does not get what is in the opportunity set, but has to choose from it. In fact, the standard theory implicitly assumes that he or she can choose one element, only. Thus standard theory does not discuss what will be the ranking of the opportunity sets A and B, if A contains a larger degree of freedom than B, but the decision maker can pick two elements from B but only one of from A. In the now classical approach to measuring freedom decision makers only enter the scene in the discussion of the different rankings of opportunity sets and the principles from which these rankings derive. However, it is not that difficult to incorporate decisions into the structure because we need only ask the question 'who controls the opportunity sets?' Control obviously implies power and the control of opportunity sets relates, therefore, to the social interaction of decision makers and the forming of coalitions. This suggests that when we want to make comparisons of freedom of choice we should rank the impact of individual agents on the social outcome and not the opportunity sets. One of the implications of this step is that we can link the concepts of freedom of choice and power to responsibility because membership of controlling coalitions can be interpreted as a proxy of the responsibility of the individual decision maker for the social outcome.

There are immediate theoretical applications for this measure of responsibility. In particular, this approach can be seen as an alternative to welfare calculation and utility maximization which seems to dominate the Law and Economics literature. The approach to responsibility that is suggested here accounts for the observation that people often compare social states and social systems with respect to the degree of freedom and the distribution of power and responsibility independent of preferences and welfare calculations. It also takes care of theoretical arguments which suggest that power and responsibility should be evaluated without reference to preferences.[1] The binding nature of law is not because it matches the agent's preferences but because it concurs with the agent's capacity to fulfil an obligation. In fact, the capacity to act creates the obligation and the related freedom of choice is the basis of the corresponding responsibility to which the law refers. This, for example, applies to the support of relatives of first degree in accordance with the German law: if your parents are in need and you have the means then you have to support them, irrespective of your preferences.

To many economists the emphasis on freedom of choice instead of welfare perhaps seems out of focus. But this narrow focus may be misplaced. Today's political climate stresses freedom, thereby unfortunately largely neglecting the well-being of nations and individuals. It seems that discussion of the attribution of guilt for actions and revenge are not outdated.

Advertising for privatization also stresses choices. Even judges cannot resist the temptation of following this track. At the Juristentag in September 2004, Udo di Fabio, a judge at the Bundesverfassungsgericht,[2] proposed to abolish all laws that protect consumers, minorities or environment. Social diversity, he says, is the result of freedom and thus has to be accepted, and not regulated. Perhaps, he argues, this does not guarantee a better society but permits better laws.

The aim of the following analysis is to combine the set-based concept of freedom of choice with the agent-based concept of power. From this we will derive a conceptual and formal apparatus for the discussion of responsibility. The next section reviews two standard approaches to the ranking opportunity sets in order to illustrate the implications and limitations of the freedom of choice theory. In the third section, we will discuss the possibility of specifying the ranking by introducing potential preferences. As an alternative, in the fourth section, we will relate the freedom of choice to the power of the decision makers as measured by the Public Good Index. An illustration of the results with application to problems of responsibility will follow in the fifth section.

THE ORTHODOX APPROACH TO FREEDOM OF CHOICE

The orthodox approach of freedom consists of comparing decision situations as expressed by the sets of alternatives which describe these situations, that is, it is strictly set-based and decision makers are considered as irrelevant for this comparison.

Let's assume X, a universal finite set of alternatives, and Z, the set of non-empty subsets of X. Elements of Z are called opportunity sets. Pattanaik and Xu (1990) propose three axioms that uniquely characterize an *ordering* R on the (opportunity) sets in Z. R is reflexive and transitive binary relation comparing sets which reads as follows: If A and B are elements of Z then ARB expresses that the degree of freedom of choice of A is *at least* as large as the degree of freedom of B. If ARB and BRA, then AIB says that the degree of freedom of choice of A is as large as the degree of freedom of B. On the other hand, if ARB and *not* BRA, then APB expresses that the degree of freedom of choice of A is *larger than* the degree of freedom of B.

The axioms proposed by Pattanaik and Xu (1990) are:

Property 2.1. For all alternatives x, y in X, we have $\{x\}I\{y\}$.
This axiom express the indifference between no choice situations. If opportunity sets contain one element only, then they are 'equivalent', irrespective of what specific elements they contain.

Property 2.2. For all distinct x, y in X, if follows $\{x, y\}P\{x\}$.
This axiom expresses strict monotonicity comparing a no choice situation with an opportunity set which expresses the possibility for a choice.

Property 2.3. For all A, B in Z and for all x in $X\backslash(A \cup B)$, we have $[ARB \Leftrightarrow A \cup \{x\} RB \cup \{x\}]$.
This is an independence property. If we 'add' an additional element x to the two sets A and B under comparison, then the relation between the extended sets is identical to the relation between A and B. This also applies if we 'subtract' from the extended sets the element x. Note that 'adding' and 'subtracting' refers to the set $\{x\}$, however, this only a set-theoretical detail.

Pattanaik and Xu (1990) prove that if we denote the cardinality of a set A of alternatives by $\#A$ and define an ordering $R_\#$ such that, for all A, B in Z, it holds that $AR_\#B$ if $\#A \geq \#B$, then the following theorem applies:

Theorem 2.1. $R_\#$ is the unique reflexive and transitive relation that satisfies Properties 2.1, 2.2 and 2.3.

Thus $R_\#$ is an ordering which allows us to compare all subsets of X, that is, all elements of Z, by the number of elements they contain. The relation $R_\#$ merely suggests the counting of elements: if A contains more elements than B then A ranks higher than B.

Obviously, $R_\#$ ranks opportunity sets without reference to the individuals who control those sets. It also abstracts from any relationship between the elements in the opportunity sets. Elements could be substitutes or complements, or strongly or weakly related in perception, connected, more or less diverse, and so on. Needless to say the $R_\#$ relation triggered a series of critical comments and objections. More specifically, it has been argued that:

(a) $R_\#$ ignores the preferences of the individuals to whom the set of alternatives are allocated. If individual i's opportunity set contains a bottle of beer and a can of Coke, it has been argued that i's freedom of choice should not be affected if the bottle breaks to pieces and the beer pours to the ground, given that i can choose one item, only, and dislikes beer.

(b) $R_\#$ does not consider complementary and substitutional relationships among the alternatives. If the only difference between two tins of Coke is given by the bar code then, it seems, that they do not really represent different alternatives when it comes to choosing an element of the corresponding opportunity set, given only one element can be selected. On the other hand, if the alternatives are highly unconnected such that they cannot be compared by the decision maker, a larger opportunity set, measured in terms of the number of elements, does not necessarily allow a larger number of choices. (This argument refers to cognitive problems, for example, as pointed out by Dewey (1979 [1938]) in his educational blueprint.)

(c) $R_{\#}$ does not take care of the fact that the alternatives in X have different values either from a social or individual point of view. To some extent this argument generalizes (a) and (b). However, alternatives may have different social values, which are independent of individual preferences or cognitive limits, which could be taken into account when comparing alternative opportunity sets.

A possible way to deal with these three objections is to qualify the equal weight assumption implied by $R_{\#}$ and to apply a weight function to the alternatives of an opportunity set. Marlies Klemisch-Ahlert (1993) defines an ordering R_α such that:

$$AR_\alpha B \Leftrightarrow \sum_{x \in A} \alpha(x) \geq \sum_{x \in B} \alpha(x) \quad \text{for all } A, B \text{ in } Z \tag{2.1}$$

In Equation 2.1, α is a mapping that assigns a (positive) weight $\alpha(x) > 0$ to every element x in X. More specifically, it is assumed that $\alpha: X \rightarrow]0,\infty[$. Thus Equation 2.1 implies that we rank the sets A and B with respect to freedom of choice by adding up the values of $\alpha-$weighted elements of the two sets and comparing the sums.

An ordering which satisfies Equation 2.1 is called an α-ordering. It is straightforward that R_α satisfies Property 2.1 only if $\alpha(x) = \alpha(y)$, which is in general not the case.

If we substitute Property 2.1 by its 'modification':

Property 2.4. For all x, y in X, $\{x\}R\{y\}$ implies $\alpha(x) \geq \alpha(y)$,
then it can be demonstrated that R_α satisfies Properties 2.2, 2.3, and 2.4. (For a proof, see Klemisch-Ahlert, 1993.)

Take any two subsets A and B of X: Alternative specifications of $\alpha(x)$ can lead to different orderings, that is, the ordering R_α is not unique. On the other hand, there may exist more than one specification of α such that the corresponding R_α gives the same ordering over the elements in Z. Klemisch-Ahlert (1993) proves that:

$$\text{if } B \subset A \text{ then } \sum_{x \in A} \alpha(x) \geq \sum_{x \in B} \alpha(x) \text{ and thus } AR_\alpha B \text{ for all } \alpha: X \rightarrow]0,\infty[\tag{2.2}$$

In other words, if B is a subset of A then A is ranked higher than B, irrespective of the specification of the mapping α, given that $\alpha: X \rightarrow]0,\infty[$. This, of course, holds for all sets A and B such that B is included in A. Therefore,

Lemma 2.1. The inclusion relation $R_{\subseteq}$ is the intersection of *all* α-orderings R_{α}. In other words, the inclusion relation $R_{\subseteq}$ implies that for all A, B in Z and $A \supset B$, we have ARB. Of course, $R_{\subseteq}$ defines an incomplete ordering over the elements in Z, as not all elements, that is, opportunity sets, can be ordered in the form of subsets (or supersets) to each other. *Lemma 2.1* is an interesting result, however, the range of its application is rather narrow.[3] If inclusion does not hold and the lemma does not apply, then the ranking of A and B depends on the specification of the α-mapping. In the next section we will discuss alternative approaches specifying the α-mapping.

SOCIAL WEIGHTS AND INDIVIDUAL PREFERENCES

There are two main approaches to specify the α-mapping: (a) assigning social values to the elements of the alternative opportunity sets; or (b) to refer to the decision maker and apply her preferences. In the second case, it has to be decided whether these preferences represent i's social preferences (that is, i's social values) or i's individual preferences.[4] In the latter case, we may argue that the α-values add up to 1. An α-value α_j represents the probability (or potential) that i will be able to enjoy (receive or accomplish) a specific x_j, which is an element of the opportunity set A of i, and the sum $\Sigma\alpha_j u_i(x_j)$ expresses i's expected value of A. The weight α_j could also be assumed to express i's perception of x_j: i could be more aware of some alternative x_j than of alternative x_k, then $\alpha_j > \alpha_k$ follows.[5] $u_i(.)$ is utility function describing i's subjective preferences.

It seems adequate to assume that $u_i(.)$ captures the intensity by which i prefers alternative x_k to that of x_j, or vice-versa. However, how can an outsider observe and measure this? Decision maker i might argue that his freedom of choice as given by an opportunity set A is larger than that of B. By a backward induction argument, i can maintain that this is because $u_i(x_k) > u_i(x_j)$. But how can an observer decide whether $\alpha_j > \alpha_k$ or $\alpha_j < \alpha_k$ applies? A comparison of the freedom of choice seems even more vacuous, if set A is controlled by decision maker i and opportunity set B is controlled by h.

If the comparison of freedom of choice in A and B is based on decision maker i's individual social preferences, then the *intensity* of liking alternative x_k and disliking alternative x_j should not matter for the ranking of opportunity sets. Individual social preferences resemble judgements over social states; it is assumed that the person does not see herself personally involved, but chooses a third person's perspective. In developed democracies there is ample empirical evidence of how people (for example, socio-economic groups) evaluate alternative social states. If we then assume that the α-mapping expresses the perceptual salience which is reflected in the process of collecting data, then, in principle, a comparison of the freedom of choice related to opportunity sets A and B seems appropriate and feasible. In a way, this is what is actually done when the social status of members of different socio-economic groups are compared with respect to school and university education, employment, number of children and their education/employment, structure and volume of property, and so on (which is a routine operation of social scientists).

One might well argue that it is a small step from the assumption and application of individual social preferences to assigning social values to the elements of the alternative opportunity sets. Here, I will not dive into the discussion of what social values are and where they come from. Indeed, I will simply borrow Binmore's idea of empathy equilibrium in order to illustrate the application of social values to freedom of choice and the specification of the α-mapping. Binmore (1994, 1998a)[6] proposed a theory of justice in morality that is described as a means of co-ordination:

> Just as it is actually within our power to move a bishop like a knight when playing Chess, so we can steal, defraud, break promises, tell lies, jump lines, talk too much, or eat peas with our knives when playing a morality game. But rational folk choose not to cheat for much the same reason that they obey traffic signals. (1998a, p. 6)

Here morality reflects social values and, of course, co-ordination works only if these values are widely shared. Binmore assumes an evolutionary process by which the empathetic preferences[7] of the members of the society converge to common ratios which express the social 'worth'.[8] However, if there is a common ratio which allows one to compare the worth or well-being of different individuals, then it should be possible to assign 'widely shared' values to alternative social states which can be thought of as being the result of evolutionary evaluation process. This is the case if individuals with deviating evaluations of social states will be alienated and perhaps become socially isolated. In the end, such individuals will revise their value system if they suffer too much, or they or their behaviours will socially 'die out'.

There could be a lot of 'trading on false prices' before society achieves an evolution equilibrium, or even comes near to it. More likely, however, evolution will result in a polymorphical society with subgroups of members that share common values. These values can also be said to characterize the different subgroups in a society. As a result, for a coalition S the opportunity set A could express a higher degree of freedom (of choice) than the opportunity set B while to the disjoint coalition T the opposite evaluation applies. If, however, S and T are not disjoint, what values apply to the members in the intersection? And what attitudes will members of S and T, who are outside the intersection, develop towards the intersection members?

Without S and T being disjoint sets it might be difficult to assume evaluation equilibria which allow for comparing freedom of choice. Sen's Liberal Paradox sheds light on the problem which may result if individual preferences on subsets of X form part of the social preferences on the elements of X. Either transitivity of social preferences or Pareto optimality has to be sacrificed in some social situations when we apply Sen's notion of liberalism. The following standard example illustrates this problem (see Sen, 1983). The decision is on whether to read *Lady Chatterley's Lover*, a book which, at the time, was considered as pornography. There are two decision makers: Prude and Lewd. Prude considers the book to be 'bad' whereas Lewd is keen on the book. The preferences are:

Prude	Lewd
o	*b*
p	*p*
l	*l*
b	*o*

That is, there are four possible outcomes considered: *o* says that neither reads the book; *p* means Prude alone reads the book; *l* means Lewd alone reads the book; and *b* implies both read the book. Perhaps it seems to be strange that Lewd prefers *p* to *l*, however, Lewd might think that the book could have a better effect on Prude. In any case, we cannot exclude the listed preferences from the list of possible preferences, especially if we do not want to unduly restrict the domain of the social evaluation which derives from them.

Now, how should the society decide on these four alternatives? Sen (1983) proposes to test how liberalism can answer this question such that individual liberty implies some power of the respective individual to determine social judgements or social decisions over his or her personal sphere: if two social states x and y are different only by the colour of agent i's shirt and i prefers x to y then the state x is socially preferred to y. Liberty, in this case, can be interpreted to require that agent i shall have the power to determine the choice between x and y in line with his or her preferences. An individual i's *personal sphere* contains some choices that directly affect the way i lives, but does not directly affect others, and if others are affected at all they are affected only because of their attitudes towards the personal lives of those who are directly affected.

Sen weakens this condition by introducing the concept of minimal liberty (ML) which presupposes 'at least two persons each having non-empty personal sphere over which they respectively have such powers' (Sen, 1983: 208). Of course, one could ask 'which powers' but power is not actually the issue here. It seems more important to clarify the private spheres of the decision makers. It could be argued that Prude's and Lewd's private spheres are characterized by the decision between p and o and l and o, respectively. Here the assumption is that nobody can be forced to read the book but society may decide to prevent the reading of the book.

If Prude should decide on p and o then o should be judged to be socially preferred to p. We express these preferences by $o>p$. If Lewd should decide on l and o, then l should be put over o. We write $l>o$, to express Lewd's preferences. An application of the Pareto criterion tells us that p should be socially preferred to l, that is, $p>l$. Assuming ML, then we have the social preferences $o>p> l>o$ which form a cycle. Thus, there is no consistent social ranking under the given assumptions, that is, a social preference ordering cannot be derived if ML and Pareto optimality are postulated.

The generalization of this result is called the Liberal Paradox or, with reference to Arrow's Impossibility Theorem, the Impossibility of a Paretian Liberal.[9] Note this theorem does not say that there is always a conflict between Pareto optimality and liberalism. If a society is rather homogeneous then the liberalism as described above can work: assume that two individuals, both having Prude's preferences, decide on the three alternatives o, p and b. (Note there is no l to rank.) The ordering is the well-determined and o will be the Pareto optimal outcome.

Is there a convergence of individual preferences to a common ranking? This is quite a different problem to Binmore's evolution of an evaluation equilibrium as the latter refers to empathetic preferences.[10] Who is responsible for an inefficient outcome? Liberalism, the designers of a liberal constitution, or the decision makers who contribute divergent preferences? If we relate responsibility to power, then the latter's preferences are the source of the problem. Then a social preference order does not exist which allows one to rank every pair of states with respect to their 'value' for the society. This outcome concurs with the case of two different α-mapping when inclusion does not work: then there is no guarantee that we can compare two opportunity sets by applying the R_α relationship.

Instead of hoping for an evolutionary convergence of the individual values to an evaluation equilibrium *à la* Binmore, society could rely on a deliberation process which supports a measure for freedom of choice. Sudgen (1998: 323) argues: 'It is a mistake . . . to try to base a measure of opportunity on an individual's *actual* preferences. To make sense of the concept of opportunity, we need to consider potential preferences – the range of preferences that the individual might have had in the relevant circumstances.'[11] This is not because we do not know the preferences, but because the measurement of freedom of choice implies an evaluation of an opportunity and not of a particular state. Opportunities are counterfactual inasmuch as they constitute a potential but not an actual situation. Therefore, Sudgen argues, the preferences that we apply for the evaluation of these opportunities have to be counterfactual as well. This justifies the application of potential preferences to evaluate opportunity sets.

In the light of potential preferences, the 'opportunity of autonomy' of Prude increases when the book is available, although, in the light of any actual preferences, Prude would be more happy about 'no book' than 'read the book'. However, for this kind of happiness the alternative 'no book' has to be in his (and Lewd's) opportunity set. Moreover, it would be peculiar if the responsibility of a decision maker depends on any actual preferences like 'I did not want to break the law'. But how to specify potential preferences? Sudgen (1998: 324) admits that 'there seems to be no way of avoiding appeal to contestable ideas of "normal", "reasonable" or "natural" preferences'. This, however, presupposes a value consensus or process which brings about agreement within the society on what the values are. This agreement might be easier to find if we talk about opportunities than about available alternatives. It might be easier to agree on the distribution of a million euros among your friends and relatives that you might win in a lottery 'some day' than to distribute the million which the deceased has actually given to you and your relatives.

To conclude, it is more likely that we agree on potential preferences, to apply to opportunities, than on a social welfare function which evaluates actual alternatives. But this still does not say that potential preferences are available whenever we have to compare opportunity sets. There will be periods in which there will be a consensus in a society on what are 'normal', 'reasonable' or 'natural' and periods when such a consensus does not exist. Of course, this also depends on what we consider the relevant society. Even if we have solved this problem we still have to decide whether we consider the preferences over the elements of opportunity sets or over the opportunity sets themselves.

THE POWER OF MAKING DECISIONS

One way to get rid of the preference problem is to link freedom of choice with power (and from this we will arrive at 'responsibility'). In the second section, we introduced the concept of freedom of choice for a given set of alternatives X and the corresponding set of opportunity sets Z. There was neither reference made to the agents who control the alternative opportunity sets nor was there any discussion of the institutional setting which substantiates control. For instance, is the freedom of choice of an individual i determined by the set of alternatives, A, which i can guarantee himself 'despite resistance' or by the participation in powerful alliances (winning coalitions) with other members of the society? Is A an opportunity set, that is, a potential, or a set of alternatives which i can consume? Can a powerful coalition S choose a particular subset of X as outcome or is its capacity constrained to the selection of an opportunity set, that is, an element of Z, which describes the freedom of choice of the members of S?

To clarify some of these problems, I suggest the following thought experiment. We describe a social choice situation ν by its set of agents (players) $N=\{1,2,3,4,5\}$, its set of minimum winning coalitions (MWC): $M(\nu)=\{\{1,2\},\{1,3,4\},\{1,3,5\},\{1,4,5\},\{2,3,4,5\}\}$, and a set of alternatives X. $M(\nu)$ gives a full description of the coalitions which have the power to decide in the given society: any superset of the elements in $M(\nu)$ will be a winning coalition, however, a true superset S' will contain at least one surplus player, that is, a player who is not relevant for the coalition S' to accomplish its aim.[12]

Let us assume that a winning coalition has the power to pick a specific element of X. Further, let us assume that x' is the element which coalition $\{1,2\}$ will pick if it forms. Should we expect that $\{1,2,4\}$ will pick an element y' although, by the definition of $M(\nu)$, player 4 is a surplus player? If $\{1,2,4\}$ has the power to pick y', then, of course, $\{1,2\}$ has also the power to pick y'. However, if $\{1,2\}$ decides to pick x' instead then y' and the coalition $\{1,2,4\}$ are irrelevant alternatives. Correspondingly, we call the coalitions in $M(\nu)$ decisive sets.

If we assume that each decisive set picks (or can pick) a different alternative x in X, then i's membership in decisive sets seems to be a 'reasonable' proxy for i's freedom of choice. For example, player 1 is member of four and player 2 is member of two decisive sets. Is it appropriate to conclude that freedom of choice of player 1 is two times 'larger' than the freedom of choice of player 2?

Note, however, that there is no member of N who is in every coalition in $M(\nu)$. Thus, it could well be that a winning coalition forms and player 1 is not part of it. Only after a winning coalition formed can a member have control of the outcome (if the member is not a surplus player). Thus the counting of membership in decisive sets only expresses a potential freedom of choice.

So far a winning coalition implied that it can pick any element of X. Thus X is not only the set of alternatives it is as well the opportunity set for winning coalitions. This specification is due to the voting game interpretation of $M(v)$. However, we could assign to each coalition S in $M(v)$ a different subset of X that describes the opportunities of S, thus S picking not an element of X but an opportunity set. If we are serious about the notion of winning coalition then each S in $M(v)$ can choose every element of Z, and measuring freedom of choice reduces to the question of whether i is a member of the winning coalition or not. However, the potential of being a member of a winning coalition which is a decisive set is captured by $M(v)$. Thus, we are back to counting the decisive sets in which player i is a member.

To illustrate the social decision situation v underlying this counting, we assume that it can be represented by a weighted voting game $v = (d, w)$ with decision rule $d = 51$ and a vector of weights $w = (w_i) = (w_1, w_2, w_3, w_4, w_5) = (35, 20, 15, 15, 15)$ such that $w_1 = 35$ is the voting weight of player 1. The set of minimal winning coalitions of this weighted voting game is $M(v) = \{\{1,2\}, \{1,3,4\}, \{1,3,5\}, \{1,4,5\}, \{2,3,4,5\}\}$. Thus, $v = (d, w)$ specifies the decision situation which we discussed. An interpretation of the minimal winning coalitions as decisive sets (deciding on the selection of x out of X) and counting of memberships gives the following vector of decisiveness of game v: $c(v) = (c_1, c_2, c_3, c_4, c_5) = (4,2,3,3,3)$. If we normalize these values by dividing them by $\Sigma c_i = 15$ we get $h(v) = (4/15, 2/15, 3/15, 3/15, 3/15)$.

Vector $h(v)$ is identical with the Public Good Index (PGI) of the weighted voting game $v = (d, w)$. Obviously, the index $h(v)$ is nonmonotonic in voting weights (for example, seats in a parliament), that is, it violates *Local Monotonicity* which says that for every two voters i and j the power values π_i and π_j satisfy $\pi_i \geq \pi_j$ if $w_i > w_j$. This fact has been widely discussed.[13] If we accept this result then we have to admit that voting weights are a poor proxy for voting power and thus for responsibility if we argue that responsibility concurs with the decision makers' potential to determine the outcome.

PERSONAL VERSUS SOCIAL RESPONSIBILITY

What looks like adding up of individual responsibility, when we apply the Public Good Index to express social responsibility, turns out to be of rather different quality: social responsibility is (just like power) a potential while individual responsibility derives from choices. In other words, social responsibility is dispositional while individual responsibility is episodic.[14] An agent i is socially responsible for a social outcome because i has power and thus a potential impact on the social outcome. An agent i is individually responsible for an outcome because i has decided to act (or not to act) and this decision, together with possible decisions of other agents, determined the social outcome. Social responsibility does not assume a decision (or presuppose an action).

There are (at least) two interpretations for the PGI which seem of relevance for the responsibility interpretation:

1. Each MWC stands for winning a majority and thus for the determination of the social outcome. This is about demand for public goods.
2. Each MWC represents a different public good. This is about the supply side of public goods.

What are the consequences that follow from these interpretations with respect to responsibility? There is a notion of responsibility which derives an obligation from the potential to act. This ties responsibility to power and freedom of choice.

If we equate i's responsibility with power and power with freedom of choice, then i has full responsibility only if i is a dictator. If X is i's opportunity set then i can choose any element x to be the outcome. X represents a maximum of freedom of choice. However, is X a given set? If we argue that each MWC represents a different public good then a dictatorial social decision situation (that is, a dictatorship) has a minimum set of alternatives: a dictatorial social decision situation is fully characterized by the single MWC {i} where i is the dictator. In fact, real-life dictatorships seem to suffer from a reduced set of alternatives. Often dictators try to form coalitions to enrich their set of alternatives. In principle, this implies that they have to give up some power. This effect has been analysed by North and Weingast (1989) in their account of the Glorious Revolution in England. 'The Glorious Revolution made it possible for the English King to obtain loans as the English parliament controlled the purse and therefore could make the King's promise to repay credible.' Wintrobe (2004: 188) concludes: 'No such revolution had occurred in France.' He argues: 'One interpretation of this "Irony of Absolutism" is that the fewer constraints on the King's power, the less power he may actually have.'

> By giving up power [Louis XVI] hoped to gain revenue in the same way that the English King had. However, a bandwagon effect developed, possibly due to the constitutional crisis and the economic crisis, amplified by the uncertainties about which direction the regime was moving, and opposition to the regime snowballed. (Wintrobe, 2004, p. 191f)

And in the end the French King lost his royal head. This way he was 'made' responsible.

As social power and individual power coincide, responsibility seems obvious in a dictatorship, while in a non-dictatorial situation the equating of responsibility and power, and power and freedom of choice raises a series of questions. In the voting game (d,w) above, is player 1 responsible for the outcome x' if coalition {2,3,4,5} forms and picks an outcome x' from X? It might be difficult to assign personal responsibility to this player, however, one could argue that player 1 has a social responsibility which derives from his power. A power value of 4/15 (as measured by PGI) says that, in principle, player 1 had a relatively high potential to influence the social outcome. If the potential to influence the outcome does not show in its realization then player 1 failed to exert power – which does not, however, set him free from responsibility. We could call this social responsibility while personal responsibility holds for the dictator i or the members of the winning coalition {2,3,4,5}. Note that even when coalition {2,3,4,5} forms, the responsibility of player 1 in the voting game (d,w) is different from the responsibility of the dummy players in the dictator game in which i holds all the power and thus full personal and social responsibility. A dummy player is not a member of a coalition in $M(v)$ and thus has no power and therefore has no responsibility if we follow the principle: a player with no power has no responsibility. On the other hand, it is obvious from the set $M(v)$ that player 1 had the potential to offer members of coalition {2,3,4,5} to form a coalition with him/her. This defines player 1's power and social responsibility.

There could be more or less social responsibility in a society – a fact that does not show in the PGI because of its normalization. Haradau and Napel (2005) demonstrate that the nonnormalized version of the PGI,[15] introduced in Holler and Li (1995), admits a potential as defined in Hart and Mas-Colell (1988, 1989).[16] They prove that:

$$P^{\mathbf{h}^0}(N, v) = \sum_{S \in M(v)} v(S) \tag{2.3}$$

Here $P^{\mathbf{h}^0}(N, v)$ expresses the potential of the nonnormalized PGI. Therefore the value of the nonnormalized PGI for player i, $\mathbf{h}_i^0$, satisfies

$$\mathbf{h}_i^0 = P^{\mathbf{h}^0}(N, v) - P^{\mathbf{h}^0}(N \backslash \{i\}, v) \tag{2.4}$$

As Hart and Mas-Colell prove that the Shapley value is the unique value which is efficient *and* admits a potential, it is immediate that the normalized form of the PGI (the Holler-Packel index) does not admit a potential – because it is efficient.[17]

For simple games and, more specially, weighted voting games we have $v(S) = 1$ if S is a winning coalition. Thus the potential $P^{\mathbf{h}^0}(N, v)$ simply equals the number of minimum winning coalitions of the game. This is different from summing up decisiveness, that is, the measure Σc_i. The potential gives equal weight to each MWC, whereas in Σc_i the representation of an MWC is proportional to the cardinality of its members. If we assume that each MWC produces a different public good then it seems more plausible to take the potential as a measure of overall power than to suggest Σc_i: the potential $P^{h^0}(N, v)$ is a proxy for the set of alternative outcomes which are 'in the game'. However, one might argue that Σc_i summarizes the possible participation in the production of public goods, inasmuch as participation is crucial,[18] and thus captures responsibility.[19]

The concept of responsibility and its relationship with power suggests a further argument why to consider MWCs, that is, the set $M(v)$, when measuring power. For example, in the above weighted voting game (d, w): why should player 3 be held responsible for the outcome x' which has been decided by the coalition {1,2,3}? Note that {1,2} is in $M(v)$ and 3 is a surplus player. Another question is whether the responsibility of {1,2} increases when player 3 joins 1 and 2 to form coalition {1,2,3}. A possible answer is as follows: given outcome x' determined by {1,2} is a public good (or a good of substantial external effects), player 3 will suffer or benefit from x' irrespective of whether x' has been decided by {1,2,3} or {1,2}.

In the light of this argument we may rethink why we consider minimum winning coalitions only. Let us assume that v is a simple game. If the players in a winning coalition S consider the value $v(S) = 1$ as a public good there should be no rivalry in consumption and each member of S will enjoy this value if coalition S is formed. Further, if there are no entry costs or transaction costs of coalition formation, S will be formed – given that S is a coalition in $M(v)$ and therefore S does not contain a surplus player j who can benefit from S without supporting this coalition. However, if T forms which has the winning coalition S as a true subset, then this is by luck,[20] and not because of the power of its members. Coalition T allows at least one member to leave the coalition without risking a different outcome. (Of course, free-riding is more likely if members of T have to pay contributions and membership becomes costly.)

This was about winning or losing. If, however, we assume that each MWC represents a different public good then there are opportunity costs to player 1 if he joins with player 2 to form the MWC {1,2}: player 1 cannot simultaneously form the MWC {1,3,4} which 'produces' a public good which differs from the public good related to {1,2}.

Thus, if we list both coalitions {1,2} and {1,3,4} in $M(v)$, then this expresses a potential or a capacity. As preferences are considered irrelevant for measuring power (see Braham and Holler, 2005a, 2005b), the operation of measuring power basically boils down to counting the non-weighted elements in set $M(\nu)$ and assigning them to those who have to give their support in case a specific element has to be put into reality. The relationship to counting relation $R_{\#}$, discussed above, seems obvious. However, when it comes to power we refer to the agents. To implement a particular α-ordering we could think of a corresponding weighting of the players, for example, to increase the power of player i and thus to increase the chance that the outcome will concur with i's (unspecified) preferences. In some cases, a revision of the decision rule could be sufficient to erase a particular coalition from $M(\nu)$ and thus redistribute power.

RESPONSIBILITY AND GUILT

One might argue that the 'power to' relation captured by power indices is not adequate to be related with the freedom of choice concept, discussed in the second section. It seems that the 'power to' does not necessarily imply that i can exercise power and constrain the opportunity set of j. It does not imply that i has 'power over' j.

According to Kristjansson (1992: 134), the extensions of 'exercising power over' and 'constraining freedom' are best seen as coinciding.[21] He claims that 'the expression "exercising power over" is the most basic one when dealing with power as a social relation (but not as ability to do things in general)' (p. 136): 'we exercise power over somebody when we constrain his freedom, and vice versa' (p. 137). Both 'exercising power over' and 'constraining freedom' are exercise-concepts while 'having power over' is an opportunity-concept. The latter comes close to the power we measure by the Public Good Index. This power concept, however, does not express the capacity of constraining the freedom of decision makers, but the potential to achieve specific outcomes (that is, public goods). Inasmuch as the realization of these outcomes by a coalition S excludes that alternative outcome being put into reality it constrains the opportunity set of decision makers not in S.

On the other hand, constraining another person's freedom, that is restricting his opportunity set, also implies a 'power to' relation. Kristjansson (1992: 129) concedes that 'if A is to have B's hands tied up, he must be able to tie them up himself or have the authority and the means of communication to order someone else to do it'. This relates his responsibility view of (negative) freedom, based on 'power over', to the 'power to' concept as operationalized by the Public Good Index. Yet, how the responsibility view of freedom can be linked to moral responsibility is not straightforward. We can hope that a further discussion of this relationship will clarify who is responsible for Auschwitz and what responsibility we share. Who is 'we' and who are the surplus and dummy players in this game?

There is of course a well-developed discussion of collective responsibility and collective guilt, especially in the context of Nazi German history. In order to derive a measure of responsibility, Zvie Bar-on (1991) discusses Karl Jasper's four categories of guilt:

- *criminal guilt* which corresponds to our individual responsibility and derives from action;
- *political guilt* which follows from the conclusion that 'every citizen of a modern state is responsible for the action of its government and administration, unless he speaks and acts openly against them' (Zvie Bar-on, 1991: 265);
- *moral guilt* which is based on 'all those actions and defaults of the German citizen which implied his support of the criminal regime, whatever the reasons, sincerely, and effectiveness of his support' (Zvie Bar-on, 1991: 266);
- *metaphysical guilt* which derives from 'the solidarity among men as human beings that makes each co-responsible for every wrong and every injustice in the world, especially for crimes committed in his presence or with his knowledge. If I fail to do whatever I can to prevent them, I too am guilty' (Karl Jaspers quoted in Zvie Bar-on, 1991: 266). Obviously, metaphysical guilt does not presuppose power; if guilt derives from responsibility then it postulates responsibility without power.

Zvie Bar-on (1991: 270) concludes that 'the overall result of Jaspers' argument is unequivocal: every German who lived in Germany during the Nazi rule and did not actively oppose the regime, bears responsibility for the lot of the victims of that regime'. When it comes to metaphysical guilt and perhaps even the case of moral guilt, it is however not obvious why responsibility should be reserved for 'every German who lived in Germany during the Nazi rule'. Moreover, why should political guilt be limited to citizens who perhaps even suffer from the dictatorship of their government, and not include those persons and institutions who support or tolerate this state from outside?

In an article, first published in 1945, Hannah Arendt (1991[1945]) writes: 'the idea of humanity, when purged of all sentimentality, has the very serious consequence that in one form or another men must assume responsibility for all crimes committed by men and that all nations share the onus of evil committed by all others. Shame at being a human is the purely individual and still non-political expression of this insight'. In fact, when I first saw the Abu Ghraib pictures, the Hooded Man and the Leashed Man, I felt shame, irrespective of the fact that the German government was explicit in not supporting the US war in Iraq. Does shame follow guilt? Obviously, Jaspers' concept of political guilt shifts responsibility also to those citizens who suffer from their state. A recourse to power and its relationship to responsibility could help to clarify some of these questions in the future. For example, the power analysis suggests that the political parties which hold some power in the 1933 Reichstag, whether they colluded with the NSDAP or whether they rejected the idea of forming a coalition without this party, are, at least to some degree, responsible for what followed. Of course, it might be difficult to assign 'guilt' to political parties, but they have power and we can assign responsibility to them. Hitler's NSDAP had no absolute majority in the German Reichstag when he became Reichskanzler and head of a coalition in 1933. Obviously, there were other majority coalitions possible in 1932 and 1933, and parties which had power in this very Reichstag have to admit responsibility for what happened then. One could argue that they valued their political ideologies and targets higher than their responsibility to prevent the rise of Hitler and his regime.

Here we speak of political power, but we may well argue that purchasing power can also be the basis of responsibility. Not only is the potential of the rich to influence the outcome of markets and politics more substantial than the potential of the poor, voting by feet becomes a more realistic alternative: the past and the present show that, in general, rich people are more welcome than poor ones. We should not ignore this freedom of choice when we try to measure responsibility.

ACKNOWLEDGEMENTS

The author presented joint work with Sebastiano Bavetta on the relationship of power and the freedom of choice at the European Public Choice Conference at Paris, April 2001. He would like to thank Matthew Braham and the participants of the Bergamo Seminar for helpful comments.

NOTES

1. See Braham and Holler (2005a, 2005b) and Napel and Widgrén (2004, 2005) for a recent discussion on power and preferences.
2. The Constitutional Court of Germany.
3. This parallels the range of application of similar results which derive for effectivity functions with respect to inclusion rankings. (See Vannucci, 2002.)
4. See Harsanyi (1955) for individual private preferences and individual social preferences.
5. For an application of perception to alternatives in opportunity sets, see Ahlert (2005).
6. See Holler and Napel (2001, 2003) for an interpretation of Binmore's Theory of Justice.

7. In Binmore (1994, 1998a) empathetic preferences are individual i's evaluations with respect to individuals j and k, that is, the measure by which i compares the well-being of j to the well-being of k. Individual i is assumed not be emotional involved with respect to j and k and thus in the role of an impartial spectator.
8. The evolutionary empathy equilibrium in Binmore (1994, 1998a), expressed by the ratio U/V, gives a possible underpinning to the social worth parameters, w_A and w_B, in Binmore (1998b).
9. For an early critical, but widely ignored comment, see Hillinger and Lapham (1971).
10. Is it really a different problem? Sen says himself that certain types of ethical thinking are the 'solution'.
11. See also Jones and Sudgen (1982) for this approach.
12. Note that the power set of N has 2^n elements, that is, winning and losing coalitions.
13. For a summary of this discussion, see Holler and Napel (2004a, 2004b). For the given game, the violation of Local Monotonicity follows from the fact that the game is not decisive (it is improper): the complement of a losing coalition is not always a winning coalition. The PGI indicates this problem while more popular power measures such as the Shapley-Shubik index or the Banzhaf index satisfy Local Monotonicity and thus do not show any particularity if the game is not decisive.
14. Kristjansson (1992: 130) argues that the locution 'having power over' . . . 'tends to denote relations of a *dispositional*, rather than *episodic*, nature'.
15. Haradau and Napel (2005) use the name of Holler-Packel index for PGI.
16. 'A potential function summarizes a game by one real number. A player i's power or expected payoff in a game (as identified by some index or value with a potential) is simply the difference between this number and the corresponding number of the reduced game in which only players $j \neq i$ participate.' (Haradau and Napel, 2005: 1). This is how, recursively, the potential of a power measure with respect to a specific game v can be calculated.
17. That is, its values $h_i(v)$ sum up to $v(N)$ with $v(N) = 1$.
18. 'Crucial ' here refers to the membership in a MWC where participation is necessary and sufficient.
19. One might argue that $P^{h^0}(N, v)$ represents the demand side and Σc_i represents the possibility to produce public goods in a particular game (N, v).
20. This refers to Barry's question 'Is it better to be powerful or lucky?' (Barry, 1980).
21. 'A exercises power over B if and only if A is morally responsible for the creation or non-removal of an obstacle O that restricts B's options – and hence that the extensions of "constraining B's freedom" and "exercising power over B" are to be seen coinciding. This defines power as a *relation* and not as a *capacity*. It is "power over" and not "power to" ' (Kristjansson, 1992: 128).

REFERENCES

Ahlert, M. (2005), 'A new approach to procedural freedom of game forms', paper presented at the colloquium on 'Freedom: Philosophical and Economic Aspects', University of Bayreuth, 10 February.

Arendt, H. (1991[1945]), 'Organized guilt and universal responsibility', in L. May and S. Hoffman (eds), *Collective Responsibility: Five Decades of Debate in Theoretical and Applied Ethics*, Savage, MD: Rowman & Littlefield.

Barry, B. (1980), 'Is it better to be powerful or lucky: part I and part II', *Political Studies*, **28**, 183–94 and 338–52.

Binmore, K. (1994), *Playing Fair, Game Theory and the Social Contract, Volume I*, Cambridge, MA and London: The MIT Press.

Binmore, K. (1998a), *Just Playing, Game Theory and the Social Contract, Volume II*, Cambridge, MA and London: The MIT Press.

Binmore, K. (1998b), 'The evolution of fairness norms', *Rationality and Society*, **10**, 275–301.
Braham, M. and M. J. Holler (2005a), 'The impossibility of a preference-based power index', *Journal of Theoretical Politics*, **17**, 137–57.
Braham, M. and M. J. Holler (2005b), 'Power and preferences again: a reply to Napel and Widgrén', *Journal of Theoretical Politics*, **17**, 389–95.
Dewey, J. (1979 [1938]), *Experience & Education*, New York: Collier Books.
Felsenthal, D. and M. Machover (1995), 'Postulates and paradoxes of relative voting power – a critical appraisal', *Theory and Decision*, **38**, 195–229.
Felsenthal, D. and M. Machover (1998), *The Measurement of Voting Power. Theory and Practice, Problems and Paradoxes*, Cheltenham, UK and Lyme, US: Edward Elgar.
Haradau, R. and S. Napel (2005), 'Holler-Packel value and index – a new characterization', *Beiträge der Wirtschaftsforschung*, no. 140, Institute of SocioEconomics, University of Hamburg.
Harsanyi, J. C. (1955), 'Cardinal welfare, individualistic ethics, and the interpersonal comparison of utility', *Journal of Political Economy*, **63**, 309–21.
Hart, S. and A. Mas-Colell (1988), 'The potential of the Shapley value', in A. E. Roth (ed.), *The Shapley Value: Essays in Honor of Lloyd S. Shapley*, Cambridge, MA: Cambridge University Press, pp. 127–37.
Hart, S. and A. Mas-Colell (1989), 'Potential, value, and consistency', *Econometrica*, **57**, 589–614.
Hillinger, C. and V. Lapham (1971), 'The impossibility of a Paretian liberal: comment by two who are unreconstructed', *Journal of Political Economy*, **79**, 1403–5.
Holler, M. J. (1982), 'Forming coalitions and measuring voting power', *Political Studies*, **30**, 262–71.
Holler, M. J. (1984), 'The public good index', in M. J. Holler (ed.), *Coalitions and Collective Action*, Würzburg and Vienna: Physica-Verlag.
Holler, M. J. and X. Li (1995), 'From public good index to public value: an axiomatic approach and generalization', *Control and Cybernetics*, **24**, 257–70.
Holler, M. J. and S. Napel (2001), 'On interpersonal comparison of value', in K. Nevalainen (ed.), *Justice, Charity, and the Welfare State*, Helsinki: Philosophica Fennica, pp. 119–38.
Holler, M. J. and S. Napel (2003), 'A pragmatic interpretation of Ken Binmore's theory of justice', in V. Kanniainen and Matti Sintonen (eds), *Etiika ja Talous*, Helsinki: WSOY, pp. 177–98.
Holler, M. J. and S. Napel (2004a), 'Local monotonicity of power: axiom or just a property', *Quality and Quantity*, **38**, 637–47.
Holler, M. J . and S. Napel (2004b), 'Monotonicity of power and power measures', *Theory and Decision*, **56**, 93–111.
Holler, M. J. and E. W. Packel (1983), 'Power, luck and the right index', *Zeitschrift für Nationalökonomie* (*Journal of Economics*), **43**, 21–9.
Holler, M. J., and M. Widgrén (1999), 'The value of a coalition is power', *Homo Oeconomicus*, **15**, 497–511.
Jones, P. and R. Sudgen (1982), 'Evaluating choice', *International Review of Law and Economics*, **2**, 47–65.
Klemisch-Ahlert, M. (1993), 'Freedom of choice: a comparison of different rankings of opportunity sets', *Social Choice and Welfare*, **10**, 189–207.
Kristjansson, K. (1992a), ' "Constraining freedom" and "exercising power over" ', *International Journal of Moral and Social Studies*, **7**, 127–38.

Napel, S. (1999), 'The Holler-Packel axiomatization of the public good index completed', *Homo Oeconomicus*, **15**, 513–21.
Napel, S. and M. Widgrén (2004), 'Power measurement as sensitivity analysis – a unified approach', *Journal of Theoretical Politics*, **16,** 517–38.
Napel, S. and M. Widgrén (2005), 'The possibility of a preference-based power index', *Journal of Theoretical Politics*, **17**, 377–87.
North, D. and B. Weingast (1989), 'Constitutions and commitment: the evolution of institutions governing public choice in seventeenth century England', *Journal of Economic History*, **49**, 808–32.
Pattanaik, P. K. and Y. Xu (1990), 'On ranking opportunity sets in terms of freedom of choice', *Recherches Economiques de Louvain*, **56**, 383–90.
Pattanaik, P. K. and Y. Xu (1998), 'On preferences and freedom', *Theory and Decision*, **44**, 173–98.
Sen, A. K. (1970), 'The impossibility of a Paretian liberal', *Journal of Political Economy*, **78**, 152–7.
Sen, A. K. (1983), 'Liberty as control: an appraisal', *Mid-West Studies in Philosophy*, **7**, 207–21.
Sen, A. K. (1988), 'Freedom of choice: concept and content', *European Economic Review*, **32**, 269–94.
Sen, A. K. (1991), 'Welfare, preference and freedom', *Journal of Econometrics*, **50**, 15–29.
Sudgen, R. (1998), 'The metric of opportunity', *Economics and Philosophy*, **14**, 307–37.
Vannucci, S. (2002), 'Effectivity functions, opportunity rankings, and generalized desirability relations', *Homo Oeconomicus*, **19**, 451–67.
Weber, M. (1947), *The Theory of Social and Economic Organization*, T. Parsons (ed.), New York: Free Press.
Wintrobe, R. (2004), 'Rational revolution', in M. Ferrero (ed.), *The Rationale of Revolutions* (*Homo Oeconomicus 21*), Munich: Accedo Verlag, pp. 171–96.
Zvie Bar-on, A. (1991[1985]), 'Measuring responsibility', in L. May and S. Hoffman (eds), *Collective Responsibility: Five Decades of Debate in Theoretical and Applied Ethics*, Savage, MD: Rowman & Littlefield.

APPENDIX: AXIOMATIZATION OF THE PUBLIC GOOD INDEX

An axiomatization of the Public Good Index (PGI) is given in Holler and Packel (1993) and 'completed' in Napel (1999).

First, we define a simple game such that $v(S)=1$ if S is a winning coalition and $v(S)=0$ if S is losing. S is a subset of the set of players N. The set strict minimum winning coalitions (that is, decisive sets) is given by:

$$M(v)=\{S \subseteq N | v(S) = 1 \text{ and } v(T) = 0 \text{ if } T \subset S \text{ and } T \neq S\} \quad (2.A1)$$

Note that for any coalition $R \subseteq N$ such that $v(R)=1$ and $R \notin M(v)$, there exists a coalition $S \in M(v)$ such that $S \subset R$, that is, T can be contracted into a $S \in M(v)$.

Definition 2.A1: Let $c_i(v)$ the number of coalitions S such that $S \in M(v)$ and $i \in S$ in the simple game (N,v), that is, $c_i(v)$ expresses the decisiveness of player i in the simple game (N,v). Then

$$\mathbf{h}_i(v) = \frac{c_i}{\sum_{i=1}^{n} c_i} \text{ so that } \sum_{i=1}^{n} \mathbf{h}_i(v) = 1 \quad (2.A2)$$

defines the value of the *Public Good Index.*[1]

The axiomatization of this measure refers to the sum and mergeability of simple games.

Definition 2.A2: The sum of two simple games u and v, expressed as $u \oplus v$, is defined such that

$$\text{for any } S \subseteq N, \text{ we have } (u \oplus v)(S) = \begin{cases} 1 \text{ if } u(S) = 1 \text{ or } v(S) = 1 \\ 0 \text{ otherwise} \end{cases}$$

Definition 2.A3: Two simple games u and v are mergeable if, for any two coalitions S_1 and S_2, $S_1 \in M(u)$ and $S_2 \in M(v)$ implies $S_1 \not\subset S_2$, $S_2 \not\subset S_1$, $S_1 \neq S_2$, that is, $M(u) \cap M(v) = \emptyset$.

That is, u and v are mergeable if each strict minimum winning coalition (MWC) related to one of the two games contributes to the game $u \oplus v$ inasmuch as it supports a winning coalition in the sum game which would otherwise not exist for this game. In other words, u and v are mergeable if the MWCs related to individual games u and v are also MWCs for the sum game $u \oplus v$.

Remark: It is easy to see that if u and v are mergeable then $c_i(u \oplus v) = c_i(u) + c_i(v)$ where $c_i(u)$ and $c_i(v)$ are the numbers of MWCs containing i in $M(u)$ and $M(v)$, respectively.
Now we can give the Holler-Packel axioms which define the Public Good Index.

Definition 2.A4: Let the index h be a map from the collection of all n-person simple games to the n-dimensional Euclidean space $\Re^n$. Then h is the PGI if it satisfies the following four axioms:

HP1: If i is an excess player, then $h_i(v) = 0$.
HP2: $\sum_{i=1}^{n} h_i(v) = 1$.
HP3: If π is a permutation, then $h_{\pi(i)}(\pi v) = h_i(v)$. Here πv is the game defined by $\pi v(S) = v(\pi(S))$ for all $S \subseteq N$.
HP4: If u and v are mergeable, then for any $i \in N$ we have
$h_i(u \oplus v) = [c(u)\, h_i(u) + c(v)\, h_i(v)]/[c(u) + c(v)]$
where $c(u) = \sum_{i=1}^{n} c_i(u)$ and $c(v) = \sum_{i=1}^{n} c_i(v)$.

Discussion of axioms: HP1 says that players who are not members of an MWC have no power. HP2 normalizes the PGI. Consequently, $h_i(v)$ expresses some relative power only. This normalization seems necessary and adequate if we want to compare the values $h_i(v)$ to the values of i which result from other normalized power measures such as the Shapley value, the normalized Banzhaf index and the Deegan-Packel index.[2] However, it complicates the axiomatization of the Public Good Index for general games (see Holler and Li, 1995.) HP3 guarantees that the power measure is independent of the label or name of the player. HP4 looks quite complex and perhaps difficult to justify. Moreover, it causes problems when we try to generalize the Public Good Index from simple games to general games. It seems straightforward to substitute HP2 and HP4 by less restrictive axioms when we apply the Public Good Index to general games.[3]

Theorem: The Public Good Index $h(v)$, defined in Equation 2.A2 is the unique value which satisfies the axioms HP1, HP2, HP3, and HP4. (For the proof, see Holler and Packel, 1983.)

APPENDIX NOTES

1. The *Public Good Index* has been introduced in Holler (1982, 1984) and axiomatized in Holler and Packel (1983).
2. See Felsenthal and Machover (1995, 1998) for these measures.
3. This is the background of the *Public Value*, introduced in Holler and Li (1995). However, there is still a series of open questions related to the application of the *Public Good Index* to general games.

3. Hayek and economic policy (the Austrian road to the Third Way)

Enrico Colombatto

ON HAYEK'S VIEW OF ECONOMIC POLICY

The debate on the scope and moral foundations of economic policy began as soon as economics strived to become something more than just a branch of political philosophy and attempted to acquire its own identity as a social science. By and large, its Founding Fathers characterized this discipline as being concerned with how individuals behave and interact in order to enhance their well-being. This justified the use of the term 'political economy', to emphasize the role of the institutional context within which human action takes place. Towards the end of the eighteenth century prominent authors went further and suggested that political economists should not be confined to the mere description and explanation of human action. Nor should they refrain from recommending how institutions ought to be designed and modified in order to enhance welfare.[1] Adam Smith was of course a leading and effective supporter of this approach,[2] which actually owed much to Galiani and, to a lesser extent, Quesnay.

At the beginning of the nineteenth century Say forcefully advocated the need for a sharper partition between the realms of political economy and of policy, the former referring to the study of human action under given institutional rules; the latter to the rules of the game. He did not exclude the importance of normative economics. Still, this branch was to remain an exercise in simulation, with little or no room for decision-making by the economist. Later on, the same perspective was also typical of Walras and of a number of more recent authors. Lionel Robbins, for instance, understood policy-making to be dependent on moral judgement; and thus unacceptable if economics was conceived as a way of reasoning and an instrument to understand individual or group behaviour. Indeed, he argued that it would make little sense to use a logical tool in order to derive normative prescriptions. In Harry Johnson's words, it would be unreasonable and probably counterproductive (see Mackintosh, 1950; Tyszynski, 1955).

Contrary to Say, Hayek chose not to consider normative economics as a mere exercise in simulation with little practical relevance. At the same time, however, he was also unwilling to accept the technocratic approach based on descriptive, a-theoretical economics and scenarios. Not surprisingly, while trying to find out a suitable compromise between socialist planning and (unconditional) free-market capitalism, he stumbled into a dilemma. On the one hand he could draw on the early foundations of political economy and follow the 'constitutional economics' approach. As made explicit by Buchanan (1979) and, more generally, by most of the public-choice and the ordoliberal schools, since economic action takes place within an institutional framework, the economist should analyse the features of an optimal context, so as to enhance voluntary exchange and widen the choices available to the agents. In other words, economy policy should propose constitutional solutions aimed at reducing transaction costs, while leaving individuals more or less free to adopt or reject such solutions. When the notion of social contract is added – which implies that it exists, that its elements are well specified and that all the members of a community are required to act in accordance with them – this a-moral version of policy-making develops into normative prescriptions for the production of the goods and services described in the social contract.

Another possibility open to Hayek was related to the existence of social norms, informal behavioural patterns that have emerged over long time periods and are generally subject to varying degrees of enforcement. In some cases norms have become ways through which individuals identify their position in society (for example manners). In other cases – and more important for the scope of these pages – they are a means to reduce the cost of cooperation within a community of interacting individuals. In the past informal arrangements were characterized by repeated trial-and-error experiences within relatively close communities. Tradition and customs would thus gradually reveal the nature and stringency of social norms. Surely, little room was left for ambiguity or to the discretion of the would-be policy-maker. If anything, politics was just a synonym for the procedure through which selected individuals were given the power to enforce compliance with the social norms.

Predictably, the conceptual gap separating social norms from policy-making is hard to bridge, even for Hayek. Whereas social norms do reflect an informal social contract originating from repeated voluntary interaction and trial-and-error processes, policy-making at its best is a way to anticipate the results of the social contract that individuals would subscribe to if they had enough time to appreciate its terms.[3] In other words, policy-making at its best is about guessing the terms of the social contract and – in an ideal world – conjecturing about those who would be willing to sign it.

In the end, and for reasons that remain largely unexplained,[4] Hayek opts for a view of economic policy which consists of a set of spontaneous rules supplemented by artificial norms created by government and cleared by 'legislators'.[5] Their purpose is to replicate – or, rather, anticipate – social norms. Although he does not frequently mention it with the clarity that the subject deserves, this argument refers to the so-called 'acceleration of time'.[6] This situation materializes as informal institutions tend to come to the surface only gradually, so that their evaluation through a trial-and-error process becomes too slow to be of significant use, especially when the features of the problems to be solved through individual interactions change rapidly. Under such circumstances, timely top-down rule making (policy-making) can be desirable and replaces slow bottom-up rules. Hence, the Hayekian enriched version of constitutional economics does not preclude freedom to choose, but admits coercion when geared to reproducing a social contract that the acceleration of time makes hard to perceive.

By and large, this defines Hayek's project for a liberal society, away from *laissez-faire* and – in his view – strong enough to resist socialist attacks. And also explains why from the end of the 1930s Hayek tried to find ways to replicate/anticipate a plausible social contract, and then to justify it without using constructivism. The pages that follow examine these efforts in some detail and conclude that the results attained are far from persuasive. Economic policy always requires the definition of the shared goals and priorities, of the tools to be employed and of the policy-maker in charge of implementation. Unfortunately, Hayek's work remains somewhat wanting on the legitimacy of both the instruments and the actors; and thus ambiguous. If so 'he has no complete theory of the social order to back up his liberal recommendations', which contributes to making 'modern liberalism vulnerable to erosion and invasion by incompatible elements' (De Jasay, 1996: 107).

HAYEK'S VIEWS ON POLICY ACTION

Consistent with the Austrian tradition, Hayek deals with economic policy as a social philosopher, rather than as an economic technocrat or a political theorist. In particular, he focuses on the aims of policy-making in a society where human dignity and thus liberty are supposed to be the primary moral components, and proposes to 'design the most rational permanent framework within which the various activities would be conducted by different persons according to their individual plans' (1944 [1979]: 26). It is therefore manifest since the beginning of his intellectual journey that although some elements of such a framework are the legacy of the past (customs, traditions, implicit contracts), Hayek also considers other elements, which stem from human design and are conceived through a procedure of 'consensus behind a veil of ignorance', whereby the social designer cannot act in order to benefit or damage specific individuals or groups deliberately. Compliance with this procedure provides legitimacy to policies, so as to protect and/or reproduce the results generated by the appropriate set of long-term, stable social norms that would have emerged spontaneously if agents had not been hindered by transaction costs or surprised by the acceleration of time, as aired earlier.

In fact, Hayek's offensive against economic policy is weaker and less comprehensive than may appear at first sight. It is a Third Way between *dirigisme* and *laissez faire* where the state plays two roles: (a) it provides a framework where individual action develops; and (b) it meets those social needs that the market fails to satisfy because of externalities.[7] It happens to be illegitimate only when it becomes the instrument of discretionary bureaucratic interference with the social norms (loosely understood as a synonym for social contract) – both directly, through rules issued by the bureaucrats themselves; and indirectly, when bureaucrats arbitrarily enforce the rules conceived by the social philosophers or by the politicians.[8] Although this is surely an important limitation, it is not enough to deter Hayek from advocating state funds in favour of generalized education, sanitation, minimum-income legislation, adequate infrastructure, information, quality control, sporting and cultural activities, collective insurance *vis-à-vis* catastrophic, unpredictable events.[9] And also behavioural rules that should not replace individual preferences (1973 [1983]: 51), but nevertheless shape human action and make it easier to predict. In short, the state is 'a piece of utilitarian machinery intended to help individuals in the fullest development of their individual personality' (1944 [1979]: 57). Unfortunately, one does not know how to distinguish between cases where the state helps spontaneous development and cases where it drives such development: 'Unlike classical liberalism that confines the state to the provision of a single public good, law enforcement, Hayek's social order is less, rather than more, clear-cut: it permits, if not positively mandates, the state to produce any number in any quantity' (De Jasay, 1996: 113).

Put differently, although Hayek emphasizes the crucial role of liberty, he reasons that nothing useful can come to birth in a vacuum (which he wrongly considers a synonym for *laissez faire*). And hastens to fill in the vacuum by appealing to common sense, search for compromise, expediency, but not rationalism.[10] By holding on to these two arguments (individual liberty and horror vacui) and carefully avoiding the discussion of the intrinsic conflicts,

Hayek's well-known condemnation of scientism actually excludes bad policy-making, rather than policy-making *per se*; and leaves plenty of room for social, piecemeal engineering, to be carried out by enlightened political action applied to economic activities. He therefore succeeds in attracting consensus from the anti-socialist ranks when attacking scientism and positivism, that is historicism, objectivism and the foundations of socialism (Saint-Simon and Comte) – and in enticing those who believe in the existence of the common interest, a notion that Hayek believes can be defined by means of an idealized version of majoritarian democracy.[11] It is hard to say whether Hayek himself was aware of the blurred border between general rules (constitutional law making by enlightened, possibly arrogant political philosophers)[12] and detailed rules (scientism by rational and selfish bureaucrats or shortsighted politicians). He must have had serious fears, though; since after (1960 [1978]) he repeatedly tried to keep the two categories apart and explain – without much success, in our view – why public-choice analysis applies to the latter but not to the former.

BETWEEN BAD SOCIALISM AND GOOD POLICY-MAKING

As the previous pages suggest, according to the main thesis put forward in this chapter Hayek's view on economic policy depends heavily on his idea of a society of free individuals protected by super constitutional arrangements. These arrangements should be the absolute barrier against socialism and the growing conviction that governments ought to play a major part in shaping people's daily life (1944 [1979]: 9).[13] This is little more than a façade, though. For in Hayek's view the real problem with socialism is not so much the violation of individual freedom, as collectivization. This approach has two consequences. It does not oblige Hayek to confront natural rights and the sacredness of private property (which he is not willing to accept, as recalled earlier on); and leaves the door open to non-socialist coercion, to be applied whenever the results are not satisfactory:

> in the ordering of our affairs we should make as much use as possible of the spontaneous forces of society, and resort as little as possible to coercion . . . There is . . . all the difference between deliberately creating a system within which competition will work as beneficially as possible, and passively accepting institutions as they are. Probably nothing has done so much harm to the liberal cause as the wooden insistence of some liberals on certain rough rules of thumb, above all the principle of *laissez-faire*. Yet in a sense this was necessary and unavoidable . . . Nothing short of some hard-and-fast rule would have been effective. And since a strong presumption in favour of industrial liberty had been

> established the temptation to present it as a rule which knew no exceptions was too strong always to be resisted. (ibid., p. 13)

and

> There were many tasks . . . where there could be no doubt that the government possessed enormous powers for good and evil; and there was every reason to expect that with a better understanding of the problems we should some day be able to use these powers successfully. (ibid., p. 14)

Unfortunately, Hayek does not attempt to clarify who has to decide about the features and desirability of the exceptions, or how the decision-making process should take place. Nor does he explain when better knowledge of the problems legitimizes government to use its coercive powers.[14] For instance, after having warned the reader about the dangers of government intervention, he makes it explicit that 'where it is impossible to create the conditions necessary to make competition effective, we must resort to other methods of guiding economic activity' (ibid., p. 27), even if that implies expropriation or compulsory purchase (1979 [1981]: 62–3).[15] The same applies to monopolies (ibid., pp. 29 and 147) as well as to a variety of other situations.

Hayek's view about economic policy is thus characterized by two essential and persistent elements: the need to develop some kind of constitutional engineering and to adjust for externalities, which justify state coercion, as explained at length in (1960 [1978]). The former turns out to be not only desirable, but also necessary, if a market economy is to generate the best possible results. The latter is always welcome, as long as intervention remains within the boundaries set by the rule of law.[16] In a word, as long as the rule of law is not violated, government intervention is admitted and leads to the production of goods and services (for example insurance services against catastrophic events and unemployment), the redistribution of income by means of taxation (including substantial inheritance taxes) and the regulation of production (1944 [1979]: 60).[17]

The core question then clearly revolves around Hayek's notion of the rule of law, defined as a set of 'rules fixed and announced beforehand – rules which make it possible to foresee with fair certainty how the authority will use its coercive powers in given circumstances, and to plan one's individual affairs on the basis of this knowledge' (see for instance 1944 [1979]: 54 and 1973 [1983]: 108). Apparently this definition does not include freedom of contract, since

> to limit working hours or to require certain sanitary arrangements is fully compatible with the preservation of competition . . . nor is the preservation of competition incompatible with an extensive system of social services – so long

> as the organisation of these services is not designed in such a way as to make competition ineffective over wide fields. (1944 [1979]: 28)

Hayek will indeed modify his view later on, when the emphasis moves from certainty and predictability to the notion of just conduct, 'as a means for assisting in the pursuit of a great variety of individual purposes'.[18] But his argument basically remains an attack against privileges or burdens for selected interest groups known in advance,[19] and an appeal for a political system that creates stable rules behind a veil of ignorance.[20] Sometimes the veil drops, though. For Hayek also conceives an ideal world where a set of desirable features must be in place (including the absence of externalities). The lack of such features is characterized as market failures, and the state is called upon to fill the gap and cover the costs through taxation: 'far from advocating . . . a minimal state, we find unquestionable that in an advanced society government ought to use its power of raising funds by taxation to provide a number of services which for various reasons cannot be provided, or cannot be provided adequately, by the market' (1979 [1981]: 41). Furthermore, 'There are common needs that can be satisfied only by collective action and which can thus be provided for without restricting individual liberty', and 'There is no reason why the volume of these pure service activities should not increase with the general level of wealth' (1960 [1978]: 257). As a result, Hayek's spontaneous order is no longer an alternative to constructivism, but a desirable situation where repeated interactions may have given birth to patterns of predictable behaviour and where order (that is predictable behaviour) has to be enhanced on a case by case basis, whenever it does not appear spontaneously.[21] As De Jasay (2004) has recently pointed out, in Hayek's view

> the market, law and its enforcement must first secure property and contract against violation, and then the market order will spontaneously emerge as a result of individual interactions within this framework of safety and predictability. [Put differently,] law is a product of collective choice and so is its enforcement . . . Hayek's spontaneous order, then, is not spontaneous, for it includes the government as a necessary condition, and government action is purposive.

Surely, Hayek is well aware of the fact that extensive state action might distort individual behaviour. But he is inclined to elude the problem by arguing that when this happens, then it means that privileges are being created and the rule of law violated. Put differently, on the one hand the reader is being told that economic policy is welcome when the market fails. On the other hand he is warned that economic policy is not acceptable when it creates winners and losers and thus distorts incentives.

HAYEK'S NEED FOR A SOCIAL CONTRACT

As mentioned in the previous paragraphs, from the late 1930s Hayek was suggesting that market-oriented economic policy was to be preferred to central planning. But the need for economic policy, and for sensible policy-making as a whole, was not questioned.

More generally, Hayek criticized the Middle Way, but also hurried up to recommend allegedly neutral, state solutions to hypothetical market failures. Unfortunately, he did not see that such failures called for property-rights solutions. This blindness prevented him from grasping the notion of externality,[22] deprived his conception of rule of law of the only intellectual anchor it could count on – the principles of 'private property and freedom of contract' (ibid., p. 28) – and forced him to apply the rule of law according to rather questionable common-sense principles (opinion and 'universalizability', to be explained shortly). As one may have noticed, Hayek correctly refrains from referring to spontaneous order; for it would be incompatible with not so spontaneous rules of the game, which are however desirable according to the Hayekian vision. Once again, when discussing competition he adds that 'we cannot, within the scope of this book enter into a discussion of the very necessary planning which is required to make competition as effective and beneficial as possible' (ibid., p. 31). And when arguing for redistribution and a minimum welfare state, he is not sure whether they should be justified in order to buy consensus against special interest (ibid., p. 156),[23] or just because not having it is a deficiency:

> some security is essential if freedom is to be preserved (1944 [1979]: 99);
>
> adequate security . . . will have to be one of the main goals of policy. (ibid., pp. 98–9)
>
> capitalism as it exists today has many remediable defects that an intelligent policy of freedom ought to correct. A system which relies on the spontaneous ordering of forces of the market, once it has reached a certain level of wealth, is also by no means incompatible with government providing, outside the market, some security against severe deprivation. (1976 [1978]: 136)

The logical weakness of this position can only be overcome by introducing new conceptual tools. Authors like Leoni (1961 [1991]) and de Jasay (1985 [1998]) clearly perceived that the only instrument that social scientists can use in order to reach a compromise is the social contract. Indeed, Buchanan's success owes a great deal to having assumed a social contract, irrespective of its moral foundations (legitimacy). Hayek never mentions it explicitly and actually denies its validity.[24] In fact, he replaced the social contract with the rule of law, the difference between the two being the same as that between a state ruled by bureaucrats with discretionary power[25] and one composed by social philosophers (politicians) with the monopoly of violence. More subtly, by sidestepping the discussion on the social contract, Hayek could actually treat it as a fact, rather than a serious concern for the social philosopher: 'constitutions are based on, or presuppose, an underlying agreement on more fundamental principles – principles which may never have been explicitly expressed, yet which make possible and precede the consent and the written fundamental laws' (1960 [1978]: 181).

As a by-product, this 'underlying agreement' explains and justifies the state monopoly of violence: 'Coercion, however, cannot be altogether avoided because the only way to prevent it is by the threat of coercion. Free society has met this problem by conferring the monopoly of coercion on the state' (ibid., p. 21).[26] And legitimacy is now maintained by reference both to the veil of ignorance, following the lines already sketched in the *Road to Serfdom*:

> Even where coercion is not avoidable, it is . . . being made impersonal and dependent upon general, abstract rules, whose effects on particular individuals cannot be foreseen at the time they are laid down. . . . Coercion . . . then becomes an instrument assisting the individuals in the pursuit of their own ends and not a means to be used for the ends of others. (ibid.)

and to a new concept – opinion – defined as

> a common tendency to approve of some particular acts of will and to disapprove of others, according to whether they do or do not possess certain attributes which those who hold a given opinion usually will not be able to specify. So long as the legislator satisfies the expectation that what he resolves will possess those attributes, he will be free. (1973 [1983]: 92)[27]

A MANIFESTO AGAINST FREEDOM

When encouraging policy-makers to intervene and enhance the acquisition of knowledge, improve on bad past legislation, question defective traditions and gain consensus, Hayek did perceive the problem of the misuse of power:

> restraints . . . on the power of the legislator could, of course, be made more effective and more promptly operative if the criteria were explicitly stated by which it can be determined whether a particular decision can be a law. But the restraints which in fact have long operated on the legislatures have hardly ever been adequately expressed in words. (1973 [1983]: 93)[28]

Still, his call for explicit rules defies centuries of political history, while his proposal to submit the legitimacy of the new rules to the test of 'universalizability' remains elusive.[29] For either the policy-maker is in fact just proposing social arrangements that may reduce the cost of human interaction and that individuals are free to accept or reject, possibly through a trial-and-error process characterized by competition in an evolutionary context. Or the policy-maker has the right to impose such social arrangements as long as they may be qualified as moral.[30]

One can of course answer by arguing that all the arrangements conceived behind a veil of ignorance are welcome by agents. Which is hardly credible, even from a purely Hayekian viewpoint. It doesn't take much to see that the politician does not necessarily use his power of coercion to minimize transaction costs in a society, that he never operates behind a veil of ignorance, let alone his knowing how people would behave and what they would choose behind the veil. Another possibility to avoid choosing is to claim that institutions come from the past, as a result of tradition and spontaneously-developed rules. Following our previous terminology, from this viewpoint the social contract has not been agreed upon, but has been revealed through history (1960 [1978] chapter 4). Therefore, one may infer that the policy-maker is not a social philosopher designing social arrangements, but one interpreting and enforcing the allegedly revealed social contract by transforming it into a law. Unfortunately, it is not clear what happens if different social scientists have different perceptions as regards revelation. And not many classical liberals would agree with Hayek's notion whereby 'liberalism regards it as desirable that only what the majority accepts should in fact be law' (ibid., p. 103).[31]

Similar remarks apply to the notion of individual freedom, often quoted as the bulwark against arbitrary policy-making. In this case Hayek departs from the classical–liberal position based on the familiar notion of 'freedom from coercion'[32] and refers instead to the concept of responsibility: 'freedom, namely a state in which each can use his knowledge for his purposes' (1973 [1983]: 55, 56). In particular, 'the argument for liberty . . . presupposes that a person is capable of learning from experience and of guiding his actions by knowledge thus acquired' (1960 [1978]: 77). Thus, liberty is no longer a (natural) right, but almost becomes part of a social contract, whereby in order to deserve it, one must show that he/she is able to profit from it. Once again, the policy-maker creeps in through the back door to assess whether individual behaviour is consistent with a contract that also requires that 'in our decisions as to whether a person is to be his own master or be subject to the will of another, we must regard him as . . . either having or not having the right to act in a manner that may be unintelligible, unpredictable or unwelcome to others' (ibid., p. 78).[33]

This departure from Austrian subjectivism plays an important role, since it allows Hayek to cry out against coercion and still favour constitutional constructivism. For in Hayek's world individual A is subject to coercion not only if other individuals exercise physical or psychological violence towards him, but also if they refuse to act according to A's wishes and such a refusal can jeopardize A's existence (ibid., p. 136). This statement has important implications. First, it means that individual freedom is not valuable *per se*, but only if it is compatible with other agents' basic needs. How basic a basic need is remains of course a matter open to debate. For instance Hayek mentions the owner of a spring in an oasis and claims that free water should be offered to all those who cannot pay and are about to die. The owner of the spring may indeed decide to do so out of compassion. But the owner cannot be obliged to do so – as Hayek advocates – unless one violates the principle of private property. And also two other principles. One is responsibility, since those who adventure in the desert without enough water should take responsibility for their poor organization or sheer bad luck. The second is the principle of entrepreneurship (and the ethics of profit), which would make sure that agents strive to find new wells, look after the existing oases, possibly establish a network of relief stations in the desert.[34]

Other examples of the effects implied by Hayek's notion of coercion apply to monopoly power and the labour market. In the former case regulation is required whenever 'a monopolist is in a position to withhold an indispensable supply' – be such an action a fact, or just a possibility (ibid., p. 136). It is easy to observe that this idea is very close to that of 'dominant position', which today pervades mainstream economics: 'whenever there is a danger of a monopolist's acquiring coercive power, the most expedient and effective method of preventing this is probably to require him to treat all customers alike, i.e. to insist that his prices be the same for all and to prohibit all discrimination on his part' (ibid., p. 136).[35] In the latter case Hayek welcomes regulation 'in periods of acute unemployment', when workers may be induced to accept unfair contracts (ibid., p. 137).

In short, individual liberty for Hayek means protection against coercion, and coercion means not only violence as commonly understood, but also resistance to the rule of law and need. And since for Hayek (1960 [1978]) taxation and compulsory military service are the outcome of – or at least compatible with – the rule of law, resistance against both turns out to be an act of coercion.[36] Put differently, the difference between the Hayekian and the socialist versions of acceptable coercion turns out to depend on how the social welfare function is defined. In the former case state intervention is justified when it enforces rules (of just conduct) or dominant-position conditions are feared;[37] while in the latter intervention is legitimate whenever it is consistent with the social welfare function in general. But one suspects that the Hayekian definitions of rules or of potential dominant position are almost as arbitrary as is any other.

To conclude, Hayek's recipe to make policy-making subject to the rule of law and to rely on state violence in order to eliminate coercion is not very persuasive. In his view the rule of law is in fact equivalent to a mix between constitutional straitjackets to restrain ordinary legislation, plus decision-making behind a veil of ignorance and according to general principles, with the purpose of inducing individuals to behave in a predictable way. The fragility of the veil of ignorance has already been mentioned earlier on. As regards general principles, Hayek (1960 [1978] chapter 10) argues that they should not be created, but just discovered, since 'they have grown through a gradual process of trial and error in which the experience of successive generations has helped to make them what they are' (ibid., p. 157).[38] This is the task of the legal scholars, whereas legislators *stricto sensu* should play the role of the benevolent policeman, and 'create conditions in which an orderly arrangement can establish and ever renew itself' (ibid., p. 161). In fact, Hayek replaces collectivism with some kind of enlightened policy-making, where neoclassical technocrats are to assist legal scholars, and legal scholars are supposed to establish what the rule of law is and make it explicit. In particular, they define when individuals are subject to state coercion. On the other hand, technocrats are meant to think of effective remedies when deviations from the rule of law are to be corrected and to enforce such amendments.[39]

POLICY-MAKING BEYOND THE RULE OF LAW

Contrary to common belief, the role of state intervention in a Hayekian world is not confined to enforcing the rule of law and restraining the use of violence (coercion) by ordinary legislators and technocrats at large. Although one wonders whether state authorities would actually listen to legal scholars telling them what they can and what they cannot do (and hope that legal scholars all share the same opinion and resist the temptation to please state authorities), Hayek goes further and emphasizes that coercive activities 'will never be the only functions of government . . . [I]nfringements of the private sphere will be allowed . . . in instances where the public gain is clearly greater than the harm done by the disappointment of normal individual expectations' (1960 [1978]: 206, 218).[40] The implications are not really clarified or examined in any detail.

Indeed, while Hayek squeezes the debate on the aims and legitimacy of economic policy into a question of rule of law, he says almost nothing about the instruments through which policy is to be carried out.[41] He therefore reduces normative economics to a matter of personal judgement by the social philosopher. In turn, economic policy acquires strong social-democratic connotations, as rules must 'tell people which expectations they can count on and which not', but 'it is clearly impossible to protect all expectations . . . which expectations must be protected must . . . depend on how we can maximise the fulfilment of expectations as a whole' (1973 [1983]: 102–3). In Hayek's view that seems to be enough to justify breach of contract *vis-à-vis* employers (pickets and strikes),[42] taxation (to finance poverty-relief programmes, social security, compulsory health insurance, agricultural improvements[43] and constitutional design).

Hayek does try to draw the line between the socialist welfare state and his own: the former being one where takers decide about the amount of redistribution, whereas the latter is one where the givers do.[44] But of course, it is not clear what happens if a giver decides to give relatively little – or nothing at all; nor is it clear whether the Hayekian system is compatible with a democratic regime.[45] In the end, Hayek seems to be less hostile to planning than meets the eye,[46] as long as good planning is enforced and bad planning rejected. In the case of town planning, for instance,[47] good planners help the functioning of the market, operate through equitable compensation mechanisms and set reasonable standards, whereas bad planners enforce rules (without compensation) and engage in arbitrary decision-making. After all, that is what a constructivist would argue: bad outcomes are the product of bad planners, rather than of the very attempt to plan human activity.

CONCLUDING REMARKS

During the twentieth century the economic profession grew more and more interested in exercises in social efficiency, whereby the economic policy-maker was to define sets of efficient solutions to assigned problems, and the politicians were supposed to choose the best option. The illusion of the benevolent policy-maker and the true nature of the relation between redistribution, incentives and economic performance were exposed only in relatively recent times.

Still, the lesson has not been learnt, let alone applied (Nelson, 1987). This contribution has tried to argue that Hayek himself bore some responsibility in this intellectual defeat, for his recipes were based on an enlightened version of economic policy (to be driven by suitable social philosophers), more or less restrained by a new constitutional order.[48] More important, Hayek did not centre his research programme on a clear and well-founded justification for policy-making, but rather on the constant effort to confine policy-making within reasonable, common sense boundaries. Such boundaries are of course Hayek's definition of the rule of law, which however proves to be unsatisfactory on two accounts. On the one hand, Hayek fails to provide a proper characterization: as a consequence, the rule of law turns out to be little more than a set of principles defined behind a veil of ignorance, possibly in accordance with a curious version of the freedom-from-coercion principle. The term 'possibly' should remind the reader that the Hayekian rule of law is in fact compatible with some redistribution, taxation, state production of goods and services and equitable compensation. When commenting on Hayek's view of the welfare state, De Jasay (1991: 15–16) is thus justified in claiming that 'here is a clear call . . . to re-create something like the "Swedish model" under the liberal banner. Horrified as Hayek would be by the imputation of such a proposal, his exposition is fully consistent with it, and must be classed as "loosely liberal" for that reason.' On the other hand he denies the principle of spontaneous order when spontaneity is not adequate or desirable: 'there can be no justification for representing the rules of just conduct as natural in the sense they are part of an external and eternal order of things, or permanently implanted in an unalterable nature of man' (1976 [1978]: 59–60). As for assessing whether the rules of the game are appropriate or consistent with just conduct, his reference to legitimacy being based on public opinion cannot be taken seriously.[49]

Of course, by looking at today's world one can maintain that both Hayek's and Chicago-style liberalism describe an ideal, utopian picture. The first boils down to some kind of benevolent elite of social philosophers in charge of policy-making, while the latter is obsessed by the notion of equilibrium and overlooks transaction costs and entrepreneurship. Still, whereas the Chicago approach is wrong, but consistent, Hayek's world of constitutional engineering is fragile from the very beginning, for it is rooted in the same rules of the game that legitimate and therefore lead to discretionary power. To deny this is equivalent to denying the very behavioural hypotheses of human action, which Hayek observed in Western Culture and learnt from Mises (1948 [1963]). As we know, the alternative is a world featuring institutional competition, ultimately based on a notion of freedom originating from natural-right principles. Unfortunately, this is a vision to which Hayek sometimes agrees when advocating methodological individualism and – even more – Austrian subjectivism, but which he eventually neglects in order to be able to engage in 'constitutional economics'.

In this respect, Hayek's divergence from Mises is hard to explain. Hayek's ongoing efforts not to confront Mises on major issues don't help, either.[50] Perhaps, Hayek may have wanted to stop short of shocking his readers or the policy-makers as a whole, and thus avoid the very mistake with which he reproached the classical liberals and the *laissez-faire* school. This is surely a feature throughout the *Road to Serfdom*, where he fails to elaborate a persuasive criterion to evaluate the legitimacy of economic policy,[51] and becomes explicit in the 1970s, when he claimed that 'attempts to push a principle further than general sentiment is yet ready to support it is apt to produce a reaction which may make impossible for a considerable period even what more modest attempts might have achieved' (1976 [1978]: 58). One wonders, however, whether an alleged champion of liberal thought should advocate accuracy and cohesion, or settle for political suitability and offer some kind of a Third Way composed of a piecemeal list of government actions to meet specific goals in the economic sphere, the only perceptible policy criterion being one of consistency with the prevailing notion of just conduct. The price Hayek paid was however high. Not only was he forced time and again to appeal to expediency within a microeconomic context, and to go as far as denying some 50 years of Austrian business cycle economics by claiming that 'it is merely common sense that government . . . will step in when private investment flags, and thereby employ resources for public investment at the least cost and with the greatest benefit to society' (1979 [1981]: 59). More important, 'the effect of leaving out pieces from the jigsaw puzzle of social theory is that the vacuum is only too naturally filled by a false conception of the state. This conception is hardly compatible with liberal principles. Indeed, it is hardly compatible with the very market order that Hayek wants to be spontaneous' (De Jasay, 1996: 118).

ACKNOWLEDGEMENTS

I am grateful to Carlo Lottieri, Anthony de Jasay, Henry Manne, Alberto Mingardi and Miro Prokopijevic for many insightful comments and helpful suggestions on a previous draft of this paper. Helpful comments were also offered by seminar participants at the Schools of Economics of the Universities of Podgorica and of Lisbon (Universidade Nova); at the Schools of Law of the Universities of Paris (Panthéon-Assas) and of Reims.

NOTES

1. See Fontaine (1996). As will be clarified later on, Hayek (1960 [1978]) definitely subscribed to this view. More recently, a similar approach was also advocated by Buchanan (1979), who insisted on the notion of economics as a system of voluntary exchange generated by – and giving origin to – agreed-upon rules. These rules are named institutions and represent an essential feature of economic analysis.

2. Smith's vision is not entirely clear, though. For instance, Grampp (2000) argues that Adam Smith supported a free market system because he believed this to be the best way to promote the social good – in his case the accumulation of national wealth and military power. As a matter of fact, this would explain why Smith did not hesitate to claim that natural rights and individual freedom should be set aside when the public good – for example national power or even fairness – is at stake. Hayek devotes the whole Epilogue of (1979 [1981]) to justifying his rejection of a natural-right approach.
3. Note that this notion of the social contract is different from that advocated by Buchanan (1979). According to the argument developed in the text, Hayekian policy-making reflects a social contract that would have emerged as a consequence of a spontaneous, time-consuming process leading to a social norm. On the other hand, in Buchanan's view the social contract is what the individuals would have chosen had they been behind a veil of ignorance.

   This view presents two major weaknesses, though. First, policy-makers cannot possibly know what individuals would choose behind the veil of ignorance. Second, people do not choose behind a veil of ignorance; indeed, the history of mankind can be described as the continuous effort to reduce the size of the veil before taking a decision.
4. Even Caldwell (2004) provides very little information on this account.
5. See Hayek's notions of 'Legislative Assembly' and of 'Constitutional Court' at (1979 [1981] chapter 17): the former is formed by the constitutional law-makers, the latter by their controllers. It is not clear how or by whom these should be appointed, though.
6. See Hayek (1973 [1983]: 88–9; 1960 [1978]: 286) and, more generally, Denzau and North (1994) and Fiori (2002).
7. Indeed, Hayek often failed to distinguish between an externality *stricto sensu* and a residual explanation for why allegedly desirable states of the world fail to materialize. Therefore, since he believed that direct state intervention is justified – if not required – whenever externalities are relevant and widely recognized, government intervention ends up by being appropriate whenever the state of the world could be improved with no obvious costs. More on this at note 21.
8. According to Hayek (1960 [1978]: 112–15) the politician does not have ideas and should merely represent conventional thought: 'His task in a democracy is to find out what the opinions held by the largest number are, not to give currency to new opinions which may become the majority view in some distant future' (ibid. at p. 112). On the contrary, the social philosopher is an intellectual innovator who conceives new, possibly welfare-enhancing ideas or general principles that agents may or may not accept.
9. See Hayek (1944 [1979]: 89–90, 1960 [1978]: 141, 144, 223, 257, 258, 364, 365, 375, 383, 1979 [1981] chapter 14). See also Hoppe (1994) for a clear account of Hayek's view on government intervention. On the other hand, some doubts on the existence of natural state monopolies are aired in (1979 [1981]: 147).
10. See on this Hoppe (1994), who emphasizes the incongruous results generated by Hayek's rejection of rationalism, despite Mises' teachings.
11. Hayek seems to have mixed feelings about democracy, that vary from unqualified praise (see the Constitution of Liberty) to scepticism. He will then solve his doubts by distancing himself from the current version of democracy (cum unlimited governmental powers) and suggesting a concept closer to that predating the French Revolution – demarchy (cum constrained governmental powers). His ideal political construction is fully detailed in Hayek (1979 [1981]), where democracy is somewhat naively described as 'a certain framework for arriving at political decisions, and tells us nothing about what the aims of government ought to be' (p. 98).
12. In some cases the Constitution should spell out and thus impose principles that are 'too unfamiliar to expect courts to comprehend' (1979 [1981]: 148–9).
13. Hayek held *laissez-faire* responsible for this state of affairs. He maintained that its alleged success in the nineteenth century led people to take the results of market forces for granted and concentrate on collective goals (ibid., p. 15).

    Curiously enough, a few years later Hayek's connection between *laissez faire* and socialism disappeared, and a large part of the Counter-Revolution of Science was actually devoted to showing the links between rationalism, positivism and ultimately socialism. Hayek (1960 [1978]: 60) finally closed the circle by saving the classical–liberal school. He followed Renan's view on liberalism and maintained that *laissez faire* actually originated from Rationalism 'as the very words show' – rather than from the classical–liberal tradition. Did Hayek truly believe that the radical Austrian school was a by-product of the French Revolution?

14. As we know, the challenge had already been raised by the libertarian school – from Rothbard to de Jasay and Hoppe – and it involved the difference between Saint-Simon's Council of Newton on the one hand, and Hayek's custodians of the rule of law on the other. Hayek's reply was elusive. In the *Road to Serfdom* (ch. XV) he believed that an international authority should take care of drafting and enforcing proper rules at a supra-national level (constitutional engineering once again). He later addressed the question at a national scale, but the answer provided in (1979 [1981]) – elected assemblies of highly paid representatives – defined the nature of the problem once more. Surely, it did not solve it. He also favoured moderate decentralization among competing local agencies in the provision of public services, subject however to centralized control as regards legitimacy. Both the central and the local agencies are also expected to compete with the private sector (1979 [1981]: 47, 49), except for the fact that the latter has no right to cover costs through taxation.
15. This position is not too far from what the Saint-Simonians were advocating a little more than a century earlier. Indeed, although Hayek strongly opposed the Saint-Simonian attitude towards private property (1952 [1979] chapter 13), when it comes to choosing between freedom and expropriation he opts for the latter. His justification is that 'we still lack adequate theoretical principles for a satisfactory solution of some of the problems which arise in this field' (1979 [1981]: 63).

    More generally, Hayek sometimes does not seem to have a very clear idea about free-market principles. When it comes to inheritance taxes, for instance, it is obvious that the liberal argument against taxation focuses on the fact that taxation interferes with the parents' desire to sacrifice their own consumption in order to enhance their children's welfare. Taxation is indeed a tax on altruism or family affection. Surprisingly, however, Hayek criticizes inheritance taxes by referring to their inefficiency, rather than their immorality (1960 [1978] chapter 6). Other examples are provided by his view of competition, which is unfair if a successful producer 'keeps out a potential competitor by offering specially favourable terms to customers only in the limited region in which a newcomer at first will be able to compete' (1979 [1981]: 84). Or by his support for progressive income taxation based on the fact that indirect taxation is necessarily regressive (1979 [1981]: 127).
16. See Rothbard (1982 [1998] chapter 28) and Hoppe (1994) for an in-depth criticism of the Hayekian notions of freedom and coercion.
17. The third part of (1960 [1978]) and (1979 [1981] chapter 14) offer a complete list of Hayek's public goods, which includes even entrepreneurship ('certain experimental developments' to use his own words). Hayek (1960 [1978] chapter 6) will subsequently change his mind about inheritance taxes. And he will also deny that being part of a national group justifies compulsory income transfers (ibid., pp. 101–2).
18. See also (1976 [1978]: 5, 37): 'The chief function of rules of just conduct is thus to tell each what he can count upon, what material objects or services he can use for his purposes, and what is the range of actions open to him'. Hayek (1973 [1983]: 2–3) was aware of the fact that the rule of law raised some problems as an operational device, but attributed them to a lack of understanding, rather than to the conceptual weakness of the very notion.
19. See for instance (1976 [1978]: 137).
20. See also (1976 [1978]: 132). Of course, even the abolition of a bad rule – for instance trade barriers – would violate Hayek's notion of the rule of law, for it would provoke damages to selected strata of the population. Not even Hayek could deny that the victims and the beneficiaries of a transition to a free trade regime would be clearly identified. In fact, Buchanan's position is easier to understand, in that he introduces the veil of ignorance

not to justify economic policy, but to justify the social contract that implies economic policy. There is no doubt that the veil of ignorance is a more effective rhetoric device to justify the ends of the individual signing the social contract, rather than to explain the ends and means of government intervention.

21. See (1973 [1983]: 36 and chapter 5) and (1973 [1983] chapter 2). A similar logical twist also characterizes Hayek's view of the welfare state as compatible with (his version of) the rule of law and thus with free-market principles, including subjectivism (1944 [1979]: 89–91). This approach is of course rejected by the orthodox Austrians *à la* Mises who are critical of top-down government action; and also by the Ordoliberals, who criticize his piecemeal approach – see in particular Vanberg (1996).

    More generally, Hoppe (1994) has rightly pointed out that the Hayekian concept of unconscious spontaneous order is simply wrong, miles away from the Austrian fundamentals (Menger and Mises) and leads to a meaningless theory of social evolution.
22. In Hayek's view an externality is the effect of one's action on other individuals (see 1979 [1981]: 43–4). Since he could not argue that all actions provoking disappointment or envy need to be regulated or require compensation, compliance with his notion of the rule of law needed to be assessed case by case, following common sense. Surprisingly, Hayek never refers to a negative externality as an encroachment on somebody else's property right.
23. Oddly enough, Hayek does not perceive the contradiction embedded in his argument. If the beneficiaries of the welfare state can be classified as 'special interest', then the Hayekian welfare state is in contrast with Hayek's fundamental rule-of-law criterion. On the other hand, if the beneficiaries are not special interests, it is not clear why traditional pressure groups should be satisfied by the welfare state and feel that no more rent-seeking activities should be pursued.
24. See (1960 [1978] chapter 4) where Hayek states that the very notion of social contract is the fruit of Rationalism, and thus unacceptable for any follower of the Scottish Enlightenment – including Hayek himself, of course.
25. See also Hayek (1960 [1978] chapter 13).
26. This view brings Hayek much closer to Hobbes and away from the classical liberals. Indeed, a classical liberal or a libertarian would never believe that a politician or a bureaucrat could pursue the private interest better than the individual involved and independent of the individual's opinions on the matter.
27. See also (1976 [1978]: 14), where the concept of opinion is suggested as the driving principle to evaluate the legitimacy of policy action, that is to draw the line between arbitrary interference and intervention within the rule of law.
28. See also (1976 [1978]: 28–9).
29. The test of 'universalizability amounts to a test of compatibility with the whole system of accepted rules . . . which may either lead to a clear "yes" or "no" answer or may show that, if the system of rules is to give definite guidance, some of the rules will have to be modified' (1976 [1978]: 28–9).
30. Hayek (1960 [1978]) explains that institutions are 'convention and customs of human intercourse', which involve a moral code as well as general and 'unconscious adherence to moral rules'. Therefore, coercion is not necessary only 'when individuals can be expected as a rule to conform voluntarily to certain principles' (p. 62). At the same time, Hayek is aware that coercive rules are deplorable and are not conducive to desirable evolution. This is why they 'can be broken by individuals who feel that they have strong reasons to brave the censure of their fellows' (p. 63). Indeed, the author could not have done better to confuse his readers. See also ibid. at pp. 67, 146–7 for yet other views of the same subject.
31. The fact that he also writes that 'it is not obvious that this same majority must also be entitled to determine what it is competent to do' or that liberalism 'accepts majority rule as a method of deciding, but not as an authority for what the decision ought to be' hardly contributes to clarifying matters. See ibid. at pp. 107 and 104.
32. Hayek (1973 [1983]: 61, 62) justifies his departure from the classical liberal lines by claiming that they were too vague to serve any operational purpose: '*Laissez-faire* . . .

never provided a criterion by which one could decide what were the proper functions of government'.

33. Hayek suggests infants and idiots as examples of individuals that do not deserve liberty. Nevertheless, the notion of learning from experience and guidance of actions is much wider and goes well beyond those categories.
34. Both principles recur frequently in Hayek's works. But they seem to be forgotten when it comes to their policy implications.
35. See also (1979 [1981]: 84–5), where the need for government action against price discrimination is argued forcefully. It may be worth pointing out that today not even socialist policy-makers would object to price discrimination.
36. See ibid., p. 143 and also De Jasay (1995 [2002]: 87), who observes that 'Hayek, in making this singular distinction between coercive and noncoercive government actions, appears to be classifying taxation as noncoercive, a judgement that has an obvious bearing on his position regarding redistribution'.
37. For some unexplained reason, this also applies to roads and sanitation (ibid., p. 141), information (ibid., p. 144), some kind of education and the advancement of knowledge in certain fields (ibid., p. 223), which Hayek treats as if they were public goods and thus 'a recognised field of public effort'. See also (ibid., pp. 222–3) for the government production of public goods through general taxation, as long as the benefits cover the cost and 'provide a favourable framework for individual decisions'.
38. The reader may observe that Hayek also claims that at times traditional conventions and norms can be broken, for they should not be considered binding, after all. Unfortunately, Hayek provides no clear indication as for when a tradition is non-binding and when it is rule of law. Hence, although the idea of the legislator as a finder is appealing, it still begs the question of establishing the nature of what the finder has actually ascertained.
39. Indeed, Hayek does not ignore that history has provided plenty of examples whereby constitutions have degenerated, also thanks to having introduced the separation of powers, as he notes when discussing the French and German cases (1960 [1978] chapters 12–13). Still, rather than drawing the obvious consequences about the impossibility of constitutional constructivism, he simply concludes that such examples demonstrate the need for further safeguards.
40. Quite astonishingly, Hayek (1960 [1978]: 218) suggests that the willingness of the public administration to compensate the individual is an acceptable criterion to compare private losses and public gains. He seems to forget both that civil servants carry out compensation by using somebody else's money and that fair compensation is actually established by the buyer (the civil service). As a matter of fact, Hayek seems to be more interested in 'fair socialism', rather than individual freedom.

    See also De Jasay (1995 [2002]) for a critical analysis of Hayek's position and ambiguities on redistribution and the welfare state.
41. True enough, Hayek does claim that policy action should not tamper with prices or quantities. That is hardly satisfactory, though. Income taxes do affect the relative price of human capital, while it is difficult to accept that according to a free-market approach 'subsidies are a legitimate tool of policy, not as a means of income distribution, but only as a means of using the market to provide services which cannot be confined to those who individually pay for them' (1960 [1978]: 264). Indeed, Hayek is advocating redistributive justice within a market system steered by allegedly wise policy-makers caring for the common good and possibly constrained by general rules set by equally wise legislators.
42. See (1960 [1978]: 275).
43. According to Hayek (1960 [1978] chapter 23), farmers should be subsidized, since they lack access to good information. And 'We all have an interest in our fellow citizens' being put in a position to choose wisely . . .; the question as to which of these services will be worth while and to what extent they should be carried is one of expediency and raises no fundamental issues' (ibid., p. 366).
44. Up to a point, though, for Hayek seems to replace socialism with populist pragmatisms: 'the defraying out of the common purse of the costs of services which will benefit only some of those who have contributed to it will usually be agreed upon by the rest only on

the understanding that other requirements of theirs will be met in the same manner, so that a rough correspondence of burdens to benefits will result' (1973 [1983]: 140). The same concept is repeated, for instance, in (1976 [1978]: 7).

45. Hayek is of course for democracy, as long as people are reasonably well educated by institutions free from political interference. Still, rather than being an argument supporting democracy, it sounds more like one for compulsory education financed by taxpayers' money, or for lifetime employment for state teachers (1960 [1978] chapter 24). See also (1973 [1983]: 3) and, more generally, (1979 [1981]), where Hayek mentions the broken promises of democracy. Nevertheless, the obvious and somewhat troubling consequences are not drawn. He offers instead a 'better' political constitution.
46. Caldwell (2004: 238) already noted Hayek's early inclinations beyond individual planning, which make him sound 'suspiciously like what the later Hayek would consider a social constructivist or, at the very least, a constitutional political economist'.
47. See (1960 [1978] chapter 22).
48. As Caldwell (2004: 206, 289) notes, Hayek thought this to be one of his major achievements, and the answer to Keynes' objections to his work in the area of political philosophy.
49. 'The power of the legislator [being derived] from a state of widespread opinion concerning the kind of rules he is authorized to lay down' (1976 [1978]: 60).
50. See Caldwell (2004).
51. Even his rule-of-law criterion starts to shake when he recommends that most wartime restrictions be kept in place for years to come (p. 155), without even bothering to explain why.

REFERENCES

Buchanan, J. (1979), *What Should Economists Do?*, Indianapolis, IN: Liberty Press.

Caldwell, B. (2004), *Hayek's Challenge. An Intellectual Biography of F.A. Hayek*, Chicago and London: The University of Chicago Press.

De Jasay, A. (1985), *The State*, Oxford: Basil Blackwell, reprinted 1998, Indianapolis, IN: Liberty Fund.

De Jasay, A. (1991), *Choice, Contract and Consent: A Restatement of Liberalism*, London: Institute of Economic Affairs.

De Jasay, A. (1995), 'On redistribution', *Advances in Austrian Economics*, 2A, 153–78, reprinted (2002) in A. De Jasay, *Justice and its Surroundings*, Indianapolis, IN: Liberty Fund.

De Jasay, A. (1996), 'Hayek: some missing pieces', *Review of Austrian Economics*, **9** (1), 107–18.

De Jasay, A. (unpublished), 'A dilemma of democracy'.

Denzau, A. and D. North (1994), 'Shared mental models: ideologies and institutions', *Kyklos*, **47** (1), 3–31.

Fiori, S. (2002), 'Alternative visions of change in Douglass North's new institutionalism', *Journal of Economic Issues*, **36** (4), 1025–43.

Fontaine, P. (1996), 'The French economists and politics, 1750–1859: the science and art of political economy', *The Canadian Journal of Economics*, **29** (2), 379–93.

Grampp, W. (2000), 'What did Smith mean by the Invisible Hand?', *The Journal of Political Economy*, **108** (3), 441–65.

Hayek, F. A. (1944), *The Road to Serfdom*, reprinted 1979, London and Henley: Routledge & Kegan Paul.

Hayek, F. A. (1952), *The Counter-revolution of Science*, Glencoe: The Free Press, reprinted 1979, Indianapolis: the Liberty Fund.
Hayek, F. A. (1960), *The Constitution of Liberty*, paperback edition 1978, Chicago: The University of Chicago Press.
Hayek, F, A. (1973), *Law Legislation and Liberty – Rules and Order*, paperback edition 1983, Chicago: The University of Chicago Press.
Hayek, F. A. (1976), *Law Legislation and Liberty – The Mirage of Social Justice*, paperback edition 1978, Chicago: The University of Chicago Press.
Hayek, F. A. (1979), *Law Legislation and Liberty – The Political Order of a Free People*, paperback edition 1981, Chicago: The University of Chicago Press.
Hoppe, H. H. (1994), 'F. A. Hayek on government and social evolution: a critique', *The Review of Austrian Economics*, **7** (1), 67–93.
Leoni, B. (1961), *Freedom and the Law*, Princeton, NJ: D. Van Nostrand Co., reprinted 1991, Indianapolis, IN: Liberty Fund.
Mackintosh W. A. (1950), 'Government economic policy: scope and principles', *The Canadian Journal of Economics and Political Science*, **16** (3), 314–26.
Mises, L. (1949), *Human Action*, New Haven, CT: Yale University Press, reprinted 1963 in cooperation with the Foundation for Economic Education, San Francisco: Fox and Wilkes.
Nelson, R. (1987), 'The economics profession and the making of public policy', *Journal of Economic Literature*, **25** (1), 49–91.
Rothbard, M. (1982), *The Ethics of Liberty*, Atlantic Highlands, NJ: Humanities Press, reprinted 1998, New York: New York University Press.
Tyszynski, H. (1955), 'Economic theory as a guide to policy: some suggestions for re-appraisal', *The Economic Journal*, **65** (258), 195–215.
Vanberg, V. (1996), 'Institutional evolution within constraints', *Journal of Institutional and Theoretical Economics*, **152** (4), 690–96.

PART 2

Is legitimate coercion really legitimate?

4. Defining economic democracy: a challenge. An institutionalist framework

Christian Barrère

> This recognition of democracy as a universally relevant system, which moves in the direction of its acceptance as a universal value, is a major revolution in thinking, and one of the main contributions of the twentieth century. (Amartya Sen[1])

THE PROBLEM OF ECONOMIC DEMOCRACY

Is 'economic democracy' an oxymoron? When she heard that the Moulinex factory in Alençon where she had worked for 30 years was soon to close down, Monique protested: 'They have exploited us for years and now they want shut of us. Every day we wait for news, hoping it won't be too bad. Its racking my nerves. I can't stand it. I feel cut off from the world, from society, left out of everything. Our lives have been put on hold.'[2]

Her protest echoes the words of the Abbé Sieyès' two centuries before: 'What is the Third Estate today? Nothing.' Except that Sieyès was challenging the forms of political power while the factory worker Monique contests the forms of economic power. In the economic sphere, rights are not distributed, granted or held by any egalitarian or democratic procedure. This, though, is not a concern for the many people for whom economics implies private property (and so owner power exclusively) and market-allocation of resources (and so unequal entitlement to power).

This attitude derives from the way we model society dichotomously as political machinery and economic machinery. In one set of models (mainly Greek and Roman political philosophy, and the models of Hobbes and Rousseau) society has a political foundation, whether in the form of a community (Plato and Aristotle) or of a social contract based either on fear and constraint (Hobbes) or on will and liberty (Rousseau). It also has some form of incentive be it virtue or reason. The most important issue is the organization of sovereignty, that is the distribution of political power, in relation to the type of incentive; the ensuing debates concern political democracy. In the other set of models, society has an economic foundation in trade, social production or the division of labour. Individuals act for motives of utility or profit and power derives from the economic workings of markets. Economic matters remain separate from democratic concerns. Accordingly, the economic analysis of democracy is confined within the bounds of political democracy as in the 'public choice' approach (see for instance Breton *et al.*, 2003).

A different approach is adopted in this chapter. It is argued that democracy and the workings of the political market are problems that cannot be studied independently of the organization and workings of the economic market. Therefore, the theory of political democracy (that is, of the distribution of political power and rights) requires an analysis of economic organization (that is, of the distribution of economic power and rights). This is a theoretical matter but also an empirical problem. If economics is indifferent to or, worse still, opposed to democratic organization, then the scope for democracy will be restricted in societies where the economic dimension is expanding. Limiting republican or democratic means of organization to the very classical political sphere leads to them being reduced to formal denominations, with social relations largely slipping away from their control and into the realm of market management. Can democracy withstand any form of devolution of economic power? One can interpret the crisis in politics as a symptom of this phenomenon: if the important things slip out of the political sphere to be taken over by the market, then why pretend to believe there is any point in political confrontation? As Ferguson (1799) and Tocqueville (*De la démocratie en Amérique*, 1835 and 1840) pointed out two centuries ago, the development of the market economy promotes concern for individual interests to the detriment of the common interest and may pose a threat to democracies. In our own times Amartya Sen (1987b) proposes to heal the fracture between ethics and economics by connecting politics and economics and by discussing the goals of economic management by governments. For Sen, freedom is a fundamental entitlement implying not only basic civil rights and equal opportunities but also equal satisfaction of certain basic needs such as being properly nourished or having self-respect and dignity. Accordingly, an attempt is made here to define economic democracy,[3] in other words, to study the connection between the traditional subject matter of political science (republic and democracy) and economics, and especially the market dimension of contemporary societies.

Some economists have studied how political democracy relates to economic performance (Barro, 1991, 1995, 1997; Lipset, 1959, 1994; Lipset *et al.*, 1993; Sen, 1984, 1987a, b, 1993). However, this does not provide us with a theory of economic democracy and the question of democracy remains within the realm of politics. Such thinking is similar to that of other social scientists who consider that modern societies include different social domains which have to be managed by different criteria. Ethical criteria concern the ethical dimension, democracy is a problem of the political sphere and economics works with efficiency criteria, regardless of any ethical or political considerations (see for instance A. Comte-Sponville, 2004). Fukuyama (1992), through the idea of the 'end of history', considers that everyone has now agreed to the market and democracy forming the two pillars of every modern organization, but he overlooks the incompleteness of democracy. Democracy has extended beyond the political domain to take in fields such as the family (women's rights, children's rights, and so on), schools, the armed forces, . . . and economics. Even if rights are mainly defined in this domain as social rights and not as economic rights, it is still essential to point out the terms and conditions on which they are granted and held and the consequences they entail.

It is not a good idea to consider the market and democracy as two necessarily opposing institutions. Some commentators imagine that the growth of the democratic domain implies a corresponding contraction in the market domain. It is argued here that the market is one of the conquests of 'modernity' and the problem is not its existence but the forms it takes. This chapter discusses, then, the strictly democratic (or non-democratic) component of economic organization. If, like Rosanvallon (2000: 11), we use the standard definition of democracy as 'the implementation of popular sovereignty',[4] what of the organization of popular sovereignty in economics or in the management of the economic sphere? And is the question meaningful? In the 1960s and the 1970s, theories critical of capitalist and communist societies developed different models of alternative organization within the framework of self-organization (for instance Kolm, 1977). Debates arose with the standard theory or the libertarian approach (Lepage, 1978) but disappeared with the globalization of markets and the expansion of free-market economies. Even so, the questions remain. Obviously, this chapter cannot cover the whole range of issues in economic democracy. It focuses on the basis for the distribution of economic rights and powers.

THE ANALYTICAL FRAMEWORK

The standard political concepts can be used in studying this problem, but a special-purpose tool is required for analysing the economic dimension. Fortunately economic theory provides us with a powerful tool in 'property rights' theory. It enables us to study entitlement to property rights and their distribution, and hence the distribution of economic power and the consequences thereof. Democracy, then, refers to the definition and distribution of such rights and may take the form of republican democracy; can one speak, by analogy, of market democracy? More specifically, an attempt is made here to define economic democracy by combining property rights theory and an institutionalist framework.

It is standard practice to distinguish among political models of society between *societas* models (society is an association of individuals) and *communitas* models (society has a unity pre-existing individuals) using an organic conception of society. Here too we shall try to interpret economic society as a *communitas*, in the line of theories of republican political democracy. Property rights shall be considered as institutions that have been built up over time by individuals and groups in relation with other organizations and institutions (mainly markets and firms) and not just as some procedure for temporary exchange relations between autonomous individuals. This chapter does not consider the whole range of problems related to economic democracy but focuses on the foundations of the distribution of economic power.

This approach is based on three postulates. First, modern societies are societies of individuals (Elias, 1973). This invalidates ancient models of democracy, such as the Greek or Roman ones, and requires their principles to be reformulated. Nevertheless, it implies that consideration of the social unit, the social conditions in which individuals act, should not be omitted. Political philosophy of the sixteenth, seventeenth and eighteenth centuries distinguished between individual and collective interests, the interests of individuals and the interests of society. Society's interests are more than just the sum of individual interests because society reproduces itself over time on a different time-scale from individuals. Moreover, individuals' interests are simultaneously interests related to their individual personalities and interests as members of a collective organization. The classical theory shows that the dynamics of modern societies, in political and economic terms, are at the same time the consequence of this dual status of individuals: individuals as autonomous entities and centres of decision-making powers, individuals as members of a political society and of a cooperative market society. Individual autonomy is the precondition for innovation and for the possibility of seizing the opportunities the market creates, and it is the factor that distinguishes 'cold' from 'hot' societies (Lévi-Strauss); by belonging to a collective entity its members benefit from cooperation and the organization of collective power over nature and society.

The second postulate is that property rights in modern societies are based on the existence of two orders, the republican order and the market order, and are organized within these two contexts (Barrère, 2005: 295–300).

From an institutionalist point of view, both orders define systems of social constraint: the legal system represents the collective framework of each individual's action (effect of the inclusion of the individual in society) and the price system also represents the collective framework of each individual's action, but in the economic sphere (Samuels, 1971). Each order acts as a system. Each order implies constraints, incentives and opportunities, interdependence and autonomy. Each order defines powers and rights and entitlement to them. How are rights to participate in defining each of these constraining systems distributed? This is the question of democracy, which obviously comes close to the question of freedom because the distribution of rights is also the distribution of powers and liberties.

The third postulate is that social institutions and organizations, such as markets, firms and conventions, create a collective heritage that is handed down over time (Barrère *et al.*, 2004). Individuals and groups produce their output using present inputs but also thanks to such institutions and common resources. Societies operate in a temporal dimension of their own.

Political models that discuss the issues of democracy and the organization of political rights and powers are founded on a distinction between private (individual) and public (common) interests. The major models dealing with the various kinds of political power, and especially with the topics of democracy, can be characterized as *communitas* models and *societas* models.[5] *Communitas* models, based on the Greek conception of political power, use a positive conception of freedom: democracy and freedom, as opposed to dictatorship and tyranny, imply the possibility of participating in collective decision making about common policies (opting for war or peace, defining social institutions, and so on). As Montesquieu wrote 'It is a fundamental law of democracy that it is the people alone who make the laws.'[6] These models involve a social claim to participate in collective decision making. They are republican models, the *res publica* defining the welfare of the *communitas*. *Societas* models conceive of society as a collection of individuals able to bargain for inter-individual contracts and use a negative conception of freedom:[7] democracy and freedom are concerned with the protection and enforcement of such contracts and with the protection of individuals against the state and collective powers. These models lead to the theory of the rule of law. They purport to protect individuals' privacy and autonomy. Modern discussions of democracy seek to combine both negative and positive conceptions of freedom,[8] defining democracy as a permanently incomplete process of 'tension' between the will to autonomy and the will to participate in social power.[9]

In my opinion, the *societas* models of political democracy are an inadequate foundation for an economic democracy because they fail to develop any theory of the distribution of rights.[10] They may propose different solutions for political organization, be it an authoritarian solution (Hobbes) or a liberal one (Locke, Harrington), but they share a common view of modern society as an association of individual owners. This view, known as 'possessive individualism' (Macpherson, 1962), claims that the individual is the sole owner of his capacities, and more than that he is 'his own man'. Individuals are not indebted to society for anything.[11] Accordingly, *societas* models mainly address two problems. One is the possibility of organizing the peaceful management of inter-individual divergences. The other is, in reaction to the models of Hobbes and Rousseau, the protection of individuals from central power. As a relation between the individual and society, as in Benjamin Constant's definition 'this quiet enjoyment of individual independence',[12] freedom is negative freedom; and the myth emerges of a society divided into private domains which never overlap and can always manage their interdependence by exchange and bargaining.

What is democracy in this scheme? It is political democracy, limited to individual and negative freedom. As society has to protect individual property, an economic democracy is a nonsense or is limited to the protection of individual property and the enforcement of contracts. In these models and in their successors, economic freedom is analysed without discussing the distribution of rights and powers emerging from the working of the market. Locke is the staunchest defender of this idea. Individual property is sacred, the state is a company, the shareholders of which are the owners and its purpose is to enforce and protect property rights (Macpherson, 1962). Friedman (1962), like the Austrian school, considers that the free market and political democracy are tightly bound together over the long term, but implicitly thinks that economic democracy is a non-sense or is identical to the free market. The distribution and organization of powers have to allow maximum freedom. However, there is no discussion of the economic conditions of freedom. And economic democracy is not a real topic because the market is organized according to property rules. One can only think of economic democracy as a problem of the enforcement of property rules and the eviction of any exogenous intervention (mainly that of the state). Obviously, liberalism can suggest rules for the distribution of wealth or property rights. But there is no connection between these rules and the conditions defining a society. One has to refer to external criteria such as ethical criteria. On the contrary, in this work, we try to build a theory of a democratic distribution of power based on the conditions for defining a modern society, a market society. This would allow us to escape from the arbitrariness of individuals' ethical choices by laying down a general principle, even if ethics recurs in its application. For that purpose, we are going to investigate the republican framework, starting from a *communitas* model of society but extending it to the market.

COMMUNITAS MODELS AND THE REPUBLICAN CONCEPTION OF POLITICAL DEMOCRACY

Some *communitas* models emphasize unity and coherence, others rivalry and conflict.

In the ancient world, in the models of Greek philosophy and Roman political philosophy, democracy was considered within the question of the proper government of the community (polis, state, empire or republic, and so on). It concerned the collective political organization emerging from the community of citizens. The ancient paradigm posited not the individual but the community as the primary category, because the community was prior to the individual and formed the background to individual life and personality (Aristotle did not define a man as an individual but as a ζοον πολιτικον, a political animal). The city (πολιζ) was conceived of along the lines of a large family. The collective project was pre-eminent. Leaders were chosen for their aptitude to ensure its pursuit and to reproduce over the ages the common inheritance handed down from their forebears and from the founders of the city before them. Good government was government that looked to the common good whereas bad government looked to particular interests; and where bad government used power in an arbitrary manner, good government meant government in accordance with the laws. Within these two categories, both republic (politically good) and democracy (politically bad, because the populace was uneducated and might be swayed by demagogues or might seek to further its own ends to the detriment of the nobles) referred to the participation of all the citizens in wielding political power (organization of the collective destiny of the community) as opposed to aristocracy and oligarchy (the power of a fraction of the community) and monarchy and tyranny (the power of a single man). Democracy meant there was no exclusion within the community of citizens because all were considered equal (this isonomy principle had the counterpart that not everyone was a citizen: women, children, foreigners, convicts, and so on). Democracy implied the right to participate actively in the government of the city. In these models, whether in Aristotle, Livy or Cicero, the common good is considered as objectively defined: beyond the diversity of opinions or private interests, there is only one common good, founded on civic morality.

Rousseau's republican model is rather similar. It defines a social contract between individuals but this contract institutes a new phenomenon, the '*corps social*'[13] which is a community and not the sum of inter-individual relations, contracts or exchanges. Accordingly the sovereignty of the *corps social* is inalienable and indivisible. The model distinguishes between private and public domains, the individual and collective domains, the domain of private individual interest and that of the general interest of individuals considered as citizens and members of the *corps social*. Reason supersedes (Condorcet, '*Cinq mémoires sur l'instruction publique*', 1791) or supplements (as in Rousseau, *Du contrat social ou Principes du droit politique*, 1762) morality as the cornerstone of the common interest. As society is not merely the sum total of individuals at any given moment but a community with its own roots, history and heritage, the common interest is not just the sum of individual interests but is founded on the historical specificity of the community and is expressed by its laws, which are the common project for organizing social development. Power is not wielded against citizens but issues from them and defending individual freedom from it is not an issue. Central power is governed by law. However, because it is a manifestation of reason, law does not limit individual freedom.[14] The break with the ancient arbitrary system is supposed to introduce pure rationality which is capable of freeing humankind. Reason abolishes factions and improves the organic unity of the nation (as Robespierre said and as shown by the worship of the Supreme Being). Accordingly, what is at stake in political organization is the rationality of law (Kriegel-Barret, 1998) and good government is *gouvernement de la raison* (government according to reason). The republic is the regime that upholds the rationality of law against privilege. The issue is one of the substance of law and popular sovereignty is the procedure ensuring this rationality.

This *corps social* introduces a new representation of society as a political entity, a community of citizens, and no longer as a *chrétienté* (christendom) or as an extended family of the prince. Equality among individuals forms the basis of their status as citizens. In this model, political institutions are responsible for organizing the pursuit of the general interest and the common good, for establishing development trends, for leading society. Political society is responsible for its self-organization, its self-government, and its future; the state becomes the leading player of society and is responsible (answerable) for its unity. Society builds an autonomous order, based on human will, and no longer a heteronomous order deriving from nature, God or ideology (Padis, 1989). The submission of all to the law ensures social cohesion.[15]

The question of democracy, defined as the question of the distribution of political power among citizens, is superseded by the question of the republic, that is, by the question of how to organize the formation of the common will for the common good and public interest and how to eliminate specific operations by the enemies of the people promoting individual and private interests. Sovereignty belongs to the people defined collectively; each member of parliament represents the whole people, the entire nation, and not just a section of the population. For Rousseau, democracy means that the people are the legislator and the supreme magistrate, being the source of legislative, executive and judicial power.

In such a framework, conflicts between groups or individuals are underestimated. They are not totally ignored but the choice of leaders by virtue or reason is supposed to preclude struggles among factions. The republican model eludes the question of individual rivalry for two complementary reasons. The separation between public and private domains leads to consideration of the problems of the general interest alone and hides inter-individual conflicts of private interests; in parallel, the economic dimension is dissimulated, and the argument is developed in the political framework of the theory of sovereignty. Accordingly the general interest looks to be common and unified.

Rousseau's model and its interpretation by the French Revolution have to be viewed in their historical context. The main opposition was between the 'aristocratic party', or the tyrannical power of the king, and the people, because the main issue was the definition of law. The focus on a frontal opposition between the Third Estate and the aristocracy meant dissensions and divergences of interests or opinions within the people were underestimated or concealed. Another reason was that competition seemed to be a distinctive feature of the *société de Cour*. Analyses postulated that the opposition of interests was limited by the abolition of privilege and by citizens having identical statuses, and because law was enough to subject individual interests to the general interest it expressed. 'The people' was a unifying category and a homogeneous phenomenon. The idea of rationalization – reason induces progress – reinforced this framework and solved the Hobbesian problem of the necessity for a sovereign. The *Ancien Régime* was irrational, so it needed a Leviathan, but the new one was rational and the republic made society transparent. The underestimation of rivalry within the people was also the effect of the absence of any economic interpretation of modern society. The model was a political one and ignored the economic dimension.[16] History was soon to show up this aporia.

The emergence of conflicting interests brought about a crisis of the republican model in the form it inherited from the French revolution. The development of the revolutionary process had soon shown the project was incomplete with the confrontations between Jacobins and Hébertistes over price regulations, the opposition between the right to existence and the right to ownership, and Jacques Roux's speeches that were to clearly show the limits of a *robespierriste* project and outline the idea of a difference between real freedom and formal freedom: 'Freedom is but a vain ghost when a group of men can with impunity starve another one. Would scoundrels' properties be more sacred than a man's life?'

The political freedom of 1789 claimed to integrate economic freedom by including the right to property among man's natural rights but the triptych of liberty, fraternity and equality soon revealed its contradictions because freedom encompasses the conflicting aspects of economic and political freedom. Economic freedom began by blowing apart political fraternity – via the development of the market and capitalistic competition – and went on to undermine equality. The equation one man equals another man was compounded or superseded by the equation one franc equals another franc. No rule extended the political principles of the republic to the production and the exchange of wealth and to the allocation of resources and no one thought out the coexistence of republican political democracy and a market economy. For a long time this republican aporia went unnoticed because of the success of economism in separating the political and the economic dimensions of social life. Liberal economism transformed the question of economic rights into a matter of respect for the free market and transformed the question of the submission to reason into one of acceptance of market logic. Marxist economism denied political democracy because class relations were determined by economics; there were no stakes in the political domain because everything came within the economic domain of the relation of exploitation. It also denied economic democracy because of the strict antagonism between labour and capital; the market and capital were to be destroyed, not reformed. Political philosophy had disappeared.

Another point is that the state wielded more power than civil society. Consequently, law appeared to be a powerful means of ensuring social cohesion. The question of the distribution of power did not arise because the problem was to ensure rational laws: the work of Montesquieu is considered as irrelevant for the new society. Kant too introduced the question of the distribution of power. In reference to Aristotle's distinction, he opposed autocracy (the power of one person), aristocracy (the power of a group) and democracy (the power of the people) as different distributions of power but he also distinguished republican (management for the common interest with separate legislative and executive powers) and despotic (management for private interests with confusion between making laws and improving them) forms of government. And the evolution of republics led to the question of the devolution of political powers among individuals and among groups. The guarantee of negative freedom has then to be examined.

History clearly shows that a republican order may take on different forms, from constitutional or non-constitutional monarchies, totalitarian republics in which the nation is confiscated by a leader, a clan, a party, or a class, to very different types of democratic republics. The republic is defined by the way the general interest is expressed and managed. The notions of general interest and the forms of its management are also highly changeable, ranging from the worship of the leader as society's guide and the person responsible for its future to forthcoming pluralist forms. The delimitation of the domain of citizenry is a first problem. In Athenian democracy, slaves, metics and women were excluded. In the Roman Republic, there was a censitary suffrage system. In the French Republic of 1793, most of the aristocracy were outside the ranks of the citizens as the *ci-devant*.

In modern republics, foreigners are excluded from the electoral system. More or less advanced forms of pluralistic democracy have been developing particularly because of the emergence of the working class, autonomously expressing its own interests. This openly illustrated the problem of the diversity of interests and opinions, of the existence of various classes and groups, mentalities and representations, and therefore of the lack of any a priori unified, general interest. Accordingly the aporia of the republican model had to consider the distribution of power and to shift from republic to democracy. This raised the question of protecting minorities and individuals. The 'Federalist papers' movement, with J. Madison, A. Hamilton and J. Jay, had already discussed the problem of factions and liberty. They showed that factions could not be eliminated and that legal procedures were required to avoid dictatorship of the majority. For them democracy was dangerous as it induced instability and the republic had to be governed by an elite through a representative procedure. In this way factions could not directly influence the government and would neutralize each other. A constitution avoids the succession of unconsidered changes by limiting political power.[17] Similarly, Benjamin Constant and the liberal conception of democracy defined a limited sovereignty: sovereignty is only relative and limited by individual rights.[18] They opened the way to the theory of the rule of law.

Defending the distinction between public and private interests and spheres, Hanna Arendt underlines another limit of the republican model. She claims that its traditional basis, the *communitas* idea, needs a social virtue that disappeared with the collapse of the 'religion–tradition–authority' trilogy, which dated from the Roman tradition whereby the leaders' authority derived from the founders of the city. This can be tied in with the Nietzschean idea of the collapse of the myth of human reason emancipating individuals and societies. Accordingly, discussions about the future of society lead on to discussion of the procedures for social decision making and so to discussion of the distribution of powers and rights.

The main political models focused on the coordination problem. In *communitas* models, democracy is the way of organizing the common will by associating all citizens in the political decision-making process. But these models ignore inter-individual rivalry. Rousseau's model ignores or underestimates the economic dimension of inter-individual rivalry, supposing that an educated people is a people without rivalry and able to lead society according to reason and, more specifically, in accordance with a rational political law. So it focuses on political organization. But, while the mainstream of *communitas* models understated rivalry, Machiavelli on the contrary focused on rivalry and conflict. Society was no longer a family as in the small societies of ancient Greece with their many formal and informal links among individuals. And there were times of struggle among the great families in the Italian cities and not only of wars against foreign enemies.

Machiavelli (*The Prince*, 1513) considers that conflicts and 'tumults' (*tumulti*) are inescapable but that they may have contrasting consequences. While conflicts in Florence degenerated into factional wars and impoverished the city, conflicts in Rome provide a strong impetus towards enrichment. So good government should not seek harmony but to manage the different moods (*umori*), especially the mood of the aristocracy and the mood of the people, through the constitution and the law.[19] Montesquieu (*De l'esprit des lois*, 1748) used a similar definition of democracy to Rousseau's and his framework is a *communitas* rather than a *societas* model. In the same sense, freedom is a consequence of law, as in the positive conception of freedom, and not the absence of law. The nature of the republic is the sovereignty of the people:[20] if the people contains the entire population it is democracy, if it is limited to a subsection of it, it is aristocracy. Virtue,[21] as the source of individual behaviour, is the principle underlying the republic. However, like Machiavelli, Montesquieu thought that conflicts provided an incentive to social development.[22] So, contrarily to Rousseau, the general interest is not an objective notion, similarly defined by every rational person, but the outcome of conflicts and struggles. In the same way Ferguson (*The History of the Progress and Termination of the Roman Republic*, 1799) thought that a market society diverted people from the debates on common interests in favour of private interests and market tranquillity, thereby weakening society. The consideration of civil conflicts led to the framework of pluralism. Tocqueville quoted Montesquieu and wrote similar commentaries, viewing conflict positively. For him, democracy 'spreads in the whole social body an anxious activity, an overabundant strength, an energy that would never exist without it, and that may create marvels, as long as circumstances are favourable'.[23]

The Hobbesian model provides harsher criticism of the conception of a pacified *communitas* and constitutes a great challenge for it. Hobbes witnessed political conflict (the civil war in England, with its violence as attested by the decapitation of Charles I just two years before publication of *The Leviathan*) and of economic conflict (the development of competition in a market society).

For Hobbes (*The Leviathan*, 1660) the state allows social peace to be organized but implies an authoritarian form of conflict management.[24] The state can even be thought of as democratic despotism if it derives from a 'republic of institution' which supposes the agreement of all – each person being equal to another – but invariably implies a loss of sovereignty for all. In this scheme virtue or reason are radically unable to ensure the unity of a 'hot' society. Freedom is much less important than security and may be sacrificed to achieve security.

This challenge is all the more important as the economic dimension of social interdependence grows. Already in Hobbes' model, the state of nature is a shadow image of competition in a market economy (Macpherson, 1962: 50). The three sources of conflict are connected with economic competition: competition results from the will to possess, defiance (defence against a potential aggression) is the corollary of competition, and glory refers to competition for symbolic benefits. Moreover, it is not necessary for everyone to have a natural instinct towards the will for power for struggles and conflicts to arise. If some people want power, others also have to claim power to protect themselves. Therefore, people with an inclination for power force others to mimic their behaviour. In a market economy (a decentralized system of allocation of scarce resources) the relation between individuals (that is, the dual status of individuals as autonomous persons and members of a social network, the market) induces two types of economic problem. The first is the problem of coordination. How can many autonomous, a priori incompatible decisions be coordinated and create economic order out of disorder? The second one is the problem of rivalry. How can the struggle of individual and opposing interests, the incompatible claims on social wealth, be overcome to achieve economic peace?

Smith was aware of both problems. Nevertheless, classical liberalism contains an economic aporia similar to the political aporia of Rousseau's model. Much as law creates a general and unified common interest transcending individual interests, so the market, through the price mechanism, creates a systemic efficiency for the benefit of all. It provides social freedom in relation to feudal bonds and privileges, and it provides economic freedom in relation to poverty and scarcity by releasing opportunities for growth: 'It is the great multiplication of the production of all the different arts, in consequence of the division of labour, which occasions, in a well-governed society, that universal opulence which extends itself to the lowest ranks of the people.'[25] In this Smithian framework the market is seen as a *communitas* that can coordinate all individual interests and allows all economic agents to participate in the growth of social wealth and its distribution. Rivalry disappears because the division of labour benefits everyone. The later liberal contractualist model considers that a free market overcomes the potential rivalry between interests by improving a system of prices that establishes a social system of economic norms and prevents anyone from violating it.

Modern republicanism (mainly Q. Skinner and P. Pettit) tries to provide a democratic answer to the Hobbesian paradox. For Pettit, democracy has to be founded on the quest for freedom defined as non-domination.

> The republican conception of liberty is akin to the negative one in maintaining that what liberty requires is the absence of something . . . It is akin to the positive conception, however, in holding that that which must be absent has to do with mastery rather than interference. Freedom consists, not in the presence of self-mastery, and not in the absence of interference by others, but in the absence of mastery by others: in the absence, as I prefer to put it, of domination, Freedom just is non-domination.[26]

Using the roman legal concept of *libertas* and the related distinction between a person *sui juris* and a person *alterius juris* (subject to his own right or to the right of another person, like a slave) Pettit defines domination thus: 'One person is dominated by another . . . to the extent that the other person has the capacity to interfere in their affairs on an arbitrary basis.'[27] For him, only arbitrary interference deprives us of liberty, but not for instance legal restrictions.[28] This is interesting because interference is inescapable in modern societies. Interference results from the social interdependence that characterizes both political and economic markets and is the source of cooperation as well as of domination.[29]

To better understand the change which results from this new definition we can relate it to the distinction drawn by Foucault between his conception of power as a relation of forces and the classical conception of power, namely theories of sovereignty, as possession of a set of rights and instruments. Power is not unique, general, abstract and centralized, but powers are multiple, local, concrete, decentralized, inherent in each relation of forces between individuals or groups. More than powers there are *relations de pouvoir* (relations of power): 'Then, there is not one unique furnace from which all the relations of power come as an emanation, but a confusion of relations of power which, finally, allows domination by a class on another class, domination by a group on another group.'[30] Surprisingly, this conception is very similar to Hobbes' conception of power. For Hobbes, power is power over someone and power is a differential reality. Power measures the excess of your capacities over the others' capacities; it is a relative quantity resulting from comparison (Macpherson, 1962: 68–9). Therefore, it implies an analysis of economic relations and not only of the political domain, although economic analysis excludes powers. If mercantilism is set at the centre of economic working rivalry, and if trade is for us war by other means, political economy has progressively moved away from this point of view. The study of cooperative results of the market has understated and concealed analysis of inter-individual and inter-group rivalry (competition, rivalry, struggle for money or power, domination, and so on). Economic analysis has tended towards the abolition of conflict (Carrier, 1993) although conflicts are the core of the other social sciences.[31] Nowadays the mainstream continues to exclude any analysis of power: for instance, Williamson proposes to exclude the idea of power because of its 'elusive' character. Obviously, there may be power relations in asymmetrical situations, mainly in hierarchical structures, but he (like Alchian and Demsetz) considers they result from free contracts and arrangements (they derive from delegations) between equals enjoying equal rights to contract.

Nevertheless, it is not easy to distinguish between a dominated relation and a cooperative relation, or between arbitrary and non-arbitrary interference: arbitrariness, for Pettit, refers to interference that ignores the preferences of the persons subjected to it. But economic relations, based on scarcity, lead to the distribution of resources and obligations. Defining arbitrariness implies defining social norms or criteria that allow us to separate 'just' or 'standard' relations and 'arbitrary' or 'dominated' relations. However, we cannot avoid these questions. They concern legal systems themselves when courts have to examine the conditions ensuring people act of their own volition. The history of the republic, in most western countries, raised the question of the forms of popular sovereignty: debates about the selection of voters among the people (is everyone entitled to participate in defining the common good?) or the kinds of representation (censitary suffrage or universal suffrage) show that political democracy may be more or less formal and more or less genuine (are lobbies, propaganda or social hierarchies able to influence individual preferences?).

The conception of democracy developed by Tocqueville (1835) provides a further incentive for considering the economic dimension of democracy. He derived the political definition of democracy (the sovereignty of the people) from a sociological property of modern societies: the equality of citizens as opposed to the hierarchy of the system of orders characterizing the *Ancien Régime* (Rosanvallon, 2000: 131). This also leads to consideration of the economic statuses of individuals.

Our examination of the republican tradition has shown the necessity for a democratic concern to discuss the economic conditions of democracy within a framework systematically introducing the questions of rivalry. History itself has raised these issues.

THE EMERGENCE OF THE QUESTION OF ECONOMIC DEMOCRACY

Instead of increasing wealth for everyone, the development of the market creates both wealth and poverty, employment and unemployment. Critical studies have denounced exclusion and exploitation, and have considered that they result from the market logic and not from market failures.[32] Smithian liberalism is then discussed and opposing theories emerge, some of which connect the workings of the economy and democratic ethics.

The first current in France to pose the problem of the economic dimension of democracy was the socialist movement. After the economic crises of the early nineteenth century a new conception of democracy arose as political and economic democracy with the idea of 'industrial democracy' (Rosanvallon, 2000: 357). The economic domain is considered as an aristocratic domain: the relationship between proletarian and employer is the same as the relationship between serf and lord. Economic emancipation has to follow political emancipation. Proudhon (1853) was the movement's leading advocate. Many models for a new economic organization emerged forming a strand of thought that would lead to the theme of workers' self-management.

The republican current tried to provide a new response to the question of political democracy. Many French republican authors such as Jules Barni (*Le Manuel Républicain*, 1872) assigned two fundamental roles to the state: organizing security to protect individual freedom, but also contributing to social welfare (a new form of common good), for instance through the provision of public utilities.

Social Catholicism also proposed an extension of the democratic principle to the economy. For instance, in France, Marc Sangnier, leader of the *Sillon*, which developed a personalist approach, wrote in 1910: 'As long as monarchy is in the firm it is impossible to have a republican society . . . Political democracy is insufficient: we don't only want the worker to have a ballot to name a political representative but also to take part in the factory in the governing of the industry he works for.'[33] After the First World War, in France as in Germany and Great Britain, there was much debate on this topic and workers won new economic and social rights. The New Deal, Keynesian policies, the development of economic regulation, the debates about public policy goals and choices led to topics of democracy being extended to the economic domain.

This extension derives not just from debates but mainly from the very organization of modern societies. These are organized principally around two forms of socialization, that is, two kinds of relations between individuals and society. The first is political socialization, with political rights for individuals defined as citizens. The second is economic socialization, with economic rights for individuals as members of the market society. The weight of market society has grown since the time of the debates about popular sovereignty. Both are specific kinds of socialization inducing diverse logics. Political socialization develops a rationale of constraint and sovereignty. Economic socialization develops a logic of exchange. The legal system is a system of coercive rules, expressing the mutual interdependence of citizens, and by the same token giving them obligations, rights and opportunities (right to property, to security, to marry, to express an opinion, and so on). It is a way to manage freedom and interdependence. The market system is another system of coercive rules, expressing mutual interdependence among economic actors, at the same time imposing constraints (prices), and providing rights and opportunities (to produce a new good, to invest in some activity, and so on). It too is a way to manage freedom and interdependence.

Then, through social struggles, the problem of economic democracy is set. How are the rights to participate in defining each of these constraining systems distributed? And, specifically, how is the distribution of rights on economic decision making and of economic wealth organized? These rights concern the present but also the future of the individual and of the communities he is a part of (clubs, nation, humankind, and so on). Democracy is one such form of devolution guaranteeing equality (one citizen is equal to the next) and autonomy (each citizen has to be protected from power, so democracy is opposed to totalitarianism). This devolution depends not only on the definition and distribution of market rights but also on the delimitation of the market sphere relative to the non-market sphere. After the Second World War, most western societies, and mainly France, Germany, Italy and Great Britain, developed mixed economies with a dichotomy between two different areas, the private sector, targeting profitability and the public sector, targeting social welfare (Barrère, 2004). Market regulation and state public regulation shared the organization of the society. Then, aside from political rights, individuals obtained recognition of their social and economic rights. Individuals enjoy entitlement as citizens, as members of a community, the nation, and therefore independently of their market status. Social rights mean rights to use resources often within a frame of public utilities: a right to health, education, transport, communication, a right to benefit from national solidarity, and so on; for instance the French Constitution, including the *Déclaration des droits de l'homme*, refers to a right to health, employment and housing. The delimitation of the market sphere relative to the non-market sphere has distributive effects. The classical views of orthodox republicanism show that the different partitions between republican logic and market logic and the change in their significance for the workings of society have social effects. Some groups take advantage of the expansion in the field of market regulation while others take advantage of its contraction to the benefit of republican socio-political regulation. Social-democratic movements point up the problems of distribution, poverty and public goods. There is therefore a contradiction and competition between entitlement by the market and entitlement by the *res publica* logic. There is also a modification of the market property through its inclusion in a special constitutional framework.

Hence, a debate arises about the relative size of the public and the private sectors. Two extreme positions appear. For proponents of the minimal state, the growing hegemony of market logic within a process of globalization means market property rights are better enforced and democracy is developed as the respect of individual preferences and choices compared with the bureaucratic regulation of society. For radical critics of the market (for example the altermondialist movement), society has to reduce the market sector in favour of the non-market one. As the Marxist myth of abundance is no longer popular, political norms of distribution of wealth and of economic power supersede economic ones. Accordingly, the main supporters of economic democracy seem to be the supporters of a minimal market. To my mind, this position is wrong for two reasons.

First, it presupposes that the market is always the same institution with the same mode of operation and the same consequences, and is invariably a bad institution. Moving towards economic democracy is not the same as reducing the market sphere to the benefit of political regulation. Instead of considering the market as an enemy which unfortunately cannot be eliminated but whose importance needs to be reduced, one can admit that the social construction of the market is a conquest of 'modernity' for what it has done in terms of efficiency and ethics. Market exchange makes possible precise management of the cost/advantage relation. Compared with the gift/counter-gift relation, it looks to deal in truncated transactions. It maintains a special form of reciprocity: a strict, measured reciprocity, under solvency conditions, consciously and explicitly calculated. Moreover, the market exchange has an ethical value and corresponds, in part, to the republican will of freedom. It is usual nowadays to contrast the beauties of the gift/counter-gift relation that forges a lasting alliance and socialization with the limits of the market exchange that cuts and isolates. Even so, these truncated transactions may have a liberating side to them. They create the formal conditions of liberation of individuals compared with a gift/counter-gift relation usually implying lasting personal dependence. The market exchange relation limits mutual dependence for it makes it possible to choose new partners for each transaction. The market contract is a forward, defined contract while the gift/counter-gift contract knows no term or an unlimited term. Hence, the market creates freedom. Moreover, the gift/counter-gift relation, in its feudal form for instance, established obligations with a hazy and uncertain content that might exceed what the co-obligees had at first envisaged. Because of his allegiance to the suzerain, the vassal might be caught up in a lengthy war. Therefore, such a relation cannot be the result of precise costs-benefit comparison of the alliance and appears rather in contexts where there is no particular choice between becoming allied or not. By contrast, the market contract clearly stipulates (within limits, of course, as neo-institutionalists Coase and Williamson showed) obligations and counter-obligations, making it possible to compare and equate them and so reducing uncertainty.

The second reason is that we are now at the end of the model of social dichotomy that characterized the post-war period. This topologic sharing model had been in a crisis for about 20 years and another model has emerged. The dividing line between domains submitted almost exclusively to a single logic is fading to the benefit of a mix of both logics. Political and public criteria slightly but surely influence market management. Conversely, economic criteria and cost-benefit considerations influence the public domain. Market regulation and republican public regulation no longer coexist side by side and sharing the society; they interpenetrate each other within new regulationist complexes. So the problem is no longer that of the position of the boundary between public and private domains. The end of this topologic model means the end of the identification of the public interest with the political sphere and of private interests with the economic sphere. In politics, as shown by the public choice approach, common interests often coincide with private or club interests; in economics, private and common interests are also mixed. The distinction is no longer between domains but between logics and principles.

A significant consequence of this is that political republican principles influence the workings of the economy. The democratic form of republican logic promotes principles of freedom and equality that cannot be identified with the formal freedom and equality of the contract, implicit or explicit, and leads to a distinction between a constrained exchange and a free exchange, an equal exchange and an exchange within a frame of dominant positions. The institutionalization of the feudal corvée (the lord/serf exchange) is opposed to the republican order much like exchanges such as slave/slave-trader, prostitute/procurer, minor/paedophile, and so on. Freedom therefore depends on the relative positions of the parties, on the balance of power before the contract, on the exchange. True freedom involves a refusal of positions of dominance. Social criticism long distinguished more or less strongly between the formal freedom and the true freedom of exchangers, even in the market contract. If it is bankrupt and negotiates in extreme conditions giving its customers massive discounts, is the firm contracting freely?[34] Is the long-term unemployed worker who finds a new job really in a position to freely negotiate his pay? Has an underdeveloped country selling its raw material to a dominant country an ounce of power compared with the dominant purchasing country? The market contract may therefore mask what we can but call an unequal exchange. It may also hide the fact that the facade of freedom to contract and to stop contracting at will is denied to some because certain contracts are but constraints: those who are not the owners of the means of production have no other option than to be on the company payroll. Moreover, the existence of unequal positions on the market may have a cumulative effect and turn the forthcoming results as demonstrated by the debates on free trade and the necessary protectionism to industrialize a new nation. This again raises the main question of the initial arbitrariness of rights. The market works on the basis of a prior definition of the rights determining the possible contracts and the positions (situations) within the balance of power, the bargaining between individuals and groups. Thus, the contradiction between market inequality and democratic republican equality remains unsolved and gets deeper. Here is a new contemporary dilemma: giving up with republic or moving from a republican model of topologically shared market sphere/republican state sphere to a democratized market model considering collective interests.

Economic democracy is also necessary because, in an information society, communication strategies become more important in choosing among a range of projects. As communication is costly, strong economic players gain an advantage over weaker ones. So economic power, through social persuasion, engenders political power and undermines political democracy.

THE MARKET AS A NEW *COMMUNITAS* WITH RIVALRY

Two types of argument justify considering the market as a *communitas* and not only as a set of partial exchanges. The first highlights the organic and institutional nature of such exchanges. The second concentrates on the connections between past and present economic situations, over time.

Organic Exchanges

The market organizes its working through inter-individual relations appearing as free and limited contracts (in terms of time and object). Ever since the classical school, economic analysis has shown the partial and illusive character of this representation.

The employee's participation in production is formally reduced to providing labour by selling hours of work. The market considers his involvement in production as a set of temporary exchanges. Nevertheless, while the relation of the firm (A) and the employee (B) may, as an inter-individual relation, be temporary, subject to renewal and individuals' choices concerning uncertainty (the employee may prefer to change jobs, the employer may change employees, and so on), it also has to be considered as part of a global and collective relation between employers and employees. The firm (A) is not defined by its singularity alone (firm A and not A′, belonging to Mr So-and-So, in this particular place, producing this particular product) but also by its belonging to the category of 'firms'; the employee (B) is not only defined by his singularity (a male, of such and such age, such and such qualification, such and such height, such and such nature) but also by his belonging to the category of 'employees'. And the global and collective employer/employee relation is but temporary and occasional as production is based on their permanent association.

The same is true for consumers. The relation between the producer and the consumer is indeed a link that comes unravelled in most cases as soon as the product or the money are provided and that only ties two anonymous persons. But it is also a relation between two groups, the group of producers and the group of consumers, each having a definite status within the economic organization. So, on the market, each inter-individual relation is always coupled with an 'inter-categories' collective relation.

A re-interpretation of market organization can now be proposed that is capable of leading to a project of economic democracy. In sociology and anthropology, the market model is usually contrasted with reciprocal and redistributive models in terms of the opposition between *status* and *contractus*. We oppose to this analysis the argument of the organic character of the market order, that is, of the fact that contracts and inter-individual relations are only meaningful within an overall framework establishing collective relations between functional groups having their own places in the processes of production, realization, consumption, financing, and so on. This organic character gives individuals participating in this order a market status that is more than the sum of their inter-individuals contracts.

A Social Link to Past and Future: a Social Heritage

Solidarism, whose main proponent was Léon Bourgeois (1902) and which influenced the French legal school of the *Service Public* (Léon Duguit, Maurice Hauriou) argues that each individual is born into a society which allows him to benefit from a social and cultural heritage (Audier, 2004). Social time is longer than individual time. Without this relation to society, no one would survive. So an implicit contract (a quasi-contract for Bourgeois) binds the individual and society: each individual has social rights (right to education, and so on) and social duties. The state too has social duties (to supply public policies, to allow each individual to survive) and rights (to use public constraint and power). For instance, the state can collect taxes that are a kind of rent for the use of social heritage and assets; as the individual earnings of this use are different, taxes may be progressive. A modern version of these ideas supports the theories of a 'universal income'.

The solidarist framework can be reinforced by considering the role of social and cultural heritage. A society produces goods and institutions. Most of these goods disappear in unproductive and productive consumption. Some remain and constitute a social and cultural heritage. Obviously, the stock of capital is an important part of this social heritage. But creative goods (artistic products, knowledge, and so on), rules, institutions and behaviour are another important part of the heritage. They have strong effects at the same time on consumption and on production, are both input and output, and are closely connected with the conditions of the economic working of present-day society. So it may be taken that social wealth depends as much on the social heritage as on the present choices of economic agents. Conversely, society has to manage this heritage (as well as the natural heritage) for future generations.

As individual exchanges are part of the overall workings of the market and as this working depends on heritage and on it being passed on, the market, like political society, is a *communitas*. This point contrasts sharply with *societas* models. In these models, society is a set of inter-individual explicit and implicit contracts between rational and omniscient individuals. The individual, then, is the source of the benefits he earns and no obligation can derive from a contract unless consciously accepted. Not all liberalists share this view. Hayek, for instance, considers society as a system and not an aggregate collection of independent individuals. And, he argues, this system has a history connecting past and present situations.

Rivalry

The market is an ambivalent phenomenon. It combines a dimension of cooperation and pacification with a dimension of competition and rivalry. Prices are social norms that do not derive from natural conditions but emerge from history and the configuration of power and economic forces. It is not only in situations of monopoly that power influences the equilibrium values, it always does so. Economic power is everywhere; as in Foucault's analysis it is a local and disseminated phenomenon. It derives from property but also from the possession of information or of specific assets. It is present in relations between producers and distributors, in vertical relations between firms, on commodities markets as well as financial ones. Markets are systems of economic forces and of relations of power. Values express social valuations that derive from a set of individual valuations but whose composition depends on the relative importance and power of each member of the market. No natural norm establishes the relative price of an hour's work for a doctor in relation to an hour's work for a plumber; none settles the national wages/profits ratio.

The Keynesian conception of the market is useful for understanding market rivalry. Unlike a classical market, a Keynesian market is not a symmetrical one where supply and demand have an equivalent and equipotent influence. Firms produce commodities but also the conditions of their demand; they can influence consumers' preferences and they determine the prices they propose for confirmation by the market. Obviously, they cannot do whatever they like, because of competition, but the bargaining process begins based on their propositions. Rivalry is also competition among firms as they seek to split up aggregate demand in their favour. Accordingly, in the marketplace, economic actors are simultaneously cooperators and rivals; politics lies within the market. This provides a new incentive for discussing the distribution of their powers and rights and imagining an economic democracy.

AN ECONOMIC FOUNDATION FOR DEMOCRATIC ECONOMIC RIGHTS

In the political domain, the first question of democracy is what is the basis of sovereignty. Does political power derive from nature, from the gods or God, or from the people alone? The republican answer is that the sole source of political power is the people, and a democratic framework adjoins the idea that the members of the people, citizens, are equal. If the domain of democracy is to be extended to the economy, we have to examine the organization of economic powers. The preliminary question is that of the foundation stone of economic powers. A traditional foundation is property. Locke, as said, suggests that the main goal of social organization is to enforce procedures for the protection of property. Nozick chooses a similar criterion: 'Whatever arises from a just situation by just steps is itself just. The means of change specified by the principle of justice in transfer preserve justice.'[35] Nevertheless, property has to be legitimate, raising the question of the original position and the institutionalist critique of the 'arbitrariness of rights'. No one can justify the child who prostitutes himself on the streets of Manila having fewer economic and social rights and powers than the child lucky enough to be born into a wealthy American family. Another line of reasoning can be explored. It consists in outlining an organizational principle as the foundation for collective economic rights instead of considering individual rights alone.

Rights Over the Market Institution

Substituting an organic conception of exchanges for the formal conception leads us to consider a new status for the individual within a society of individuals. He is not merely a citizen but also a member of the collective institution of the market. Just as the individual has political rights because he is a citizen, he has economic rights because he is a member of the market. Moreover, the individual benefits from the heritage built up by earlier generations and handed down from generation to generation. He also contributes to developing this heritage and adding to it. This common production of institutions and their efficiency can also be interpreted as a collective constitution of a social patrimony, the social patrimony of a market society. As the outcome of the participation of all, this heritage cannot be the property of a single group and the question of the rights of each individual together with the question of the rights of all considered as a group of individuals has to be asked with regard to its management. Individuals, then, because of their involvement in the market institution and because of their involvement in a social history contribute to the efficiency and systemic output of the market society, and have entitlement because of their involvement. After all, if the market is thought of as the social construction of an organization, all the constructors have rights in their common product.

By this argument, the contribution of every producing agent is twofold: a direct input of productive resource, for instance in supplying hours of labour; an indirect input through participation in the market process of production and in the surplus this form of organization allows by virtue of the participation of all. It leads to a global value of a product that varies with such contributions, with heritage and with the collective involvement of all the members of the market society. A relative measure of direct individual contributions is possible in relation to the system of prices.

On the other hand, a precise distribution between the value created by the present contributions and the value related to the heritage and to the general participation in social working is impossible. This is particularly true because the efficiency of individual contributions is strongly dependent on heritage and global conditions. For the same reasons, individuals collectively make their contributions to the global working of the market, but none of them can be isolated. They correspond to team production that cannot be divided up on the basis of individual contributions. So aside from individual rights connected to the relative value of the individual contributions in spite of their connection to global conditions, it is possible to imagine collective rights that cannot take private property rights as their model. The institutionalist framework justifies this proposition. We can also invoke Hayek's analysis. When he shows that market organization is superior to planning constructivism as the market allows everyone to create, give, receive and treat a piece of information essential for the economic dynamics, does he not show that this collective product (the social surplus obtained) is fundamentally the collective product of all the participants in the market? In a way, the market is the common property of the individuals participating in it, and social welfare is partly the collective product of the team formed by individuals engaging in exchange. In short, the market has a dimension of a new commons!

In other words, society produces a set of institutions which appears as a social heritage, the heritage of market society. Because it derives from the action of every member of the social team, this heritage cannot be appropriated by any particular group. The market is a common heritage. Beyond his private rights over purchased goods, each economic agent has organic and collective rights over the market as an institution. Their community can organize a collective management of the market, define its scope, its forms and procedures. Economic democracy can be founded on a solid basis just as political democracy was founded on the equality of citizens as members of a political *communitas*. Economic democracy is based on a new *communitas*, the market society.

Rights Over the Institution of the Firm

We now have to apply to the market of factors the principle by which the market inter-individual relation has a collective organic relation as its corollary. The firm is not only a set of inter-individual contracts, but a collective being, embedded in history. The liberal conception of power in the firm founds them on traditional property rights. It limits the employee's relation to occasional and uncertain participation in production; it reduces the employee's payment to the purchase of hours of work. It does not grant employees any property right over the common output of factors. By contrast, we consider that employees, as members of an organization, which is what the enterprise is, participate in the collective output beyond their mere submission into the immediate process of work. So, they are entitled to rights.

We start from the same framework as Demsetz and Alchian in recognizing the firm as a collective phenomenon and a production team. We add the institutionalist idea that the firm has a history and produces by using a heritage built up by its previous members. Nevertheless, we disagree with them on the conclusions. They consider that the owner of the capital has to be the sole 'residual claimant' (Demsetz, 1988). This argument refers to efficiency, regardless of considerations of equity. In this chapter, we seek an economic foundation for the distribution of economic rights. Efficiency conditions are important but do not override equity as a goal. If the structural organization of market societies implies that the collective group is the final producer, equity implies that it should be the final holder of the collective surplus.[36]

The Aristocratic Market or Equality of Individuals as Members of a Cooperative Institution

The idea of reserving economic rights to the owners of capital is an old one. A similar one was used in defining political rights and for the same reasons. In France, after the Revolution, the right to vote was reserved to property-owning citizens for reasons relating to incentives. Collective decision making fell to them because their fortune authorized them to be conscious and responsible. The organization of a monopoly of economic rights in favour of the owners of capital because they are the residual beneficiaries and so the most motivated actors makes the market into a censitary system with rights over the allocation of resources proportional to ownership and heritage.

On this view, the traditional market model appears to be an aristocratic model, in which rights (rights to appropriation and decision making) over the collective product and heritage are reserved for the production factor of capital alone. In the feudal model, the lord was the main rights holder by virtue of his power over land, which was the privileged factor of production. In modern production, capital, as a new aristocrat, has the privilege of holding exclusive rights over the collective surplus.

A democratic model of market organization is based on the recognition of the rights of all the participants in production and exchange because they all contribute to the collective surplus generated by the market organization, either through the exchange of goods and information or through production. Accordingly a new working programme starts, which is to define the scope of such rights and the means of exercising them.

Such a conception seems to be fairer and truer to republican ethics than the conception that monopolizes the rights over the product for the benefit of one particular group of actors, the owners of capital. It is right too as the owners of the capital do not directly manage firms but hire managers.

It also seems more realistic in a world in which production is no longer connected to an energy-resources paradigm (production as the transformation of human and natural energy, production considered as worker's sweat) but is increasingly connected to an informational paradigm (creation together with the management of factors give the product).[37]

Obviously that does not mean that everyone will obtain equal power over a firm or over society, or indeed that the state should become the owner and manager of the market. Procedures have to be imagined which mix individual and collective rights.

Autonomy

Hobbes' criticism can be extended to market management. For Hobbes, individuals alienate their freedom to the benefit of the law. In return, the state provides security and protection of property by improving rules and laying down political norms. In the same way, on the idea that, like the legal system, the market order is a system of constraints and opportunities, the market ensures free exchange, provides security and the protection of property and favours production and wealth by imposing a system of prices and determining economic norms but by compelling individuals to accept the system of prices instead of their own valuations. The standard answers are that the system of constraints is inescapable as it expresses scarcity, that it is the best way of managing scarcity, and that the freedom afforded by market exchange offsets the constraints it imposes. As already seen, the market exchange relation limits mutual dependence for it makes it possible to choose new partners for each transaction or to jump at opportunities. However, consideration of the organic character of exchanges qualifies that remark. For instance, the employee can change employer but cannot usually change his status as employee. Marxist or institutionalist analyses emphasize that positions in relations of exchange and production seem to be self-replicating; behind the anonymity of exchanges, it is the same groups that are invariably buyers or sellers, particularly on the labour market, reflecting a process of social segmentation of consumption and investment (especially in human capital). Such polarization of positions, with its cumulative effect, has repercussions on the conditions of political and economic democracy as it facilitates the reproduction of dominance. It contradicts the formal principles of republican equality and freedom.

Action to democratize the working of the market implies action to limit dominance in market relations. Economic actors, with their inequalities and their differences have to be reintroduced into the analysis of the workings of markets, as in Sen's capability-based perspective.[38] Obviously this does not mean strict equality but the protection of economic minorities.

The definition of the state as belonging to the rule of law gives individuals some rights and protection against collective arbitrariness. The rule of law protects the politically weak, but the same question arises for the economically weak. For Smith, a significant justification of the market was that it helped the poor. History shows this has not always been the case. As for the protection of individuals from the state in the political domain and for the protection of the weak (for example the mechanism of legal guardians) the question arises of the protection of individuals from the market in the economic domain and, mainly, of the protection of the 'market disabled'. The principal form of protection is the law because protection implies the organization of relative power. For instance, European law defines 'essential facilities' or public utilities offering a universal service, with equal access and equal treatment whatever the costs of delivery.

Accountability and Pluralism

Any democratization of the workings of the market has to consider its dimension of rivalry. Rivalry is a rivalry of interests and of opinions, particularly of individual preferences and valuations, arising in explicit markets and implicit markets (for instance to evaluate damage to the environment or irreversibility costs). Nietzsche's philosophy showed that divergences of representations and subjectivities are inevitable, that is, objective scarcity cannot be separated from subjective valuations. So, unlike in Rousseau's model, reason is not a sufficient basis for defining a single common interest and managing economics. Pluralism is not only a property of politics but also of economics. A consequence of this is that democracy requires a more transparent market, against fetishism: prices have to be seen as scarcity and preferences indicators, according to the power of each agent. In the political domain, Habermas proposes forming a public domain where debate can take place, a public forum for deliberation. Arendt also emphasizes the need in a democracy for a public political arena for discussion and deliberation. Might the same not apply in the economic domain for managing conflicts among individual or group interests? In the same way, a public forum for debate reflects the emergence of public opinion as a separate entity from political power and the state. Might economic public opinion emerge and exist independently of the market mechanism? At the same time, there arises the issue of competence to decide on economic issues. Centuries ago, Plato criticized political democracy for giving too much power to demagogues and Sophists (the men who spoke too easily). Might the same not be true of economic democracy? The matter of the procedures by which an economic democracy can be organized is a fundamental one, but this topic is still in its infancy.

CONCLUSION

I have sought here to consider the distribution of economic rights in much the same way as the standard theory of democracy considers the distribution of political rights. I have tried to derive a principle of economic democracy not from ethical or a priori choices but from the conditions of a modern society considered as a *communitas*. A republican interpretation of political democracy and the related debates have yielded important results: democracy results from equality among citizens, which is the source of popular sovereignty; it allows a distinction to be drawn between individual and social interests; it seeks to organize the workings of society so that individual and group relations escape from relations of dominance and so that minorities and individuals are protected. Autonomy adds to equality. Nevertheless, this framework tends to understate economic rivalry.

History has raised the question of economic rights according to the dualism of our societies. What is at issue is not the size of the market domain but the articulation between republican and market logics. Even then, it is necessary to characterize market logic: it is not reducible to temporary and independent exchanges but organizes organic exchanges within a global framework, imparting to the market a character of *communitas*. As a *communitas*, embedded in time, the market bestows a peculiar status on agents: they are simultaneously rivals and members of a cooperative system. This forms an economic basis for democratic economic rights, considering that all members of the collective institutions of the market and the firm have some collective rights over their workings and their output. A new theoretical programme then emerges, that of imagining the conditions and procedures for such rights.

NOTES

1. 'Democracy as a universal value', *Journal of Democracy*, **10** (3) (1999: 4).
2. *Libération*. 7/9/2001: 20.
3. Its object is not the incentive or the monitoring procedures for developing democracy. It is not mainly concerned by the working of democratic processes but by the definition of economic democracy.
4. 'La mise en oeuvre de la souveraineté du peuple.'
5. In both models, there may be a social contract, so contractualism does not suffice to distinguish them. In *societas* models, it is conceived as an inter-individual contract whereas in *communitas* models it is a central and global contract between each individual and the whole society.
6. 'C'est une loi fondamentale de la démocratie que le peuple seul fasse les lois', in *De l'esprit des lois*, Book II, Chapter II, quoted by Rosanvallon, 2000: 27. Amartya Sen uses a similar definition of freedom to include economic aspects of freedom such as the will

to cooperate and conceives of economic freedom simultaneously as a social engagement and an individual capacity.

7. According to Berlin's definition (Berlin, I., 1969, 'Two concepts of liberty', I. Berlin, *Four Essays on Liberty*, London: Oxford University Press. New edn. in Berlin 2002), founded on a distinction introduced by B. Constant between the liberty of the Ancients and of the Moderns. Negative liberty refers to a mere absence of constraints or obstacles external to the agent, whereas positive liberty refers to the presence of the possibility to act. Berlin wrote that we use the negative concept of liberty in attempting to answer the question: 'What is the area within which the subject – a person or group of persons – is or should be left to do or be what he is able to do or be, without interference by other persons?'; whereas we use the positive concept in attempting to answer the question 'What, or who, is the source of control or interference that can determine someone to do, or be, this rather than that?' (1969: 121–2).
8. Tocqueville used a conception of freedom considering both negative and positive aspects: freedom is not only a private liberty but also a political liberty, a possibility of civic participation.
9. Rosanvallon, 2000: 14. Many authors (for instance, in political philosophy Pettit, 1997 and Skinner, 1998, in philosophy MacCallum, 1967) say that freedom (in the negative meaning) is not merely the absence of constraints and the enjoyment of a sphere of non-interference but the enjoyment of certain conditions in which such non-interference is guaranteed and then the presence of a democratic constitution. Conversely, freedom (in the positive meaning) implies commitment to democratic institutions with individual guarantees. For instance, Habermas defines on one hand rights to privacy and individual autonomy and on the other rights to public participation (1997: 138–49).
10. Rawls, who focuses on the distribution of the basic rights and primary goods, develops a model of inter-individual contract that seems to be a *societas* model. However, the fiction of the veil of ignorance allows him to have undefined people whose social quality is only their belonging to society. They do not contract as separate individuals but as members of this collective institution that pre-exists social differentiation.
11. Macpherson also shows that the principle of balance introduced by Harrington connects the distribution of political power with the distribution of land ownership (absolute monarchy when a single man has more than three-quarters of the whole property, mixed monarchy when an aristocracy is in the same situation, republic when the people is the major owner).
12. 'Cette jouissance paisible de l'indépendance individuelle'. Guizot's liberalism extends this project by limiting democracy to the private sphere and abolishing the principle of popular sovereignty (Rosanvallon, 2000: 40).
13. Although the community results from a social contract, it constitutes a new phenomenon, over and above inter-individual contracts. After the social contract each individual acts not as a private and autonomous person but as a member, a component part of the community, a citizen.
14. Kant (Projet de paix perpétuelle, 1795 [1958]) wrote, in the same way, that obedience to the law is an act of freedom because the individual is both subject and legislator.
15. The idea of autonomy of the political logic of law is also underlined in the USA by the modern republican civic tradition; see Mercuro and Medema (2005).
16. Nevertheless, Rousseau wrote: 'no citizen should be rich enough to buy another, and none so poor that he has to sell himself' (Rousseau, *Social Contract*, 2.6: 87).
17. The same problem is addressed by Condorcet (Cinq Mémoires sur l'instruction publique, 1791) with the issue of education. Education is the precondition of social emancipation and of social stability (la division du travail favorisant la stupidité du peuple, 'l'instruction est le seul remède de ce mal, d'autant plus dangereux dans un Etat, que les lois y ont établi plus d'égalité', quoted by S. Audier, 2004: 41).
18. 'La souveraineté n'existe que d'une manière limitée et relative', B. Constant, quoted by Rosanvallon, 2000: 106.
19. In British Republicanism, one strand (Nedham, Neville, Sidney) takes its inspiration from Machiavelli's model and focuses on conflicts while another (Harrington) focuses on

harmony. Montesquieu, Ferguson and Tocqueville also developed the idea of the dynamic value of conflicts.
20. That of monarchy is the government of one person according to laws, and that of tyranny the government of one person without laws.
21. And not honour as in monarchy or fear as in tyranny. It is because virtue is the precondition for the smooth running of republics that Montesquieu thinks that the republican form is only possible for small societies and that a big society needs monarchy.
22. 'In a free state asking for brave people at war and shy ones when in peace is something impossible; generally speaking anytime one can see everybody being quiet in a state calling itself a republic, one can be sure that freedom is not there', *Reflections on the reasons of the Romans' rise and fall* ('Demander, dans un Etat libre, des gens hardis dans la guerre, et timides dans la paix, c'est vouloir des choses impossibles; et, pour règle générale, toutes les fois qu'on verra tout le monde tranquille dans un Etat qui se donne le nom de République, on peut être assuré que la liberté n'y est pas', 'Considérations sur les causes de la grandeur des Romains et de leur décadence', 1734).
23. La démocratie 'répand dans tout le corps social une inquiète activité, une force surabondante, une énergie qui n'existe jamais sans elle, et qui, pourvu que les circonstances soient favorables, peut enfanter des merveilles'; Tocqueville, 1986: 237, quoted by Audier, 2004: 48.
24. Rousseau would have liked to change the alienation of freedom into a conquest for freedom with the idea of a free adherence to law rationality.
25. A. Smith, *An Inquiry into the Nature and Causes of the Wealth of Nations*, 1776. Book IV, chapter 2, quoted in Combee, 1991: 73.
26. Pettit, 1999: 165.
27. Ibid.
28. In the liberal tradition J. S. Mill or A. Sen also insist on conditions of social dependency.
29. Nevertheless, Pettit understates the idea of community which was inherent to the classical conception of republic to mainly examine inter-individual or inter-groups relations (women/men, nationals/foreigners, . . .).
30. 'Il n'y a donc pas un foyer unique d'où sortirait comme par émanation toutes ses relations de pouvoir, mais un enchevêtrement de relations de pouvoir qui, au total, rend possible la domination d'une classe sur une autre, d'un groupe sur un autre', 1994, 3: 379.
31. Conflicts of subjective rights or objective rules in legal theory, group and classification conflicts in sociology, all manner of conflicts in political science and history, struggles between races, sexes, ethnic groups, generations, civilizations, power struggles, and so on.
32. In the Mercantilist period, impoverishment was connected to restrictions in competition (guilds, collusion, barriers to entry, and so on). But, now, data show that market economies are unable to prevent mass poverty (in the United States and in France approximately 10 per cent of the population lives below the poverty line and this figure has not fallen with globalization since 1980). Beyond the situation of industrialized countries, there is the mass poverty of non-industrialized countries.
33. 'On ne peut avoir la république dans la société tant qu'on a la monarchie dans l'entreprise . . . La démocratie politique est insuffisante: ce que nous voulons, c'est que le travailleur, non seulement ait un bulletin de vote pour nommer un représentant politique, mais soit, dans l'usine, capable de participer lui-même à la direction des affaires de l'industrie dans laquelle il travaille.' Quoted by P. Rosanvallon (2000: 360).
34. The fact that the French supreme court itself has been led to distinguish between formal and real freedom is very meaningful. In its judgment of 30 May 2000, the court declared that the economic constraint hanging over a contracting party may be such violence that it invalidates its consent and nullifies the contract. If the contracting party can prove that it became involved under the constraint of its economic situation because it had no other choice than to contract and accept the proposed conditions, the contract will have to be nullified. Alongside the vice related to physical violence or to moral duress the introduction of economic duress not exercised by a person but by the economic and social context can completely change contract laws.
35. Nozick (1973) 47–8.

36. Hence the legitimacy of the claim of the Moulinex worker made redundant after 30 years in refusing that the factory's future should depend on the decision of the manager and consequently countering it with the idea of rights conferred by her long-term involvement in a collective industrial undertaking.
37. This is attested, significantly by the fact that corporate management teams – and not only in Japan namely the case of stock-options for managerial staff – organize different methods of payment based on recognition of the employee's long-term contribution to the firm.
38. Positive freedom becomes a capability, that is an entitlement to rights and the capability to convert them into actual earnings.

REFERENCES

Audier, S. (2004), *Tocqueville retrouvé: genèse et enjeux du renouveau tocquevillien français*, Paris: Vrin-EHESS.

Barni, J. (1872), *Le Manuel Républicain*, Paris: Librarie Germer Bailliére.

Barrère, C. (2005), 'Law, justice and republic: the French republican model of judicial regulation', in A. Marciano and J. M. Josselin (eds), *Law and the State, A Political Economy Approach*, Cheltenham, UK and Northampton, MA, USA: Edward Elgar, pp. 283–309.

Barrère, C., D. Barthélémy, M. Nieddu, F.-D. Vivien (2004), *Réinventer le patrimoine?*, Paris: L'Harmattan.

Barro, R. J. (1991), 'Economic growth in a cross section of countries', *Quarterly Journal of Economics*, **106** (2), 407–33.

Barro, R. J. (1995), *Economic Growth*, New York: McGraw Hill.

Barro, R. J. (1997), *Determinants of Economic Growth, A Cross-Country Empirical Study*, Cambridge, MA: MIT Press.

Berlin, I. (1969), 'Two concepts of liberty', in I. Berlin, *Four Essays on Liberty*, new edn 2002, London: Oxford University Press.

Bourgeois, L. (1902), *Solidarité*, new edition 1996, Toulouse: Presses du Septentrion.

Breton, A., G. Galeotti, P. Salmon and R. Wintrobe (2003), *Rational Foundations of Democratic Politics*, Cambridge: University Press.

Carrier, B. (1993), *L'analyse économique des conflits. Eléments d'histoire des doctrines*, Paris: Publications de la Sorbonne.

Combee, J. and E. Norton (1991), *Economic Justice in Perspective*, Englewood Cliffs, NJ: Prentice Hall.

Comte-Sponville, A. (2004), *Le capitalisme est-il moral?*, Paris: Albin Michel.

Condorcet, J.-A.-N. de Caritat (1791), *Cinq mémoires sur l'instruction publique*, reprinted 1994, Paris: Flammarion.

Demsetz, H. (1988), *Ownership, Control and the Firm*, Oxford: Basil Blackwell.

Elias, N. (1973), *La civilisation des mœurs*, édition Presses Pocket, Paris: Calmann-Lévy.

Ferguson, A. (1799), *The History of the Progress and Termination of the Roman Republic*, new edition, revised and corrected, Edinburgh: Bell & Bradfute.

Foucault, M. (1961), *Histoire de la folie à l'âge classique*, Paris: Gallimard.

Foucault, M. (1975), *Surveiller et punir. Naissance de la prison*, Paris: Gallimard.

Foucault, M. (1994), *Dits et Ecrits. 1954–1988*, 4 vols, Paris: Gallimard.

Friedman, M. (1962), *Capitalism and Freedom*, Chicago, IL: University of Chicago Press.

Fukuyama, F. (1992), *The End of History and the Last Man*, New York: Free Press.
Habermas, J. (1997), *Droit et démocratie*, Paris: Gallimard.
Hobbes, T. (1660), *Leviathan*, reprinted 1998, Oxford: Oxford University Press.
Kant, E. (1795), *Projet de paix perpétuelle, traduit et réédité*, reprinted 1958, Paris: PUF.
Kriegel-Barret, B. (1998), *Philosophie de le République*, Paris: Plon.
Kolm, S.-C. (1977), *La transition socialiste: la politique économique de la gauche*, Paris: Cerf.
Lepage, H. (1978), *Autogestion et capitalisme, Réponses à l'anti-économie*, Paris: Masson.
Lipset, S. M. (1994), The social requisites of democracy revisited, *American Sociological Review*, **59**, 1–22.
Lipset, S. M. (1959), 'Some social requisites of democracy: economic development and political legitimacy', *American Political Science Review*, **53**, 69–105.
Lipset, S. M., K.-R. Seong and J. C. Torres (1993), A comparative analysis of the social requisites of democracy, *International Social Science Journal*, **136**, 155–75.
MacCallum, G. (1967), 'Negative and positive freedom', *Philosophical Review*, **76**, 312–34, reprinted in Miller (1991).
Machiavelli, N. (1513), *The Prince*, reprinted 2005, Oxford: Oxford University Press.
Macpherson, C. B. (1962), *The Political Theory of Possessive Individualism*, Oxford: Oxford University Press; French edn 1971, *La théorie politique de l'individualisme possessif, De Hobbes à Locke*, Paris: Gallimard.
Mercuro, N. and S. G. Medema (2005), *Economics and the Law, From Posner to Post-modernism and Beyond*, Princeton, NJ: Princeton University Press.
Miller, D. (ed.) (1991), *Liberty*, Oxford: Oxford University Press.
Montesquieu, C.-L. de Secondat (1734), *Considérations sur les causes de la grandeur des Romains et de leur décadence*, new edn 1852, Paris: P. Ducrocq.
Montesquieu, C.-L. de Secondat (1748), *De l'esprit des lois*, Paris: Editions Larousse.
Nozick, R. (1973), 'Distributive justice', *Philosophy and Public Affairs*, **3** (1), 45–126.
Nussbaum, M. (1990), 'Aristotelian social democracy', in R. B. Douglass, G. M. Mara and H. S. Richardson, *Liberalism and the Good*, New York and London: Routledge, pp. 203–52.
Padis, M. A. (1989), *Marcel Gauchet, la genèse de la démocratie*, Paris: Michalon.
Pettit, P. (1993), *The Common Mind. An Essay on Psychology, Society and Politics*, Oxford: Oxford University Press.
Pettit, P. (1993), 'Negative liberty, liberal and republican', *European Journal of Philosophy*, **1**, 15–38.
Pettit, P. (1997), *Republicanism. A Theory of Freedom and Government*, Oxford: Oxford University Press.
Pettit, P. (1999), 'Republican freedom and contestatory democratization', in I. Shapiro and C. Hacker-Cordon, *Democracy's Value*, New Haven, CT: Yale University Press, pp. 163–90.
Proudhon, P.-J. (1853), *Manuel du spéculateur à la Bourse*, Paris: Garnier Frères.
Rosanvallon, P. (2000), *La démocratie inachevée. Histoire de la souveraineté du peuple en France*, Paris: Gallimard.
Rousseau, J.-J. (1762), *Du contrat social ou principes du droit politique, par Jean-Jacques Rousseau, citoyen de Genève*, Amsterdam: Marc Michel Rey; *The Social Contract*, translated by Christopher Betts and reprinted 1993, Oxford: Oxford University Press.

Samuels, W. J. (1971), 'Interrelations between legal and economic processes', *Journal of Law and Economics*, **14** (October), 435–50.
Sen, A. (1984), *Choice, Welfare and Measurement*, Oxford: Blackwell; Cambridge, MA: MIT Press.
Sen, A. (1985), 'Well-being, agency and freedom: the Dewey lectures', *Journal of Philosophy*, **82**, 169–221.
Sen, A. (1987a), *The Standard of Living*, Cambridge: Cambridge University Press.
Sen, A. (1987b), *On Ethics and Economics*, Oxford: Blackwell Publishers.
Sen, A. (1993), 'Markets and freedoms: achievements and limitations of the market mechanism in promoting individual freedoms', *Oxford Economic Papers*, **45**(4), 519–41.
Skinner, Q. (1990), 'Machiavelli's "Discorsi" and the pre-humanist origins of republican ideas', in G. Bock, Q. Skinner and M. Viroli, *Machiavelli and Republicanism*, Cambridge: Cambridge University Press.
Skinner, Q. (1998), *Liberty before Liberalism*, Cambridge: Cambridge University Press.
Smith, A. (1776), *An Inquiry into the Nature and Causes of the Wealth of Nations*, edited by Edwin Cannan, new edn 1994, New York: Modern Library.
Taylor, C. (1979), 'What's wrong with negative liberty', in A. Ryan (ed.), *The Idea of Freedom*, Oxford: Oxford University Press, pp. 175–93; also in D. Miller (ed.), *Liberty*, Oxford: Clarendon Press, pp. 141–62 (1991).
Tocqueville, A. de (1835 and 1840), *De la démocratie en Amérique*, new edn 1986, Paris: Robert Laffont.
Waldron, J. (1993), 'Homelessness and the issue of freedom', in J. Waldron (ed.), *Liberal Rights*, Cambridge: Cambridge University Press, pp. 309–38.

5. The big pattern of democracy: a study of the Gastil Index

Martin Paldam

INTRODUCTION

The Gastil Index,[1] which measures the degree of democracy, is now available for 171 countries from 1972 till 2003. These data are crude, and they have often been criticized, but at present they are taken as given. They are given as two integers for each country and year, measuring democratic rights and civil liberties on a scale from 1 to 7. This chapter uses the average of the two data. They are scaled so that 1 is pure democracy, while 7 is pure dictatorship. This scaling may confuse, but the index is used as posted.

The chapter shows that democracy has increased – the index has fallen – in the average country from 4.6 to 3.2, but the underlying pattern is much more complex. Explaining the development of democracy for 171 countries over 32 years is potentially an endless job. However, the chapter only aims to study the big pattern in the index by considering three theories:

1. Lipset's Law:[2] The Grand Transition – from poor to rich[3] – leads to democracy.
2. The Reverse Lipset: Countries become rich because they are democracies.
3. The family of theories claiming that democracy is determined by culture.

All three theories can be true at the same time. 1 and 2 deal with the relation between the Gastil Index and the standard of living, while 3 considers various 'cultural' classifications of the countries. The appendix lists the 171 countries and the classifications used. The three theories are discussed only at the *operational* level as explanations of the data at hand. Evidence will be presented that 1 and 3 are both true, and it is further demonstrated that 3 is still true when controlled for 1, while little support is found for 2.

Democracy is sometimes seen as a 'Western' concept, and it has been claimed that other concepts of democracy exist which are more relevant elsewhere. The author disagrees with this line of argument. There are, of course, other ideals than democracy such as obedience to God or the Party, service of the Nation, equality, a high standard of living, and so on, but to term them 'democracy' is to confuse issues.

The next section gives a few basic observations on the data. The following section looks at the three theories, while the third section turns to the main pattern in the data. The fourth section considers the rich countries, while the fifth section looks at the Muslim exception. The sixth section deals with the historical experiment of the 33 countries that are either still Communist or in transition from socialism. The final section concludes the chapter.

A FIRST LOOK AT THE DATA: TREND AND STABILITY

The average path of the Gastil Index for all 171 countries is shown in Figure 5.1. The regression line shown (reg 6 in Table 5.3) has a significantly negative slope corresponding to the rise of about 67 percent in income (real GDP per capita) that has happened during the period. However, there was no trend before 1987 when the rule of Gorbachev in the Soviet Union started to affect the control of the center over the empire, so the graph can be alternatively interpreted as reflecting the victory of the West in the Cold War, and the resulting expansion of Western values in the world.

The standard deviations – as defined in Table 5.1 – of the Gastil Index are measures of political system stability. S_t (Figure 5.2a) shows the stability over time, while S_i looks at the stability across countries (Figure 5.2b). Not surprisingly, we note that the average $A(S_t) > A(S_i)$.

The stability over time S_t has no trend. However, the values for the 1980s are relatively high, pointing to the period as one of unusual political turmoil. It is interesting that the instability starts already in the early 1980s before it takes a systematic direction.

The cross-country stability has a characteristic parabolic shape:

$$S_i = \underset{(2.2)}{-0.953} + \underset{(12.6)}{1.112A_i} - \underset{(12.1)}{0.138A_i^2} \quad R^2 = 0.49, n = 171 \qquad (5.1)$$

numbers in parentheses are *t*-ratios.

Stability is only present at the two extremes, especially at the high democracy end. Political systems at average Gastil Scores of 3–5 are rather unstable. This corresponds to well-known observations, namely that sufficiently tough dictatorships tend to last for some time, but the most permanent

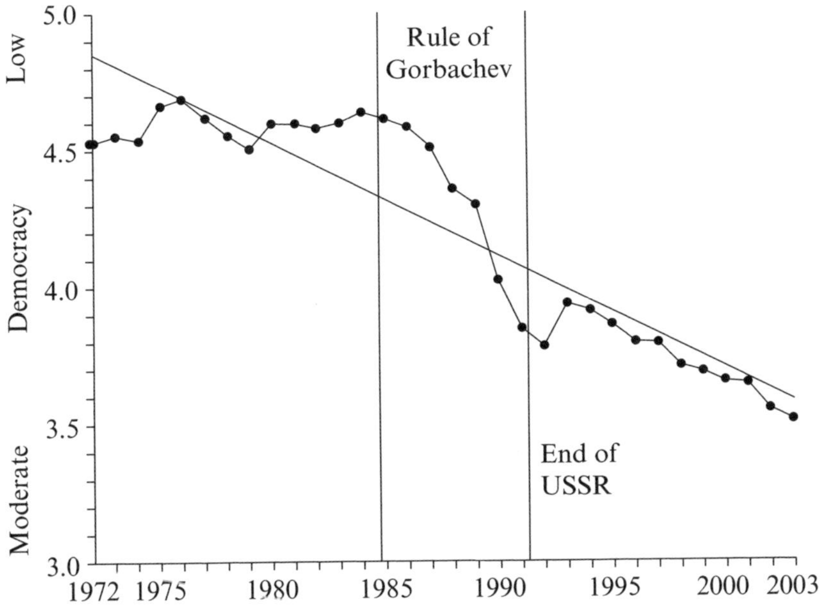

Note: Soviet power in the East Bloc loosened gradually from 1988 to 1991 when USSR was dissolved.

Figure 5.1 The average Gastil Index, A_t, *for the 171 countries 1972–2003*

system appears to be democracy once it has survived the first couple of decades. It has even been termed the 'end of history' in Fukuyama (1992). Systems of partial or steered democracy are always under pressure to change either way.[4]

THREE THEORIES

Two of the three theories listed in the introduction deal with the relation between democracy and economic development, y_{it}.[5] The third theory relates democracy to culture: it will be operationalized as a set of six 'folk' theories and ideas. Finally, some statistical problems are discussed, and the estimating equation is presented.

The Grand Transition normally lasts one to two centuries when a country starts as poor LDC, goes through low Mic (middle income) and high Mic to become a DC. The process is far more than growth[6] as it changes society profoundly: the structure of production changes, and urbanization increases. The level of education rises dramatically. Children

Table 5.1 Averages and standard deviations over time and across countries

Over	Running average	Average: $A = 4.21$	Running standard deviation	Average standard deviations
Time	$A_t = \sum_{i=1,171} \gamma_{it}/171$	$A = \sum_{t=1,32} A_t/32$	$S_t = \left(\sum_{i=1,171} (A_i - \gamma_{it})^2 \right)/170$	$A(S_t) = \sum_{i=1,32} S_t/32 = 1.99$
Country	$A_t = \sum_{t=1,32} \gamma_{it}/32$	$A = \sum_{i=1,171} A_i/171$	$S_i = \left(\sum_{t=1,32} (A_t - \gamma_{it})^2 \right)/31$	$A(S_i) = \sum_{i=1,171} S_i/171 = 0.89$

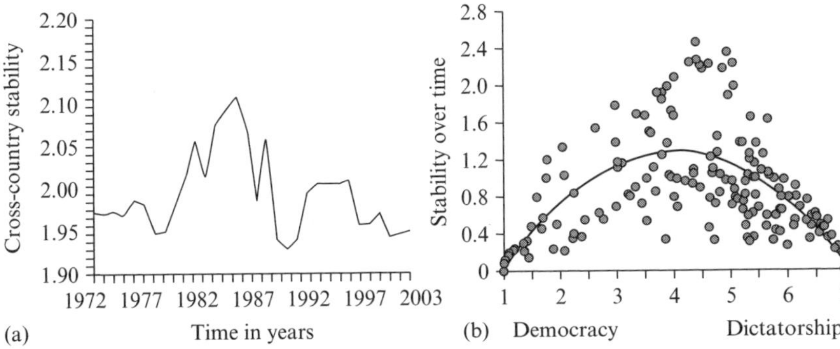

Note: The curve on Figure 5.2b is reg 1 in text. While ten countries (all Western) have perfect democracy, 1.0, for all 32 years, only one country (North Korea) has perfect dictatorship, 7.0, for all years.

Figure 5.2 Political system stability over time and across countries: (a) Over time: S_t *as a function of time; (b) Across countries:* S_i *as a function of* A_i

cease to be an economic necessity and become an expensive consumption good, and people's concept of family changes from extended to core. The income distribution becomes more equal, and so on. The process is complex, and the variables interact in a highly simultaneous way as sketched in panel A of Figure 5.3. Hence, it is very easy to present a model giving any causal structure, or the reverse one. We are looking for signs of the main direction. Our arguments and findings support the causal structure depicted on Figure 5.3.

Part of the process is the improvement of a certain group of non-material externality goods. They are social capital and honesty, civil liberties and democratic rights, security in the streets and homes, and even happiness – they appear in panel B of Figure 5.3.[7] It is strong evidence for the Lipset Law that the Grand Transition is associated with a large improvement in a whole class of similar externality goods.

The structure of causality depicted in Figure 5.3 takes the development process to be highly simultaneous, while the improvement of the various externality goods is considered to be mainly an outcome. We thus distinguish between main causality from the transition to the externality goods and the virtue-rewarded loop the other way, of which the Reverse Lipset is one member. The name given to the reverse causality indicates that it would be nice indeed if honesty, trust, low crime rates and democracy were causal factors in economic development, and not the other way round. We look for signs that this is the case. A recent meta study, Docouliagos and

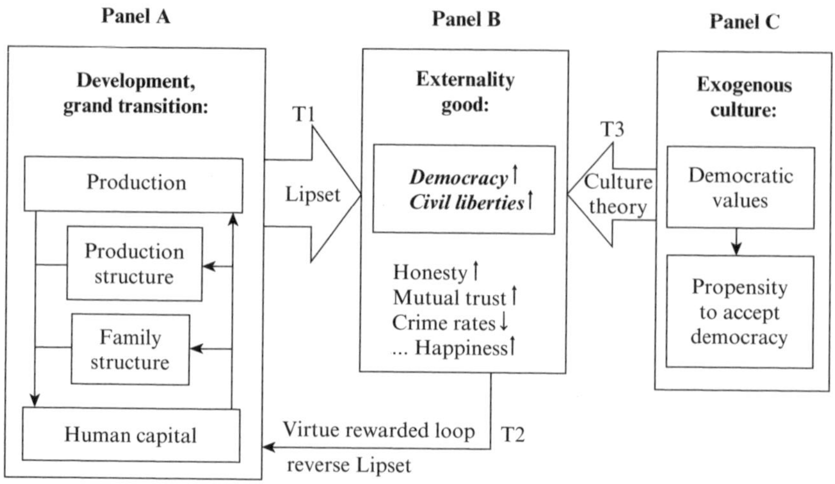

Figure 5.3 The causal structure discussed

Ulubasoglu (2005), covers 81 studies of the reverse Lipset effect and conclude that it is small but positive.[8]

The group of externality goods is indeed virtuous 'goods'. They are also fully or partly public goods (except happiness), and they are not supplied via the normal market and not even deliberately produced: they could hence be seen as positive externalities that follow from the development process. However, we know from polls as well as from much casual evidence that people value and demand these goods. Anyone who visits a corrupt society is likely to have noticed that people do not like it. Also, even in countries with no democracy, governments often take great care 'enacting' the outward shells of democracy as a way to obtain legitimacy and perhaps as homage to virtue.

The causal link from income to democracy may operate in a narrow or a broad way. The narrow version has income as the key variable: $\gamma=\gamma(y)$. The broad version has as a function of the entire transition: $\gamma=\gamma$(education, family structure, y).

The narrow theory sees the generation of these goods as purely demand driven, and the economist will explain the process of their improvement as the production of a demand driven luxury good – that is, a good with an income elasticity above 1. Studies of the pattern of consumption (since the classical study by Houthakker, 1957) find that elasticities generalize when goods are aggregated into groups. This result suggests that if the level of these goods in society is demand driven, then the elasticities are general too. This line of thought thus explains Lipset's Law by a deep parameter in human behavior, and rejects the idea that culture is the key explanation.

The broad theory sees the generation of these goods as a consequence of the whole of the Grand Transition, and thus it is closer to the externality view. It is because society changes that people come to demand more honesty and democracy. This version of the theory suffers from wooliness: the explanation should be further developed so that it becomes clear which parts of the Grand Transition explain what.

The data contains a group of oil countries that are rich due to resource rent and has not gone through the Grand Transition. They are much less democratic than other rich countries. This supports the broad theory rather than the narrow one.

A culture may be seen as a set of weights given to the values that are common to all people. A cultural theory is thus a theory that the weights differ systematically between cultures. One value is the preference for democracy. If one culture values democracy more than another, one should observe that the average Gastil Score is lower in the countries of the first group, also when the analysis is controlled for other relevant variables.

Cultural theories are empirically difficult because it is hard to find adequate measures for 'culture' to use in a formal test. This chapter therefore uses various country classifications and binary dummy variables to account for these classifications.[9] Thus, a classification is a box in which some countries are placed, and the corresponding dummy variable is set to one. If they are outside the box, the dummy is zero. The theory that the said culture matters is tested by examining if its dummy generates significant and robust coefficients in a set of regressions using different controls.

The level of analysis pursued demands cultural theories that are at the same time very general and easy to operationalize statistically. Such theories inevitably become rather like stereotypical 'folk' theories, even though books have been written about each of them. The following cultural hypotheses have been included:

1. Democracy originated in the West, and some claim it is a particularly Western value, which means that Western countries should have an unusually high propensity for accepting democracy. It is tested by including a Western dummy variable of the type described. Due to the scaling of the Gastil Index, the coefficient to the Western dummy should be negative if Western countries are more democratic. It appears that a broad agreement exists about the countries that should be termed Western. We have subdivided the West into (a) a group of Old West, and (b) a group of Convergers like Greece and Spain, which were Mic countries in the first half of the twentieth century, but have converged to become rich Western countries.

2. The Latin American countries are a distinct group of Mic countries with a culture related to the Western one. For a long time the Latin American countries pursued a special policy mix that involved economic isolation. Hence one would expect these countries to have a coefficient that deviates to the same side from the general pattern as does the West, though perhaps less so.
3. Another well-known hypothesis is that the countries in the Orient (Far East) have Asian values, which give democracy a low weight relative to economic growth and political stability. This should give the Orient dummy a positive sign. A special group of Oriental countries are the Asian Tigers, which already have a Western standard of living.
4. A popular cultural theory claims that the Muslim world is adverse to such Western values as democracy. Muslim countries are defined as countries that have a large Muslim majority and a Muslim government. Hence, Sudan, Lebanon and Indonesia are classified as Muslim, while Nigeria, Tanzania and Kenya are not. In addition, a variable for the Arab countries has been included as the original core group where Muslim culture is likely to be particularly strong.
5. A special case is the countries that were ruled by a Communist party before 1990. Of these, a few are still Communist, while the rest are the Transition countries, which have chosen new economic and political systems since 1990. They provide a fine historical experiment.
6. As already mentioned, it is important to single out the oil countries. Consequently, an oil dummy is included for countries with oil as the dominating export good.

Many countries belong to several groups: Libya is thus Muslim, Arab and an oil country, while Norway is a Western oil country, and so on. One hundred and seventy-one countries provide a fair amount of observations for tests. Appendix Table 5A.1 shows how the countries are classified for the statistical test.

Within the time span of 32 years considered, the average country has had a growth per capita of about 1.6 percent per annum or 67 percent. This is substantial, but still small compared to the Grand Transition – to analyse this, we have to use the cross-country variation. Also, 32 years is too short for major cultural change, so we take cultures to be exogenous. So, for a study of the Gastil Index it is important to sort out the variation over time from the large cross-country variation. Consequently, the following cross-country model is used for the regressions in Tables 5.3 to 5.5.

$$\gamma_i^{32} = \alpha_0^{32} + \alpha_1^{32}\log y_i + \beta_1^{32}D_{1,i} + \ldots + \beta_n^{32}D_{n,i} + u_i \qquad (5.2)$$

$$\gamma_i^{10} = \alpha_0^{10} + \alpha_1^{10}\log y_i + \beta_1^{10} D_{1,i} + \ldots + \beta_n^{10} D_{n,i} + u_i \qquad (5.3)$$

$\gamma_i^{32}, \gamma_i^{10}$, are averages of the Gastil Index, *i*, for either all 32 years or for the last ten years. Income, y_i, is gdp, that is GDP per capita. Each *D* is a binary dummy for a culture or some other country characteristic as will be explained, and u_i is residuals. The αs and βs are the coefficients estimated. Theory 2 is the claim that there is a counter causality bias in α_1. We take it for granted that there is no such bias in the βs.

The present chapter thus uses a pure cross-country approach, which assumes that all adjustments to the changes in the variables take place within the time period studied. Panel approaches are used both in Borooah and Paldam (2007) and Jensen and Paldam (2007), where the following two models are explored:

$$\gamma_{it}^1 = \alpha_0^1 + \alpha_1^1 \log y_{it} + \beta_1^1 D_{1i} + \ldots + \beta_n^1 D_{ni} + u_{it}, \quad \textit{for each } t \qquad (5.4)$$

$$\gamma_{it}^N = \alpha_0 + \alpha_1^N \log y_{it-1} + \varphi^N \gamma_{it-1} + \beta_1^N D_{1i} + \ldots + \beta_n^N D_{ni} + v_{it} \qquad (5.5)$$

Where Equation 5.4 is estimated for every year available to study the dynamics in the coefficients, and Equation 5.5 is estimated for different *N*s to catch the adjustment over time, and then the fully adjusted (steady state) coefficients $z^\infty = z^N/(1 - \varphi^N)$ can be calculated for $z = \alpha_1, \beta_1, \ldots, \beta_n$. The different approaches give rather similar results: $\alpha_1^1 \approx \alpha_1^{10} \approx \alpha_1^{32} \approx \alpha_1^\infty$, $\beta_1^1 \approx \beta_1^{10} \approx \beta_1^{32} \approx \beta_1^\infty$, and so on.[10] However, the present chapter concentrates on the cross-country pattern.

THE BIG PATTERN IN THE DATA

First, the average scores for 1972–2003 will be considered, and then the path of the average αs over time is discussed. The *y*-data have the structure given in Table 5.A2 (of the Appendix). The proper year to use for the *y*-data is initial gdp, but as the transition countries are an important case, and their data make little sense before 1998, I use final gdp instead of initial.[11]

Figure 5.4 presents the basic support for Lipset's Law. It shows the average γ-score for 1972–2003 for all 171 countries explained by the logarithm to *y*, in 2001. The figure and the averages in Table 5.2 show four points:

1. A significant downward trend appears in the observations.
2. All countries with 'full' democracy are in the rich group.

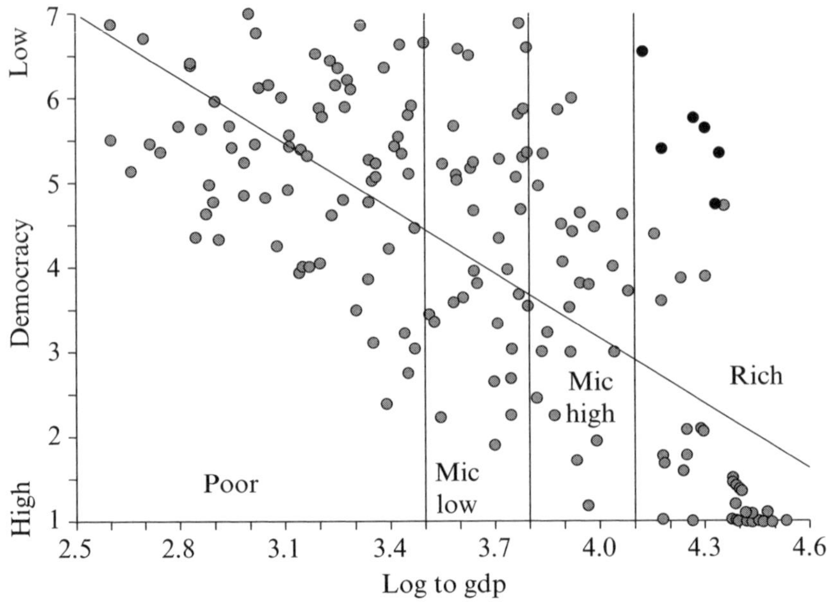

Figure 5.4 The average democracy score 1972–2003 explained by gdp 2001

3. Lipset's Law explains ⅓ of the variation in the data.
4. It is easy to suggest additional factors explaining more of the variation.

A first additional factor is suggested in the figure: seven points are extreme in being both rich and undemocratic. Six out of the seven outliers are the six richest oil countries (marked in black): Saudi Arabia, Bahrain, Brunei, Qatar, Kuwait and United Arab Emirates. The last rich outlier is Singapore. This is the first indication that the resource rent point is important. It should also be mentioned that the most extreme outlier to the other side is India, which has an unusually high level of democracy for its income level.

Table 5.2 shows various averages of the variables analysed. For now, we consider the four last columns showing averages for the Gastil Index, and how they deviate from the grand average.

5. The average score is 4.21 for all 32 years, and 3.72 for the last ten years. It is close to the middle of the scale (4 points) from no to full democracy.
6. Western countries are relatively democratic as expected. Also the Latin American group and the Asian Tigers appear relatively democratic.

Table 5.2 Average value of variables

Countries covered	Number of countries	gdp-PPP for 2001		for 32 years		for last 10 years	
		y	log *y*	Average	Δ	Average	Δ
Africa, South of Sahara	43	1727	3.10	5.26	1.05	4.60	0.88
Latin American	22	5753	3.72	3.24	−0.97	2.86	−0.86
Orient	16	8549	3.69	5.02	0.81	4.70	0.98
Of which Tigers	4	20 865	4.31	3.39	−0.82	2.63	−1.09
West	25	24 301	4.38	1.30	−2.91	1.17	−2.55
Of which old rich	15	26 658	4.42	1.07	−3.14	1.10	−2.62
Others	50	5536	3.63	4.42	0.21	3.58	−0.14
Muslim	44	5144	3.49	5.47	1.26	5.49	1.77
Of which Arab	16	8869	3.79	5.63	1.42	5.86	2.14
Communist	5	2252	3.31	6.71	2.50	6.80	3.08
Transition (ex com)	28	6364	3.71	(5.11)	(0.90)	3.59	−0.13
Oil countries	20	9886	3.86	4.99	0.78	4.99	1.27
All countries	171	7947	3.63	4.21	–	3.72	–

Note: The Δ-columns show the deviation from the average. The countries with less democracy than the average are shaded in gray. All averages are unweighted.

7. Two groups of countries have low scores: Communist and Muslim countries, where the core group of Arab countries is (even) less democratic than the average.

Communist countries have Gastil scores of 6–7. The Small Transition – the one from socialism since 1990 – provides a fine historical experiment demonstrating what political system countries prefer, given their history and income, when they have to make a new choice.

The development from 1972 to 2003 of the Gastil Index for the four income groups of countries in the World Bank classification (see Appendix) are shown in Figure 5.5. The trendless part of the aggregate curve from 1972 to 1986 is due to a small rise in the two poorest groups and a steady fall in the two richest groups. However, all four curves have a (significant) negative slope indicating that democracy increases. The increase for the average country is about 0.03 points a year or one full point on the scale over the 32 years. This corresponds to the average raise of 67 percent in real per capita income in the period.

The relative position of the four curves also supports Lipset's Law as the level of democracy for the four income groups differs precisely as predicted. The only deviation from the picture is the development of the Mic h(igh)

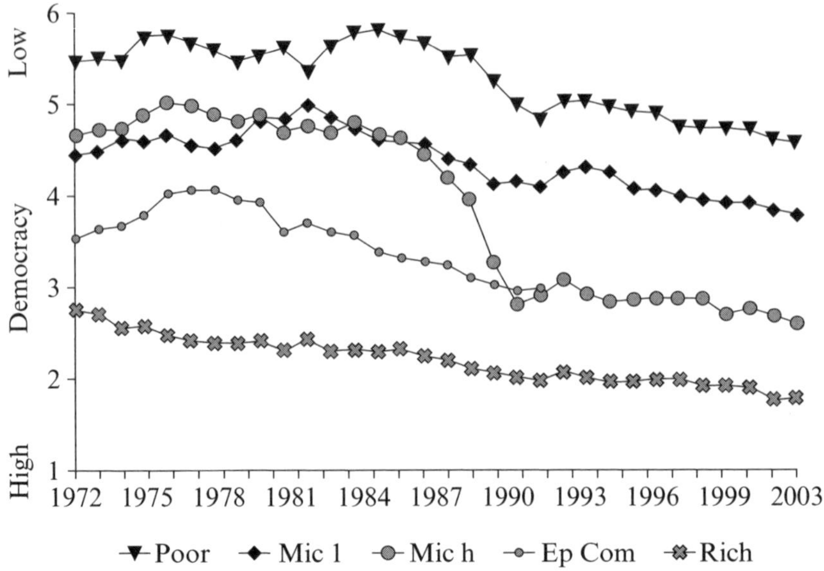

Figure 5.5 The development over time for the four main income groups of countries

group that intersects with the Mic l(ow) group before 1990. This is due to the high number (ten) of ex-Communist countries in the high Mic group now in transition. The 'Ep Com' line shows how much the high Mic curve changes when the ten Communist countries are excluded.

Some researchers – for example Przeworski *et al.* (2000) – explain the observations presented by the reverse causal structure: democracies are countries that develop particularly well and hence become rich. Here, the causality is from democracy to development. It surely would be great to see virtue rewarded, and a large number of studies have analysed the matter. The conclusion is that it has fared rather poorly as a variable explaining growth; see for example Barro and Sala-i-Martin (2003: 528–9) and Brunetti (1997).

Model 5.3 is used for the regressions of Table 5.3.[12] Lipset's Law predicts that log y_i gets a negative coefficient. It is indeed negative, always significant, and it obtains an $R^2 = 0.34$ if it is the only variable in the regression (reg. 6). The country groups included add almost as much explanatory power as Lipset's Slope, but the bulk of the extra explanation is from just two variables: Muslim and West.

Africa, Orient and Transition get insignificant coefficients. That is also the case in other combinations where these three variables are included either together or one at a time. Consequently, the countries in these groups

Table 5.3 Cross-country regressions explaining the average, 1994–2003, and y *for 2001*

	Const.	Log y	West	Muslim	Com	La Am	Trans	Africa	Orient	R^2	N
Reg 2	**7.86**	**−1.21**	**−1.40**	**1.87**	**2.85**	−0.64	−0.26	0.01	0.28	0.65	171
	(7.2)	(4.2)	(3.6)	(7.75)	(4.66)	(1.83)	(0.86)	(0.03)	(0.71)		
Reg 3	**7.92**	**−1.24**	**−1.35**	**1.87**	**3.09**	**−0.61**				0.64	171
	(9.9)	(5.4)	(4.0)	(8.4)	(5.7)	(2.1)					
Reg 4	**8.13**	**−1.33**	**−1.13**	**1.99**	**3.07**					0.63	171
	(10.1)	(5.9)	(3.5)	(9.2)	(5.6)						
Reg 5	**8.69**	**−1.45**	**−1.18**	**1.84**						0.56	171
	(10.0)	(5.9)	(3.3)	(7.8)							
Reg 6	**11.80**	**−2.23**								0.34	171
	(13.6)	(9.4)									

Note: The two numbers given in each row are the coefficient estimate and its *t*-ratio. Abbreviations: Com is Communist. La Am is Latin American. Trans is Ex-Communists. West is the old West group. Bold coefficients are significant at the 5% level, that is, where the *t*-ratio exceeds 1.9.

have the average level of democracy when controlled for their level of development. It is also the case for the Transition countries as will be discussed in the sixth section. The 'Asian Values' hypotheses find no support in these data; nor are African countries exceptional as regards democracy, but they are exceptionally poor.

Communist countries are three points less democratic relative to the Lipset Path, but the group consists of five countries only, so it does not add much to the R^2. Western countries are more than one point too democratic, and it is reflected in the Latin American group as well. Muslim countries are almost two points less democratic than they should be given their income level. This will be further analysed in the fifth section.

Table 5.4 adds the oil variable. It is significant, and the sign is always positive. Oil countries are less democratic. This once again supports the resource rent point. Clearly, it is not income alone, but also the transformation during the Grand Transition that causes democracy to rise. In Table 5.4, the Arab group is also singled out, and it appears to be less democratic than other Muslim countries even when controlled for oil and income.

THE 38 RICH COUNTRIES: IS THE WEST SPECIAL?

The data contain 38 rich countries: two are Caribbean 'tourist states', two are Transition countries discussed on pp. 119–21, five are Muslim Oil

Table 5.4 Cross-country regressions on the effect of oil on democracy

	Const.	Log *y*	Oil	West	Muslim	Arab	Com	R^2	*N*
Reg 7	**9.50**	**−1.74**	**0.88**	**−0.77**	**1.35**	**1.09**	**3.04**	0.68	171
	(11.7)	(7.6)	(2.9)	(2.4)	(5.4)	(2.8)	(5.9)		
Reg 8	**8.97**	**−1.59**	**1.11**	**−0.89**	**1.71**		**3.08**	0.66	171
	(11.1)	(7.0)	(3.7)	(2.76)	(7.66)		(5.9)		
Reg 9	**9.02**	**−1.58**		**−0.92**	**1.47**	**1.38**	**3.02**	0.66	171
	(11.1)	(6.9)		(2.9)	(5.8)	(3.6)	(5.7)		
Reg 10	**12.34**	**−2.44**	**2.10**					0.46	171
	(15.6)	(11.2)	(6.1)						

Note: See Table 5.3.

countries discussed in the next section. The remaining 30 countries are divided as listed in Table 5.A1 into: five Asian Tigers, ten Convergers and 15 Old West which are countries that were DCs already in the first half of the twentieth century – all countries in this group have been democracies for at least 50 years – most much longer.

The ideas of democracy and civil rights originally developed in the West. It is therefore arguable that they are relatively strong in the Western system of values. Figure 5.6 shows that the Old West is actually very democratic and has been so throughout the period. The Convergers are becoming more democratic as they become richer, and precisely the same applies to the Asian Tigers. This is, of course, a clear confirmation of Lipset's Law, and contrary to the Reverse Lipset idea.

We know from Table 5.2 that the Oriental countries do not deviate from the general trend, and it is interesting that the Asian Tigers, who made the Grand Transition exceptionally fast, have also had a quick transition to democracy. The regressions above suggest that they will not converge fully to the Western level, but may stop 1.25 from it as they do indeed seem to do in Figure 5.6. A closer inspection shows that the oldest Tiger – Japan – is now close to the Western level. It suggests that the transition from a 'reasonable' to a 'full' democracy takes considerable time, so perhaps the other Tigers will gradually become (even) more democratic just as the Convergers. In fact, the curve for the Tigers looks as the one for the Convergers with a delay of 15 years.

The exception to the general picture is the five rich Muslim oil countries, which have few democratic and civil rights and are moving even further away from democracy. They are all ruled by absolute monarchs, as was Europe before the French Revolution. We analyse the effect of Muslim culture on democracy in the next section.

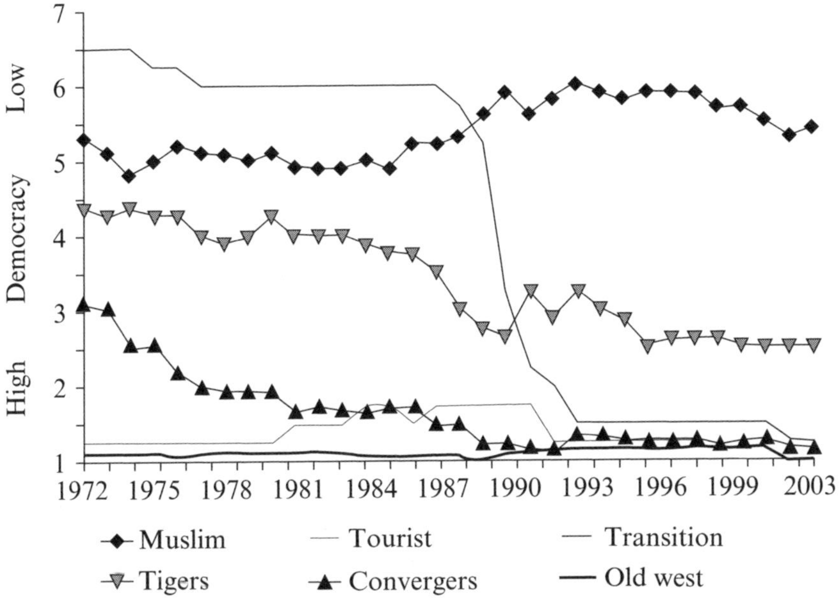

Figure 5.6 The development of democracy in the rich countries

THE MUSLIM EXCEPTION:[13] AN AVERSION TO DEMOCRACY?

The data are complete for 44 Muslim countries, with an average Gastil Score of 5.5. Table 5.2 shows that the average Arab country is 3.2 times richer than the average non-Arab Muslim country; nevertheless the average Gastil Score for the Arab group is 5.7. The Lipset Graph corresponding to Figure 5.4 is shown in Figure 5.7 for the Muslim countries separately. The average only covers the years 1994–2003 in order to allow the data to include the seven Ex-Communist countries that are (now) Muslim.

The picture in Figure 5.7 is constructed as Figure 5.4, but looks very different as there is no sign of a downward slope. The slope through the points is positive, but insignificant. Also, the average is high – there is little demand for democracy in this group of countries.

Figure 5.8 shows the development over time for the 16 Arab countries, the seven Transition countries that used to be Communist, and the remaining 21 Muslim countries. When the data for the 44 countries are examined for trends over the 32 years, only the Arab group of countries has a significant trend, and it is upwards. Table 5.5 gives five regressions to explain this sub-set of data, using model 5.1 above. The main impression

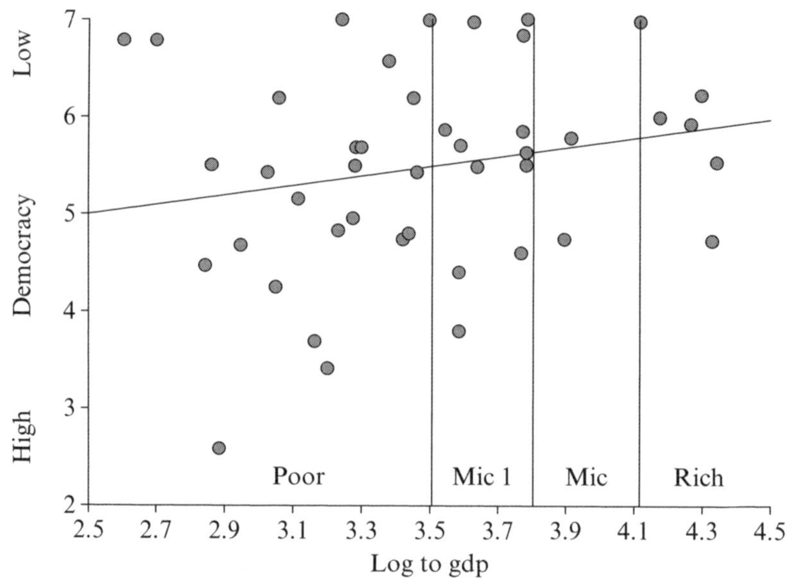

Figure 5.7 The average democracy score in 44 Muslim countries, 1994–2003

from the table is a low level of significance throughout. Only the constant is significant.

While the facts thus tell a clear story, the explanation is less obvious. The two largest religions – Christianity and Islam – are rather similar, and both emerged in the Middle East, so it is strange that one has developed cultures which are easy to combine with democracy while the other has developed cultures that are not.

Maybe it goes back to the founders of the two religions. A poor itinerant preacher founded Christianity. He never sought either wealth or power, but he was nevertheless executed. The (final) Prophet of Islam became both wealthy and powerful. He and a small circle of his early followers ruled in Mecca from about 630 and for the next half century when a major Arab/Muslim state was forged through conquest and conversion. Few more amazing success stories can be told. This period is a Muslim ideal, and the political system in this ideal state was certainly not democracy. The wave of fundamentalism that is now so prominent in the Muslim world is a reaction to modernization including democracy and other 'Western' ideas, and it expresses a wish to return to the ideal and re-establish the Caliphate, that is, to return to a medieval society. Hence, it is likely that democratic values carry relatively little weight in the Muslim culture.[14]

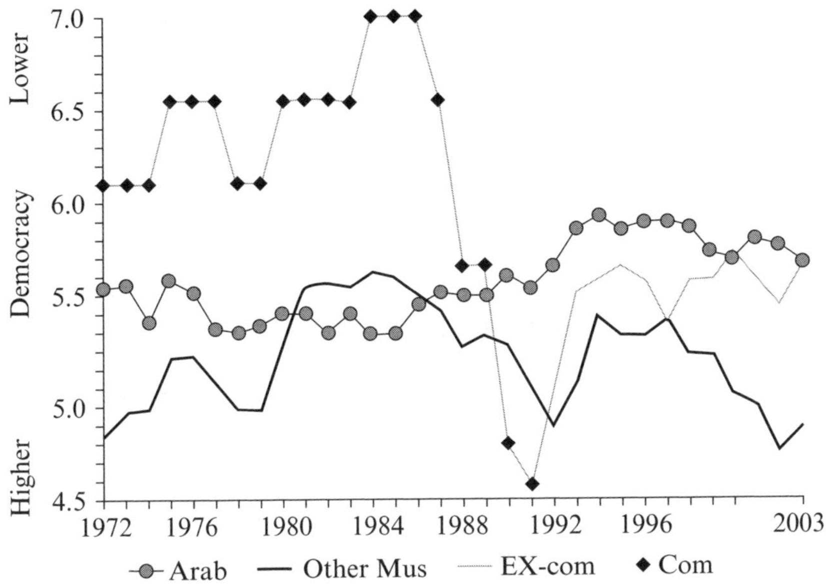

Figure 5.8 *The development over time for three groups of Muslim countries*

Table 5.5 *Regressions for the 44 Muslim countries, 1994–2003*

	Const.	log *y*	Arab	Oil	Trans	African	Orient	R^2	*N*
Reg 11	**5.82**	−0.23	0.55	0.62	0.43	0.02	−0.18	0.14	44
	(3.1)	(0.4)	(1.0)	(1.3)	(0.8)	(0.1)	(0.2)		
Reg 12	**5.99**	−0.285	0.60	0.61	0.46			0.14	44
	(3.6)	(0.6)	(0.2)	(0.2)	(0.3)				
Reg 13	**5.09**		0.51	0.46	0.42			0.13	44
	(22.4)		(1.4)	(1.3)	(0.9)				
Reg 14	**4.56**	0.22	0.48					0.08	44
	(3.3)	(0.5)	(1.3)						
Reg 15	**3.78**	0.49						0.04	44
	(3.0)	(1.4)							

THE SMALL TRANSITION: A HISTORICAL EXPERIMENT

The data include 33 countries with a Communist government before 1990. Five still have a Communist regime. The remaining 28 countries form the

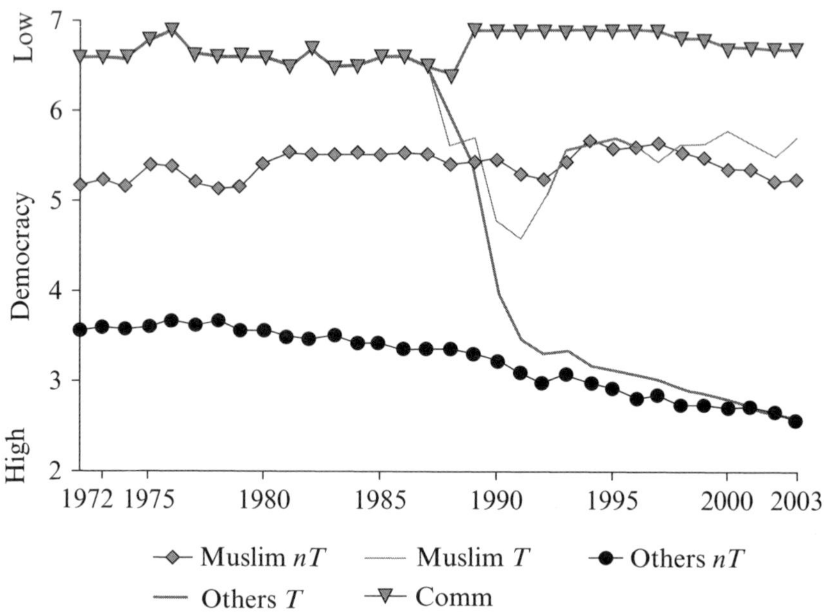

Note: *nT* means non-Transition, *T* is Transition, *others* are neither Communist nor Muslim. Finally, *Com* is Communist. To simplify all Communist countries are shown as an average from 1972 to 1987.

Figure 5.9 The small transition

Transition group, which is further divided into three groups: Muslim countries, ex-Soviet non-Muslim countries and the rest, which are all – except Mongolia – East and Central European countries.

For the countries in the Transition group, the political change in 1988–91 came in the form of a sudden collapse of the old political system and the central control. In the cases of the Soviet Union and Yugoslavia, even the state as such disintegrated. The development of the new political order in these countries thus provides a fine historical experiment.

Figure 5.9 shows what has happened. It is as could be expected from the analysis till now. The five remaining Communist countries even tighten their dictatorships – probably due to the dramatic collapse of Communism in the 28 Transition countries. The Muslim Transition countries had a short 'democratic spring' in 1990–92, and then they moved to the typical Muslim level of democracy (around 5.5). Finally, the non-Muslim transition countries moved toward the other countries in that group. The group of non-Muslim transition countries has made great strides toward democracy. The most Western countries in the group are also the richest in the group. They

Table 5.6 Regressions on 33 Communist and Transition countries, 1994–2003

	Constant	Log *y*	Muslim	Com	Oil	R^2	*N*
Reg 16	**11.51**	**−2.28**	**1.79**	**2.82**	0.78	0.74	33
	(4.0)	(3.0)	(3.2)	(4.3)	(1.1)		
Reg 17	**11.04**	**−2.14**	**2.02**	**2.84**		0.73	33
	(3.8)	(2.8)	(3.8)	(4.4)			
Reg 18	**20.23**	**−4.43**				0.51	33
	(7.1)	(5.7)					

are already at an almost Western level of democracy as seen in Figure 5.6. Consequently, the countries quickly converged to the position in the big pattern where they would have been without the previous Communist regimes.

The models from Tables 5.3 and 5.4 are reestimated on the data for the 33 countries in Table 5.6. The group contains only one Latin American and three Oriental countries so some of the regressions in Tables 5.3 and 5.4 make little sense to replicate for the 33 countries. However, the regressions that can be replicated look precisely as expected from Tables 5.3 and 5.4.

The degree of socialism, σ, can be defined as the share of GDP produced by publicly owned real capital. The Communist countries were very socialist, as σ was in the range from 0.7 to 0.95 in all these countries.[15] We know that other countries are/have been socialist as well, with σ-scores well above 0.5. However, no systematic cross-country data exists for σ. The Gastil data show that the least democratic group is the Communist group, but the author is convinced that the result generalizes to socialism in general. It is very difficult to combine socialism and democracy. The main reason is that in any system somebody has to do the nasty job of preventing the agents from maximizing costs. In a capitalist country, it is the job of the owners and the market. This leaves the state with the nice and popular job of taking care of the losers and in general of making the system milder. However, in a socialist country the state has to do the nasty job itself. This makes the state unpopular. Thus, control is needed, and this is easy to establish when the state owns everything. The result hereof is dictatorship.

CONCLUSION

The analysis above is based on the Gastil Index from the NGO Freedom House. These data are known to contain measurement errors, but they nevertheless have a very significant pattern. Three basic conclusions emerge from the above analysis of data for 171 countries over the last 32 years:

1. Lipset's Law is consistent with the data. It explains about one third of the variation in the data. There is no doubt that a democratic transition occurs as countries go through the Grand Transition.
2. Little indicates that causality may be from democracy to income. It is difficult to reject that some causality occurs from democracy to development, but the main direction of causality is surely from income to democracy.
3. Three cultural hypotheses are confirmed by the data for 1972–2003:
   (a) Communist countries are the least democratic, and it appears to be a general trait that public ownership of the means of production is difficult to combine with democracy. Fortunately, it appears that Communism is disappearing.
   (b) Muslim countries are rather undemocratic too, and they show no tendency to become more democratic when income grows. This is a worrying fact as it is an important part of the present divergence between the West and the Muslim World.
   (c) Western countries are relatively democratic, but this may be due to the simple fact that they have been relatively wealthy for a longer time than anybody else.

The reader may wonder if the findings will generalize to a longer period. In particular, we want to know if the Muslim Gap is permanent or transitory. All we can see from the data (Figure 5.9) is that the gap is large and increasing, so it is not likely to go away soon. However, in the studies of the dynamics referred to, it appears that the Muslim Gap is non-stationary. If it can grow, as it has done for the last 50 years, this would appear to suggest that it can fall too.

Several other cultural hypotheses find no support in the data: the Asian Values hypothesis is rejected, and African countries are only undemocratic because they are poor. Also, signs have been found that the Western exception may be due to history only, as democracy slowly improves once it is established, and many Western countries have been democratic for more than a century.

ACKNOWLEDGEMENTS

This chapter was presented at a workshop at Deakin University, Melbourne and at the University of Iceland, Reykjavik, as well as at the European

Public Choice Meeting in Durham, UK. It has generated many inspiring comments and proposals for further research, which is already in progress, see Jensen and Paldam (2007) and Borooah and Paldam (2007). I am especially grateful to Christian Bjørnskov, Nils Petter Gleditsch, Thorvaldur Gylfason, and Virginie Pignon.

NOTES

1. The index is published by *Freedom House*. It was developed by Raymond Gastil. He is no more in charge, but the name is still in common use. Two alternative democracy indices exist, but they build on less primary data. For the period covered, they are so correlated as to give almost the same results, see Jensen and Paldam (2006).
2. After S.M. Lipset (1959), who first suggested the connection and discussed both directions of causality.
3. The *Grand Transition* is from a poor LDC (less developed), via Mic (middle income), to a rich DC (developed). The *Small Transition* is from a socialist to a market economy.
4. The reader may wonder if the parabolic form is an artifact due to the definitions of the index and the censoring at the two ends. However, since we can give a substantial explanation, it is preferable.
5. GDP per capita measured at PPP prices, gdp. The data are for 2001 from WDI (2003) supplemented with CIA World Factbook (net) to get one observation for each country.
6. The classical study of the Grand Transition is Chenery and Syrquin (1975). It has been a hot research field in the last decade under the name of 'cross-country regressions', see Barro and Sala-i-Martin (2003). The classification of countries in four groups: Poor LDC, low Mic, high Mic, rich DC, follows the World Bank. Mic is the abbreviation for *middle income country*. See Table 5.A2 for the statistics defining the groups.
7. See Eisner (2001) on crime rates, Frey and Stutzer (2000) on happiness, Paldam (2001) on corruption, and Uslaner (2000) on trust.
8. A large body of literature discusses Lipset's Law (since Lipset, 1959) and the problems of causality. Surveys are found in Lipset (1994) and Przeworski *et al.* (2000), which is also is a prominent advocate for the virtue-rewarded idea, and so is Lambsdorff (2002).
9. This method is also used in Paldam (2002), where the argument in its favor is more detailed.
10. The one-year estimates: z^1 varies a great deal more than the long run estimates z^{32} and z^{∞}, but the variation of z^1 tends to vary around the long run estimates, so the average z^1 for the 32 years of z^{32} are typically very similar.
11. The results are very robust to the choice of year for income.
12. The same analysis has also been made using Model 5.1 – the results are virtually the same.
13. I am not, of course, the first one who has discovered the exceptional poor showing of the Muslim countries in these data, and it is also found when other attempts to measure democracy are used, see for example Weiffen (2005) for a survey of this literature, including the many attempts to explain the fact.
14. Many Muslims have other political ideals as well. A battery of questions in the World Value Surveys (see Inglehart *et al.*, 2004) analyse the values and beliefs relating to religion and politics in about 80 countries of which ten are Muslim by our classification. Muslims do express a clear preference for democracy (see E110–124), but at the same time, they also express strong preferences for having a religious factor in politics (see F63–66 and F102–105).
15. This definition goes back to Karl Marx. By the definition both China and Vietnam are now rapidly moving out of socialism.

REFERENCES

Barro, R. J. and X. Sala-i-Martin (2003), *Economic Growth* 2nd edn, Cambridge, MA: MIT Press.
Borooah, V. K. and M. Paldam (2007), 'Why is the world short of democracy? A cross-country analysis of barriers to representative government', *European Journal of Political Economy*.
Brunetti, A. (1997), 'Political variables in growth regressions', in S. Borner, and M. Paldam (eds), *The Political Dimension of Economic Growth*, Houndsmill, UK: Macmillan, pp. 117–35.
Chenery, H. and B., Syrquin (1975), *Patterns of Development 1950–1970*, Oxford: Oxford University Press.
Doucouliagos, H. and M. Ulubasoglu (2006), *Democracy and Economic Growth: a Meta-analysis*, WP School of Accounting, Economics and Finance, Faculty of Business and Law, Deakin University.
Eisner, M. (2001), 'Modernization, self-control and lethal violence. The long-term dynamics of European homicide rates in theoretical perspective', *British Journal of Criminology*, **41**, 618–38.
Frey, B. S. and A. Stutzer (2002), *Happiness & Economics*, Princeton, NJ: Princeton University Press.
Fukuyama, F. (1992), *The End of History and the Last Man*, London: Penguin.
Houthakker, H. S. (1957), 'An international comparison of household expenditure patterns, commemorating the century of Engel's law', *Econometrica*, **25**, 532–52.
Inglehart, R., M. Basáñez, H. L. Díez-Medrano and R. Luijkx (2004), *Human Beliefs and Values, a Cross-Cultural Sourcebook Based on the 1999–2002 Values Surveys*, Mexico: Siglo XXI Editores, México DF.
Jensen, P. S. and M. Paldam (2007), 'The pattern of democracy in the 20th century. A study of the Polity Index', in J. Casas and P. Schwartz (eds), *Problems of Democracy*, Cheltenham, UK and Northampton, MA, USA: Edward Elgar.
Lambsdorff, J. G. (2002), 'Corruption and rent-seeking', *Public Choice*, **113**, 97–125.
Lipset, S. M. (1959), 'Some social requisites of democracy: economic development and political legitimacy', *American Political Science Review*, **53**, 69–105.
Lipset, S. M. (1994), 'The social requisites of democracy revisited: 1993 presidential address', *American Sociological Review*, **59**, 1–22.
Paldam, M. (2001), 'Corruption and religion. Adding to the economic model', *Kyklos*, **54**, 383–414.
Paldam, M. (2002), 'The cross-country pattern of corruption: economics, culture and the seesaw dynamics', *European Journal of Political Economy*, **18**, 215–40.
Przeworski, A., M. E. Alvarez, J. A. Cheibub and F. Limongi (2000), *Democracy and Development. Political Institutions and Well-Being in the World, 1950–1990*, Cambridge, UK: Cambridge University Press.
Uslaner, E. (2002), *The Moral Foundations of Trust*, Cambridge, UK: Cambridge University Press.
World Bank (2003), *World Development Indicators*, Washington, DC: World Bank.
Weiffen, B. (2005), 'The cultural-economic syndrome: impediments to democracy in the Middle East', conference paper for EPCS 2005, Durham, UK, prepared at the Institute of Political Science, Tübingen.

Netsources

CIA World Factbook: <http://www.cia.gov/cia/publications/factbook/>
Gastil Index, available from the NGO Freedom House: <http://www. freedom-house.org/>

APPENDIX

Table 5.A1 Countries included and the classification used

	W	Typ	Rel		W	Typ	Rel		W	Typ	Rel
Afghanistan	p		M	Gambia, The	p	Af	M	Niger	p	Af	M
Albania	ml	T	M	Georgia	p	T		Nigeria	p	Af, oil	
Algeria	ml	Ar, oil	M	Germany	r	Wo		Norway	r	Wo, oil	
Angola	p	Af		Ghana	p	Af		Oman	mh	Ar, oil	M
Argentina	mh	LA		Greece	r	Wc		Pakistan	p		M
Armenia	p	T		Grenada	ml	LA		Panama	ml	LA	
Australia	r	Wo		Guatemala	ml	LA		Papua New Gui.	p		
Austria	r	Wo		Guinea	p	Af	M	Paraguay	ml	LA	
Azerbaijan	p	T, oil	M	Guinea-Bissau	p	Af		Peru	ml	LA	
Bahamas	r	Tu		Guyana	ml			Philippines	ml	O	
Bahrain	r	Ar, oil	M	Haiti	p			Poland	mh	T	
Bangladesh	p		M	Honduras	p	LA		Portugal	r	Wc	
Barbados	r	Tu		Hungary	mh	T		Qatar	r	Ar, oil	M
Belarus	mh	T		Iceland	r	Wc		Romania	ml	T	
Belgium	r	Wo		India	p			Russia	mh	T, oil	
Benin	p	Af		Indonesia	p	O, oil	M	Rwanda	p	Af	
Bhutan	p			Iran	p	O	M	Samoa	ml		
Bolivia	p	LA		Iraq	ml	Ar,oil	M	Sao Tome & Prin.	p	Af	
Bosnia-Herzeg.	ml	T		Ireland	r	Wc		Saudi Arabia	mh	Ar, oil	M
Botswana	mh	Af		Israel	r	Wc		Senegal	p	Af	M
Brazil	mh	LA		Italy	r	Wc		Serbia & Monten.	p	T	
Brunei	r	O, oil	M	Jamaica	ml	LA		Sierra Leone	p	Af	
Bulgaria	mh	T		Japan	r	Ot		Singapore	r	Ot	
Burkina Faso	p	Af	M	Jordan	ml	Ar	M	Slovakia	mh	T	
Burma	p	O		Kazakhstan	ml	T, oil	M	Slovenia	r	T	

Burundi	p	Af		Kenya	p	Af		Somalia	p	Af	M
Cambodia	p	O		Korea, North	p	O	Co	South Africa	mh	Af	
Cameroon	p	Af		Korea, South	r	Ot		Spain	r	Wc	
Canada	r	Wo		Kuwait	r	Ar, oil	M	Sri Lanka	ml		
Cape Verde	p	Af		Kyrgyzstan	p	T	M	Sudan	p	Af	M
Central Af. R.	p	Af		Laos	p	O	Co	Suriname	ml		
Chad	p	Af	M	Latvia	mh	T		Swaziland	ml	Af	
Chile	mh	LA		Lebanon	ml	Ar	M	Sweden	r	Wo	
China	ml	O	Co	Lesotho	p	Af		Switzerland	r	Wo	
Colombia	mh	LA		Liberia	p	Af		Syria	p	Ar	M
Comoros	p		M	Libya	ml	Ar, oil	M	Taiwan	r	Ot	
Congo, Braz.	p	Af		Lithuania	mh	T		Tajikistan	p	T	M
Congo, Kinsh.	p	Af		Luxembourg	r	Wo		Tanzania	p	Af	
Costa Rica	mh	LA		Macedonia	ml	T		Thailand	ml	O	
Cote d'Ivoire	p	Af		Madagascar	p	Af		Togo	p	Af	
Croatia	mh	T		Malawi	p	Af		Tonga	p		
Cuba	p	LA	Co	Malaysia	mh	O	M	Trinidad & Tobago	mh	LA, oil	
Cyprus (Greek)	r	Wc		Maldives	ml		M	Tunisia	ml	Ar	M
Czech R.	r	T		Mali	p	Af	M	Turkey	ml		M
Denmark	r	Wo		Malta	r	Wc		Turkmenistan	ml	T	M
Djibouti	p	Af	M	Mauritania	p	Af	M	Uganda	p	Af	
Dominican R.	ml	LA		Mauritius	mh			Ukraine	ml	T	
Ecuador	p	LA		Mexico	mh	LA, oil		Un. Arab Emir.	r	Ar, oil	M
Egypt	ml	Ar	M	Moldova	p	T		United Kingdom	r	Wo	
El Salvador	ml	LA		Mongolia	p	O, T		United States	r	Wo	
Equatorial Gui.	p	Af		Morocco	p	Ar	M	Uruguay	mh	LA	
Estonia	mh	T		Mozambique	p	Af		Uzbekistan	p	T	M
Ethiopia	p	Af		Nauru	ml			Venezuela	ml	LA, oil	
Fiji	ml			Nepal	p			Vietnam	p	O	Co
Finland	r	Wc		Netherlands	r	Wo		Yemen	p	Ar	M
France	r	Wo		New Zealand	r	Wo		Zambia	p	Af	
Gabon	ml	Af, oil		Nicaragua	p	LA		Zimbabwe	p	Af	

Abbreviations to Table 5.A1

Typ(es):	*Af*, south of Sahara Africa. *Ar*, Arab. *O*, Oriental or East Asia. *Ot*, are Tiger Countries. *LA*, Latin American. *Wo*, Old Western, *Wc*, Western converger. *Tu*, is used for Barbados and Bahamas, that are rich from tourism. *oil*, main export oil. *T*, in transition from a communist to a market economy since 1989.
Re(ligion or ideology):	*M*, Muslim, *Co*, Communist.
W(ealth):	*p(oor)*, *m(ic) l(ow)*, *m(ic) h(igh)*, *r(ich)*. Classification from World Bank (2003), but the limits between groups are changed from using the official exchange rate to the PPP-rate.

Table 5.A2 Main economic structure in the world 2001

US $	(1)	(2)	(3)	(4)	(5)	(6)	(7)	(8)
Country group	Population Millions	GDP-exc (exchange rate)			GDP-PPP (purchasing power)			PPP-ratio (6)/(3)
		Billions	gdp-exc	Limits	Billions	gdp-PPP	Limits	
Rich	957	25'372	26'510	9'206	25'506	26'650	12'350	1.01
High Mic	504	2'672	4'550	2'975	5'494	8'500	6'700	1.87
Low Mic	2'164	4'957	1'230	745	10'178	4'700	3'175	3.82
Poor	2'506	1'069	430		14'373	2'190		5.09
World	6'130	34'100	5'560		54'940	7'370		1.44

Note: While GDP is the macro aggregate, gdp is per capita. The PPP-limits between the groups are calculated as the same fraction of the gap as in the exchange rate case.

6. Violence and its impact on democracy in Colombia

Giorgio Brosio and Roberto Zanola

INTRODUCTION

Colombia is neither waging war against external enemies, nor has a dictatorial government engaged in a large-scale repression of insurrection. However, Colombia ranks among the most violent countries of the world. Homicides are one of the harshest forms of violence. Unfortunately in Colombia they are accompanied by every kind of violence, such as massacres, kidnappings, forced relocation of villagers, crimes against property. Drug traffickers, guerrillas, army and police forces members, paramilitary groups, rural rich and poor, young gangs and 'self righteous' citizens are all involved in violence, in addition to common criminals.

In the last decade more than 280 000 homicides have been recorded. It is as if an entire mid-sized city had been swept away. The rate of homicides has receded slightly in the most recent years, but not to too much relief to the Colombians, since other forms of violence have compensated the reduction. The number of kidnappings has tripled between 1995 and 2000 and from 2000 to 2003 more than 16 000 people were kidnapped.

One would expect that this extreme incidence of violence would impact hugely on the economy and democratic institutions. This is not the case, however, at least in comparative terms, especially in Latin America. In the recent decades Colombia neither had a revolutionary period, nor dictatorships of any kind.[1] Its economy has done comparably well in the region and its income distribution, although highly skewed in favour of the rich segments of the population, is no more unequal than that of neighbouring and more peaceful countries.

The intensity of violence, combined with the persistence of democratic institutions and the reasonably good economic performance, has attracted a large number of scholars from different disciplines – called 'violentologists' in Colombia – to study the factors originating violence and its impact on society.[2]

A sub-set of these studies is focused on the effects of violence on democracy. Colombia retains most of the formal requirements of democratic systems, such as regular and free elections. Electoral turnout is low, but has not been reduced by the outburst of violence in recent decades. To explain the survival of democracy in Colombia scholars resort to various labels. Democracy in this country has been variously labelled as 'illiberal', 'besieged' and 'suspended'. Freedom House (2005) presently qualifies Colombia as a 'partially free' country.

The aim of this chapter is to look at democracy from the opposite perspective, that is, to look at the impact of democratic government on violence. We refer to two main concepts of democratic government. According to the first concept democracy is a system for the selection of rulers through a fully competitive struggle. In the second concept a government can be considered as democratic when it is capable of providing outcomes that improve the lot of the poorest segments of the population. More democracy implies and requires, according to the first concept, higher political participation. More democracy brings in, according to the second concept, less inequality and poverty.

The main argument developed in this chapter is that improvements in democratic government along those two dimensions – more participation and less poverty and inequality – help to reduce violence in Colombia. This is also the strategy that has been started in Colombia, although with evident weaknesses and limits, with the constitutional reform of 1990, which brought a new system for the selection of the upper House and a considerably more decentralized government. We bring empirical support to our argument by using a model of determination of violence referred to Colombian Departments, between 1990 and 1999. The model explains violence in terms of addictive, not necessarily rational, behaviour and introduces electoral participation and poverty/inequality as prices of violent behaviour. According to our knowledge, additive models have not yet been used to explain violence, at least in the economic literature.

The chapter contains four sections and an Appendix. In the first section we illustrate the singularity of Colombia in the Latin American context. The most, in our judgement, distinctive features of violence in Colombia, such as the pervasiveness of its violence, the presence of every imaginable type of violent action and the changing geographical pattern of violence are presented in the second section.

The links between democracy and violence in Colombia are explored in the third section. Our interpretation of violence as addictive behaviour is presented in the fourth section, where we summarize the results of our model of the determination of violence. The model is presented with more detail in the Appendix at the end of the chapter.

Throughout this chapter we use homicides as the variable indicating violence. The choice is supported, mostly, by the recognition that underreporting of crime diminishes with the severity of crime. However, it is not synonymous, for sure. In other words, the correlation between homicides and violence is far from perfect and can create problems with reference to some determinants, such as inequality. According to the literature most of non-lethal violence takes place in low-income families, but not necessarily homicides. As our data set will expand, we intend to apply our model, and our discussion, to other indicators of violence.

THE SINGULARITY OF COLOMBIA IN THE LATIN AMERICAN CONTEXT

Colombia stands out for its singularity among Latin American countries. Although most Latin American countries have a reputation of being violent, Colombia surpasses them by far. Its homicide rate more than quadrupled between the late 1980s and the early 1990s. During this latter decade only two countries, Guatemala and El Salvador, which were engaged in a bloody civil war, surpassed Colombia. But the distance between Colombia and other traditionally violent countries, such as Brazil, Mexico and Peru, has never been so wide, as in the 1990s.

At the same time Colombia has, in Latin America, an unsurpassed tradition of democratic institutions. In recent decades, however, Colombian democratic institutions have been submitted to severe strain and there is a growing disinclination to label Colombia as a fully-fledged democracy. However, some of the most typical democratic institutions, such as regular and freely competed elections, are there. Voter turnout is the lowest in Latin America, but it is not declining. One has also to take into account that the disparity between Colombia and the rest of Latin America in electoral participation could be partly ascribed to the fact that in Colombia voting is not compulsory,[3] while this is not the case in most Latin American countries.

The economic performance of Colombia has been traditionally good. It could be claimed that the Colombian (not exceedingly high) level of per capita GDP is inflated by drug trafficking. At the same time it has also to be taken into account that huge exports of drugs exert a pressure towards the re-evaluation of the local currency, thus reducing the competitiveness of traditional exports. This is a typical manifestation of the 'Dutch disease'. There is no doubt, for example, that the Colombian textile industry has been severely affected by the revaluation of the Colombian peso.

Income and wealth inequalities are a potential factor of social disorder that can be conducive to violence. Inequality is huge in Colombia. Its Gini

Table 6.1 Homicide rates, economic and political indicators in selected Latin American countries

	Homicide rate, late 1970s/early 1980s	Homicide rate, late 1980s/ early 1990s	Gini coefficient	Per capita GNP (1999) US$	Electoral turnout in Parliamentary election (earliest in the the 1990s)
Guatemala	–	150	58.3 (2000)	1690	14.2 (1994)
El Salvador	–	150	52.0 (2000)	1930	51.1 (1994)
Colombia	20.5	89.5	57.6 (1999)	2180	40.4 (1990) 29.2 (1992) 40.1 (1998)
Jamaica	–	35.0	52.0 (2000)	2810	44.7 (1993)
Brazil	11.5	19.7	59.0 (2001)	3930	79.9 (1994)
Nicaragua	–	18.3	60.0 (2000)	710	73.3 (1990)
Mexico	18.2	17.8	54.6 (2000)	4460	50.0 (1991)
Venezuela	11.7	15.2	46.7 (2000)	3700	49.9 (1993)
Trinidad and Tobago	2.1	12.6	40.0 (2000)	4700	70.4 (1991)
Dominican Republic	–	11.9	49.7 (2000)	1950	30.6 (1994)
Peru	2.4	11.5	49.8 (2000)	2080	57.7 (1995)
Bolivia	–	–	60.1 (1999)	990	50.0 (1993)
Panama	2.1	10.9	56.3 (1999)	3730	70.1 (1994)
Ecuador	6.4	10.3	56.1 (1998)	1480	66.3 (1994)
United States	10.7	10.1	40.8 (1997)	32 270	55.1 (1992)
Honduras	–	9.4	58.4 (1999)	770	63.5 (1993)
Argentina	3.9	4.8	52.2 (2000)	7780	78.1 (1993)
Costa Rica	5.7	5.6	46.6 (2000)	3580	84.1 (1994)
Uruguay	2.6	4.4	44.6 (2000)	6320	96.1 (1994)
Paraguay	5.1	4.0	59.4 (1999)	1650	45.4 (1993)
Chile	2.6	3.0	57.1 (2000)	4730	81.9 (1993)

Sources: 1. PAHO, Health Situation Analysis Program, 1997, quoted by World Bank, 'Crime and Violence as Development Issues in Latin America and the Caribbean', 1997; 2. Gini coefficient, World Bank Development Indicators, World Bank; 3. GNI per capita, World Bank, World Development Indicators; 4. voter turnout, Idea International.

coefficient for income is very high, but it is surpassed by that of countries, such as Brazil and Chile, that have much lower levels of violence and of social unrest. It is slightly lower also than that of countries, such as Paraguay and Bolivia, that have low levels of violence, but high levels of political unrest. In other words, inequality is surely a factor that plays a part in the origins of violence in Colombia, but the link between inequality and violence in Colombia looks different from that observed in other Latin American countries.

MAIN FEATURES OF COLOMBIAN VIOLENCE

All Inclusiveness and Overlapping

Colombia exhibits almost every possible kind of violence. Violence is associated with drug production and trafficking. Large scale and countrywide guerrilla movements also produce violence. Furthermore, Colombia is afflicted by pervasive criminality and by violence inside families. Criminal, especially young people, gangs wage violence in the urban areas. Economic violence is also widespread, particularly in the rural areas, where landowners and their private police fight with landless peasants. Oil producing areas have become a magnet of every kind of violence. Reaction to violence produces further violence. The most conspicuous example is the violence produced by the paramilitary, or self-defence, groups. These organizations started to protect peasants from guerrillas and drug traffickers, but ended up with conducting large-scale massacres and extra-judicial killings. Some of these groups were started by big landowners and are still used for the protection of their estates. In the urban areas self-defence groups organized by citizens have proliferated and their activity has turned from defence into offence. Illegal chases of prostitutes, beggars and transvestites are organized by groups of citizens. As has to be expected in those circumstances the presence of the police and the army has been greatly expanded over the territory, but effective control has lessened. Large areas are 'controlled' during part of the day by the army and the police, but for the rest of the time they are left to illegal, violent control. The borderline between defence of the legal order and outright illegal activity has become blurred. Even racial violence has surged, although Colombia is one of the most ethnically homogeneous countries of Latin America.

According to the statistics common criminality accounts for the largest share of murders (Table 6.2), but there is hardly specialization in crime. Guerrillas are increasingly engaged in drug trafficking and even in common criminality, especially in kidnapping. Initially and officially this was for covering the minimum cost of their activity, but there is a large consensus that revenue now extends beyond this cost. The same applies to paramilitary and self-defence groups (Table 6.3). Illegal activities, implying also homicides, are carried out by legal uniformed bodies, not to mention citizens' groups involved in the 'moral cleansing' of the urban areas.

Table 6.2 Homicides in Colombia, by main categories, 1988–2000

Year	Political homicides	Forced disappearances	Murders of social marginals	Massacres	Common violence
1988	2738	210	273	1083	16796
1989	1978	137	364	732	20101
1990	2027	217	267	1229	21600
1991	1829	180	389	1364	25110
1992	2178	191	505	1602	25125
1993	2190	144	161	1097	24042
1994	1668	147	277	1009	23543
1995	1831	85	371	1049	22321
1996	1783	183	218	1131	23350
1997	2318	215	85	1280	23200
1998					23096
1999*	1843	291	158	1594	24358
2000**	2285	440	272	2276	26264
Total	24648	2440	3340	15446	298606

Sources: Pedro Valenzuela (2001). Original data derived from: Comisión Colombiana de Juristas (1999, 2000a, 2000b). For common homicides between 1988–2000, National Police (1999). * With the exception of common homicide, it includes data from October 1998 to September 1999. ** With the exception of common homicide, it includes data from October 1999 to September 2000.

Table 6.3 The finance of guerrillas, 1998–9

	FARC	ELN
Taxes on narcotraffickers	180	30
Ransom-kidnapping and extortion	198	40
Diversion of government resources	40	60
Assualts on financial institutions	30	20
Total	448	150

Note: Quoted from N. Richani, 2002. See also, for original sources, Granada and Rojas (1995).

Growing Spatial Spread of Violence

Although there is a concentration of violent activities in a few departments – four of them account for more than 55 per cent of the total national number of homicides and 12 departments account for 90 per cent of the total – every area is exposed to violence. During the 1990s the national average rate of homicides per 100 000 inhabitants remained over 60. Even departments that are considered peaceful, such as Chocò and Narino, have a homicide rate well above all Latin American countries (with the exception only of Guatemala and Salvador during civil war). The geography of violence shows significant variations over the years. In general, the increase in the overall rate of violence has implied and extended geographical coverage of violence. At this time, no department is immune. Changes in the localization of drug trafficking, guerrillas and their main adversary, the paramilitaries, have set the trend. The drug cartel of Medellin moved to Cali after the death of its (in)famous boss, Pablo Escobar. This was followed by a significant decrease in the homicide rate in the Department of Antioquia, (whose capital city is Medellin). However, the homicide rate continues to stay well above the national average, since guerrillas and self-defence forces that fight to share the rent from coca leaves cultivation that has replaced drug trafficking now affect the department. Guerrillas and paramilitaries are concentrated in the North Western part of the country, but are moving rapidly towards the eastern regions. Coca and poppy cultivation are concentrated in the central areas of the country, but while in 1991 only four departments had coca cultivations, their number had extended to 25 in 2003. Out of these 25, 11 departments have an area of cultivation that extends over more than 1000 ha (despite the massive efforts put into eradication). In the meantime, Colombia started the cultivation of poppies for the production of heroin, and Colombia has become one of the biggest suppliers of the drug to the US. As Table 6.A2, in the Appendix, shows there is little overlapping between coca leaves and poppy cultivation.

Violence is said to be an urban phenomenon: Colombian cities account for almost half of total homicides. But this corresponds roughly to the ratio of urban to total population. Violence in Colombia is as rural as urban: between 1996 and 1998 there were 305 *municipios* (over a total of about 1000) where the homicide rate was above the national average.

There also used to be specialization in crime. Political violence was mostly located in rural areas, while common criminality and that related to the drugs traffic took place mostly in the cities. These borders are getting blurred, as political violence tends to extend to the rural areas, while that related to drug traffic is spreading to the rural areas, where cultivation of coca and poppies takes place.

The Partial Demise of State Institutions and the Increasing Tendency of Citizens to Administer their own Justice

The Colombian state has lost control of large areas of the country and has surrendered part of its monopoly of coercion to the various criminal groups, even in those areas that remain under its nominal control. A violent competition for filling the void left by state institutions is taking place among the *narcos*, the guerrillas, the paramilitaries and the self-defence groups. While the important size of these rents – deriving basically from drug production and trade and from control of natural resources, from extortion and offences to property – is feeding a war among violent factions, no one faction seems to prevail. Large and increasing segments of society are using violence to protect and/or to advance their interests. The use of violence is spreading from the conflicts for the control of traditional illegal activities, to the illegal substitution of state institutions by groups of citizens. Even the army and police bodies are competing in the same areas, on a private and illegal basis, with violent groups for a share of the rents.

VIOLENCE AND DEMOCRACY

As mentioned in the Introduction, combining record levels of violence with the maintenance of democratic institutions – political leaders at all levels of government are selected through popular and regular elections – is a peculiar feature of Colombian society, which surprises observers. There is a wide perception among scholars that a high level of political violence is 'a contributing cause to the breakdown [of democratic regimes], but the line between cause and effect is blurred' (Linz, 1978: 14).

According to scholars and international agencies, Colombia oscillates between a democratic and semi-democratic regime. According to the classification by Mainwaring *et al.* (2001), Colombia was democratic between 1974 and 1990, but fell into the semi-democratic category thereafter. In fact, the homicide rate more than quadrupled between the late 1970s and early 1980s, and late 1980s and early 1990s (more exactly, it jumped from 20.5 per 100 000 inhabitants to 89.5).

The recognition of the fact that part of the violence, at least the most evident political component of it, was to be ascribed to the limited legitimacy of the Colombian ruling classes stood behind the constitutional reform of 1990. The reform included: (a) the change of the election system for the Senate, whereby proportional representation replaced the existing past-the-post system; and (b) the introduction of a highly decentralized system of governance (Gaitan and Moreno Ospina, 1992), based on popular election of councils and heads of subnational governments. Health and education were added to their responsibilities and a massive infusion of finance to subnational governments was started even before the devolution of the expenditures. Political participation was to be enhanced by the reform of the Senate (by reducing the power of local caudillos), the extension of local elections to the governors[4] and the introduction of other participation-fostering mechanisms, such as plebiscites and referenda. Decentralization of finance and responsibilities was meant to reduce poverty and inequalities. More generally, the reform intended to enhance the legitimacy of the Colombian political system through the creation of new political parties, on the assumption that it is easier to start a new party at the local than at the national level. We have to mention that Colombian politics has been traditionally characterized by a bipartite system, based on the Liberals and the Conservatives, whose legitimacy has been increasingly dented by corruption, monopolization of power and incapacity to represent broad sectors of the society (see, Bejarano (1992), Hoyos and Ceballos, (2004), Pizarro (1997) and Posada-Carbò (2004). The latter author has a much more optimistic view of the working of democratic institutions in Colombia).

Clearly the reform had, potentially, a positive impact on democracy in Colombia. As mentioned, there are two main definitions of democracy. The first one views democracy as a procedural mechanism. According to it, the selection of rulers through a fully competitive struggle for the people's vote characterizes a democratic system. At least, using Przeworski's words 'Democracy is a system in which parties lose elections' (p. 10). Democracy, it is advanced, is a fragile, self-enforcing mechanism. It relies on the participation of all the relevant political groups, although the democratic process may produce outcomes that severely hurt some of these groups. Quoting again Przeworski, democratic institutions have to be devised in such a way as to offer the relevant political forces 'a prospect of eventually advancing their interests that is sufficient to incite them to comply with immediately unfavorable outcomes' (Przeworski, 1991: 19).

The second definition is a substantive one referring to the outcomes of government. According to it a system can be labelled as democratic if it is able to provide to all its citizens access to a decent standard of life. This standard will vary depending on the level of development of the country concerned. It means, however, that to be labelled as democratic a government has to engage itself in reducing poverty and inequality.

This chapter cannot provide a full account of the outcomes of the reform. The literature says that they are at least partial and quite contradictory. Political competition and voter participation have increased. For example, the number of parties taking part in elections is now higher and racial minorities show an expanding participation in representative bodies, although electoral laws require that political parties satisfy minimum standards in terms of membership and votes to be admitted to elections. The voter turnout still remains low, but it has significantly increased since the inception of the reform. More precisely, only 25.6 per cent of voters turned out to vote in the presidential elections in 1991, and their participation has increased to 46.4 per cent in the 2002 election (see Table 6.A1 in the Appendix).

However, democracy requires that candidates to elections compete fearlessly, safely and freely. Candidates, however, have become an increasingly frequent target of violence, especially since the beginning of the twenty-first century. Guerrillas murder candidates to demonstrate their control of territory and the melting down of state institutions. Their victims are preferably candidates of right wing parties. The paramilitary and self-defence groups are engaged in the physical elimination of left wing candidates, that are considered as actual, or potential supporters of guerrillas. Kidnapping of candidates and intimidation is also widely used (see Garcia and Hoskin, 2003).

Detailed statistics on the number of political candidates and officials murdered are now available, showing really impressive numbers. A former Minister of Defence, Rafael Pardo, reported in 2000 that since the mid-1980s '4 presidential candidates, 200 judges and investigators, half of the Supreme Court's Justices, 1200 police officers, 151 journalists and more than 300 000 Colombians have been murdered'.[5] However, caution has to be used in the interpretation of these numbers, particularly concerning the trend that they could suggest. Before 1990 no local elections were held, and murderers targeted only candidates to national offices, such as the presidency and the congress. These 'practices' have continued, for sure.

There have been some even more worrying facts than these, such as, for example, the practical extermination of a radical opposition party, the UP (Union Patriotica). After the agreement reached in 1985 between the government and the FARC, the main guerrilla movement, the latter started its own political party, namely the UP, with a platform of incisive social and economic reforms. Members of this party and especially candidates to local and national elections, members of parliament and elected mayors have been systematically murdered.[6] Obviously, officials deny any implication in these murders, but these facts show, at least, that the chances that strongly alternative parties have to accede to power are still quite limited.

Another worrying fact is the almost systematic murder of journalists and academics,[7] who challenge official views about the extermination of political opponents, although there is no state censorship in Colombia and freedom of expression has explicit constitutional guarantee.

Albeit there are a number of studies on decentralization in Colombia,[8] it is still hard to evaluate its impacts in terms of effective service delivery. Hence, its contribution to alleviation of poverty and reduction of inequality is still uncertain. The decentralization path has been quite uneven. It started with local elections and the devolution of finance, but the transfer of responsibilities did not follow suit. Teachers and medical personnel were reluctant to be transferred to local government units, since they feared to be posted in the rural and remote areas (and also to lose their pension entitlements). One has thus to expect delays in improvements in service delivery. At the same time, the increase of local revenues, through a massive injection of transfers from central government, but without a corresponding increase in responsibilities, favoured slackness and corruption at the local level. This has been facilitated by the one term only system for the appointment of the heads of the executive bodies (from the president of the republic down to mayors). The rationale of the system of disallowing incumbents from taking part in elections is to foster competition by reducing the opportunities of building a network of clientelistic links between the elected and the voters. Unfortunately, the one term only constraint reduces accountability and stimulates corruption.

AN EXPLANATION OF VIOLENCE IN COLOMBIA: ADDICTIVE BEHAVIOUR

Recourse to violence appears so widespread and permanent in Colombia and extorts such a high cost on the country, that it suggests large sectors of the Colombian population may have become addicted to violence. In other words, observation of facts concerning violence suggests that economic models of addiction could be tested.

Addiction is a topic that has intrigued social scientists from different disciplines. There is a vast amount of literature on addiction, but the chapter will not provide a systematic overview. Instead, we use the rational addiction perspective to investigate the robustness and causality of the link between democracy and violence. According to Becker and Murphy's (1988) seminal paper, addiction is usually assumed to involve both reinforcement and tolerance. Reinforcement means that an increase in past level of consumption increases the craving for present consumption, especially in the case of a rational and far-sighted consumer, who is aware of the increasing future cost associated with rising levels of consumption. Tolerance means that the satisfaction from a given level of consumption is lower when the past level is greater. However, this upward spiral in consumption may not affect some consumers. Some consumers, described as 'myopic', may have such a high rate of preference for present consumption (and discount the future so heavily), that the impact of tolerance effects on current consumption are negligible, and positive reinforcement effects of previous consumption on the marginal utility of current consumption can cause the demand for a habit-forming good to soar to persistently high levels.

Although a number of papers have empirically investigated the rational addiction model[9] by using data referring to distinct harmful goods, one can also imagine that people could also become addicted to almost every product, or activity, independently of biological or pharmaceutical dependency, such as violence. When this occurs, present violence is expected to depend upon past and future violence levels.

To test the rational addiction model a panel-data GMM methodology is applied to a sample of 27 Colombian departments. Dynamic panel analysis allows one to investigate a rich model specification (Fajnzylber *et al.*, 2002). First, applying a dynamic panel model may control for all time-invariant variables or department-invariant variables, whose omission could bias the estimates in a typical cross-section, or time-series study. Second, by analysing the patterns of violence levels for a given department over time, it is possible to test whether there is inertia in the incidence of violence. Finally, we can control for joint endogeneity to obtain consistent estimates of the effect of various economic and social variables on violence levels.

The data we use are drawn from a wide range of sources. Appendix 6.3 provides a detailed description of the variables and their sources. Violence is represented by the rate of homicides per 100 000 inhabitants, *viol*. Past and future violence affect the present level of violence, as well as its price. The choice of the proper variable for price is a demanding task. Two different prices have been used. Since the seminal paper by Becker (1968), there has been substantial research on the determinants of crime and empirical testing of various crime models. The basic idea is that criminal acts result from a rational decision based on the expected benefits that are equal to the difference between the loot and the opportunity cost of crime. To this aim, there is an intuitively reasonable and generally accepted agreement in the literature about the notion that income inequality is a contributing factor to crime (Ehrlich, 1973). This is because the more inequality there is, the greater the number of individuals who can expect to derive a net benefit from crime. Hence, we use a weighted Gini coefficient as a measure of the inequality of income distribution, in which the weights are the ratio between the department per capita income and national per capita income, *wgini*. However, this price alone does not take into account the full meaning of violence price. In a somewhat wider interpretation of Becker's paradigm, the cost of violence might also be interpreted in terms of political participation. It is likely that when participation is higher institutions work better and deviant behaviour is more effectively sanctioned. Hence, we include voter turnout, *turn*, as a second explanatory variable defining the price of violence. It is represented by the share of actual voters on total population in Presidential elections. Due to the lack of annual observations, this variable has been estimated, for the years between elections, on the basis of a linear evolution. Finally, in order to minimize the possible bias from omitted variables on the coefficient associated with our indicator of violence, we include a number of controls. These are: the share of homicides of young people (less than 14 years old) over total homicides, *young*; the amount of extra judiciary killings per 100 000 inhabitants, *extra*; the amount of property offences per 100 000 inhabitants; number of property offences; and the share of urban homicides on total department homicides, *urban*. The empirical specification of the demand for violence is:

$$viol_{i,t} = \alpha_0 + \alpha_1 viol_{i,t-1} + \alpha_2 viol_{i,t+1} + \alpha_3 wgini_{i,t} + \alpha_4 turn_{i,t} + \alpha_5 young_{i,t} + \alpha_6 extra_{i,t} + \alpha_7 prop_{i,t} + \alpha_8 urban_{i,t} + \varepsilon_{i,t} \quad (6.1)$$

where subscripts t and i stand respectively for the department and the period considered and $\varepsilon_{i,t}$ is the error term (see Appendix 6.1 for a detailed description of the model). A panel-data GMM methodology is applied to estimate Equation (6.1).

However, the estimation of Equation (6.1) may give rise to some misleading results and some caution is necessary. First, we test whether data can be pooled by using an F-test on the null hypothesis that the coefficients for each variable in Equation (6.1) are the same for each year. The null hypothesis of equal coefficients could not be rejected in either case, therefore data can be pooled. Second, we test the stationarity of the variables included in the model by employing the IPS t-bar tests with a heterogeneous time trend in its specification. The null of unit root could not be rejected and hence the series are $I(1)$ processes, while the series in first differences appear to be stationary or $I(0)$ processes. Therefore, Equation (6.1) is estimated in the first differences. Finally, taking first differences will induce a first-order moving average process into the transformed residuals (Arellano, 1989). Hence, in order to get consistent estimates we instrument endogenous variables with three to four lagged and led levels of the dependent variable and of the variables of price. The regression results are reported in Table 6.4.

The coefficient associated with past violence is negative and statistically significant, providing dependence from the past level of violence such that past changes negatively impact on the present level. This may be interpreted as a slowing down in the incidence of violence. Is this slowing down high enough to guarantee a constant reduction of violence over time, even if no reduction strategy is followed? A way to answer this question is to look at the coefficient associated with future levels of violence. In our sample the coefficient is not statistically significant, so that violence cannot be defined as a rational addicted 'good'. When this occurs, time does not reduce satisfaction from a lower future level of violence. In other words, we can say that there exists a natural way of reducing violence

Table 6.4 Regression results

Variables	Estimated coefficient	Robust Std. Err.
hom $(t-1)$	−1.321414*	0.2413546
hom $(t+1)$	0.1466851	0.2551915
wgini	35.2057**	15.92359
turn	−421.1934**	125.6115
young	1.240148	1.039914
extra	0.056016	0.5018572
prop	0.0196696	0.0334125
urban	−21.95643**	9.589037
R^2	0.9071	
Hansen J statistic	21.953	
p-value	0.00124	

Notes: Instruments used are three and four lagged and three and four led levels of dependent variables and both prices. Regression includes $T-1$ time and $N-1$ department dummy variables but their estimates are non-reported to save space. */**/*** Significance at 0.01/0.05/0.10 levels, respectively.

consisting only in the passing of time. Hence, which is the role of active political strategies in reducing violence? Probably, they are expected to accelerate the natural reduction in violence levels. To this aim, it is useful to focus on the effects on violence of the two definitions of prices used in this chapter.

The price of violence in terms of inequality (*wgini*) is statistically significant at all common levels and displays the expected sign, meaning that an increase in inequality will increase the level of violence. Our second measure of price (*turn*) displays the expected sign meaning that an increase of democracy will reduce the number of homicides per 100 000 inhabitants. However, a word of caution is necessary due to the potential endogeneity of political participation. The direction of causation between violence and political participation is not obvious *a priori* (see also, for the case of Colombia, Hoyos and Ceballo, 2004). Political participation is clearly obstructed by violence. Intimidation of voters and murder of candidates is a daily feature of Colombian political life, as already mentioned. In their study of the 2002 parliamentary election Garcia and Hoskin (2003) show that in the municipalities controlled by the guerrillas, or the paramilitaries, the voter turnout is lower than elsewhere. However, their results also show that the same municipalities are characterized by higher poverty. It is thus difficult to ascribe lower turnout to violence. They also show that when municipalities are affected both by guerrillas and paramilitaries, the level of turnout is not lowered and that, in any case, the number of voters living in the areas is small. Thus the impact of violence on political participation does not appear to be greatly significant. On the other hand, or rather on the contrary, the fact that guerrillas, the paramilitaries and other criminal actors try to suppress political participation shows that fear has an impact on them. This adds an argument to the strategy of reducing violence though increased political participation.

Finally, the share of urban homicides over total department homicides is the only variable of control, which is statistically significant, displaying a negative sign. This may be interpreted as an indirect measure of substitution between forms of geographical location of violence.

CONCLUSION

Colombia has a unique combination of huge violence and survival of democratic institutions. The resilience of democratic institutions in Colombia is surprising and has stimulated the burgeoning of a huge literature that discusses the degree of democracy in Colombia and tries to explain its survival. This chapter has looked at the link between the two variables from the opposite perspective. That is, we have tried to show that democracy, both in procedural and substantive terms, can contribute to reducing violence. We have tried to test empirically this proposition by using a model of violence determination based on addictive behaviour. The results seem to confirm – in addition to the fact that violence can be explained in terms of addictive behaviour – that lower inequality and poverty and higher voter turnout can have a lenient impact on violence. We are conscious of the exploratory character of our main findings and of the circumscribed range of suggestions that can be derived from them. For example, higher political participation could contribute to reducing violence, but there are limits to the increase of voter turnout in Colombia if, for example, political parties offering a more radical alternative are, *de facto*, not allowed to compete.

NOTES

1. More precisely, during the nineteenth century the constitution was broken only once. Another violation of the constitution also took place in the twentieth century with the dictatorship of Rojas Pinilla. The origin of this dictatorship was the incredible wave of violence that erupted in the late 1940s and that is infamously known in Colombia as 'la violencia'.
2. In their 2000 review, Gaitan and Montenegro consider more than 70 studies. These studies are separated according to the background of their authors. Gaitan and Montenegro distinguish between six distinct disciplines: sociology, political science, psychology,

anthropology, medicine and economics. Among more recent studies by economists we have to quote Bourguignon *et al.* (2002), Brauer and Gómez-Sorzano (2002).

3. Law 403 of 1997 introduced incentives to voting. Casting a vote was rewarded with: (a) preference in the obtention of a public sector job; (b) half a day paid leave; (c) discount of 10 per cent in university fees; (d) reduction in length of mandatory military service; and (e) preference in the awarding of scholarships, housing subsidies and assignment of rural land. However, this has not resulted in a substantial increase of voter turnout.
4. Popular election of mayors was introduced in 1988 and the first election, thereafter, took place in 1988.
5. Quoted by Posada-Carbò (2004: 69).
6. Cepeda Castro and Giron Ortiz (2005).
7. One of the most respected Colombian academics and analysts of violence, Professor Jesus Antonio Bejarano, was killed in September 1999.
8. See, for example, the following web-sites: www.ard-decentralization.com/Colombia; www.iadb.org/regions; www.worldbank.org/
9. The RA model has been criticized by a number of authors because of: initiation in consumption is not explained; consumers can accurately predict future prices and other demand shifts; consumers are not only rational and forward looking, but also time consistent; consumers have no self-control problems; the model fails to explain temptation, mistaken behaviour and cue-triggered decision processes (O'Donoghue and Rabin, 1999; Gruber and Köszegi, 2001; Akerlof, 1991; Elster and Skog, 1999; Gul and Pesendorfer, 2005; Lowenstein *et al.*, 2003; Bernheim and Rangel, 2004). However, despite these criticisms, the model is still popular because it leads to a simple linear specification with testable hypothesis, which consists in approximating the instantaneous utility function in the neighbourhood of steady state by a quadratic function.

REFERENCES

Akerlof, G. (1991), 'Procrastination and obedience', *American Economic Review*, **81**(2), 1–19.

Arellano, M. (1989), 'A note on the Anderson-Hsiao estimator for panel data', *Economics Letters*, **31**(4), 337–41.

Becker, G. (1968), 'Crime and punishment: an economic approach', *Journal of Political Economy*, **76**, 169–217.

Becker, G. S. and K. M. Murphy (1988), 'A theory of rational addiction', *Journal of Political Economy*, **96** (4), 675–700.

Becker, G., M. Grossman and K. M. Murphy (1994), 'An empirical analysis of cigarette addiction', *American Economic Review*, **84** (3), 396–418.

Bejarano, A. M. (1999), 'La Constitucion de 1991: un projecto de construcción institutional', in M. Gandour and L. B. Majia (eds), *Hacia el Rediseño del Estado*, Bogota: Departamento Nacional de Planeación.

Bernheim, D. and A. Rangel (2004), 'Addiction and cue-triggered decision processes', *American Economic Review*, **94** (5), 1558–90.

Bourguignon, F., J. Nuñez and F. Sanchez (2002), 'What part of the income distribution does matter for explaining crime? The case of Colombia', paper presented at the Congress of the European Economic Association, Venice, August.

Brauer J. and A. Gómez-Sorzano (2002), 'A structural model of political murder in Colombia, 1950–1999', mimeo, May.

Castro, C., I. Giron Ortiz and C. Giron Ortiz (2005), 'Comment des militaires ont été liquidés en Colombie', *Le Monde Diplomatique*, May.

Comisón Colombiana de Juristas (1999), 'Estadísticas sobre derechos humanos en Colombia', Bogotà.

Comisión Colombiana de Juristas (2000a), 'Estadísticas sobre derechos humanos en Colombia', Bogotà.

Comisión Colombiana de Juristas (2000b), 'Ejecuciones extrajudiciales, homicidios sociopolíticos y desapariciones forzadas', Bogotà.

Echandia Castilla, C. (1999), '*Geografia del conflicto armado y de las manifestaciones de violencia en Colombia*', Bogotà: Centro de Estudios sobre Desarrollo Economico, Facultad de Economía.

Ehrlich, I. (1973), 'Participation in illegitimate activities: a theoretical and empirical investigation', *Journal of Political Economy*, **81** (3), 521–65.

Elster, J. and O. J. Skog (1999), *Getting Hooked: Rationality and Addiction*, Cambridge: Cambridge University Press.

Fajnzylber, P., D. Lederman and N. Loayza (2002), 'Inequality and violent crime', *Journal of Law and Economics*, **XLV**, 1–40.

Freedom House (2005), 'Freedom in the world, 1999, 2004', accessed at www.freedomhouse.org.

Gaitan, F. and S. Montenegro (2000), 'Un Analisis Crítico de Estudios sobre la Violencia en Colombia', paper prepared for international conference, 'Crimen y Violencia: Causas y Políticas de Prevención', Bogotá.

Gaitan, P. 'La elección popular de alcaldes: un desafío para la democracia'. *En Análisis Político*, 4 (May–August).

Gaitan, P. and C. Moreno Ospina (1992), *Poder local. Realidad y utopía de la descentralización en Colombia*, Bogotá: Iepri – Tercer Mundo Editores.

Garcia, M. and G. Hoskin (2002), 'Participación Política y Guerra en Colombia. Un Analysis de las Elecciones de 2002', in G. Hoskin, R. Masias and M. Garcia (eds), *Colombia 2002: Elecciones, Comportamiento Electoral y Democracia*, Bogotà, Corcas y Ciencia Política de la Universidad de los Andes.

Granada, C. and L. Rojas (1995), 'Los costos del conflicto armado', *Planeación y Desarrollo*, **26** (4), 119–51.

Gruber, J. and B. Köszegi (2001), 'Is addiction "rational"? Theory and evidence', *The Quarterly Journal of Economics*, **116**, 1261–303.

Gul, F. and W. Pesendorfer (forthcoming), 'Harmful addiction', *Review of Economic Studies*.

Hoyos, D. and M. Ceballos (2004), 'Electoral behaviour trends and decentralization in Colombia's municipalities', London School of Economics Crisis States Programme working paper no. 57, December.

Linz, J. (1978), *Crisis, Breakdown and Requilibration*, Baltimore, MD: Johns Hopkins University Press.

Loewenstein, G., T. O'Donoghue and M. Rabin (2003), 'Projection bias in predicting future utility', *Quarterly Journal of Economics*, **118** (4), 1209–48.

Mainwaring, S., D. Brinks and A. Pérez-Liñán (2001), 'Classifying political regimes in Latin America, 1945–1999', *Studies in Comparative International Development*, **36**, 37–65.

O'Donoghue, T. and M. Rabin (1999), 'Doing it now or later', *American Economic Review*, **89** (1), pp. 103–24.

Pizarro, E. (1997), 'Hacia un sistema multipartidista? Las terceras fuerzas en Colombia hoy', *Analisis Político* (May–August).

Posada-Carbò, E. (2004), 'Colombia's resilient democracy', *Current History*, **103** (670), 68–73.

Przeworski, A. (1991), *Democracy and the Market*, Cambridge: Cambridge University Press.
Richani, N. (2002), *Systems of Violence. The Political Economy of War and Peace in Colombia*, New York: State University of New York Press.
Valenzuela, P. (2001), 'Reflections on recent interpretations of violence in Colombia', paper presented at the seminar 'Is Poverty Structural Cause of Violence? The Case of Colombia', Uppsala, November.

APPENDIX 6.1 THE RATIONAL ADDICTION MODEL

Following Becker *et al.* (1994) the rational consumer maximizes utility under the assumption that tests are constant over time. Assuming a constant rate of time preference, σ, a concave and time-separable utility is defined as (Becker *et al.*, 1994):

$$U = \sum_{t=0}^{T} \sigma^{t-1} U(Y_t, C_t, C_{t-1}, e_t) \tag{6.1A}$$

where Y is the consumption of a non-addictive good; C is the consumption of the addictive good; and e is the stock of 'addictive capital' built up by consuming C in earlier periods.

Consumer's choices are constrained by the consumer's wealth, W, and the prices of C and Y. Assuming a constant price of the non-addictive good, treated as numeraire, and perfect capital markets, the life-time budget constraint may be written as:

$$\sum_{t=1}^{T} r^{t-1}(Y_t + P_t C_t) \leq A_0 \tag{6.2A}$$

where r is the constant real interest rate; P is the price of the addictive good; and A_0 is the initial value of assets.

Maximizing Equation 6.1A under this budget constraint, one can obtain the optimal path of consumption for Y and C. A standard technique used in literature to derive a structural demand function for consumption of C is to approximate the instantaneous utility function in the neighbourhood of steady state by a quadratic function in the arguments. Assuming a rate of time preferences equals to the market interest rate, one can derive the following difference equation:

$$C_t = \theta_1 C_{t-1} + \theta_2 C_{t+1} + \theta_3 P_t + \theta_4 e_t + \theta_5 e_{t+1}$$

with

$$\theta_2 = \delta\theta_1$$

and

$$\delta = \frac{1}{1+r} \tag{6.3A}$$

where the θs are parameters which depend on the underlying preferences. Equation 6.3A nests different behaviours. Since a good is addictive if and only if an increase in past consumption leads to an increase in current consumption, a zero value of θ_1 implies a non-addicted consumer. Only when $\theta_1 > 0$, forces that increase past or future consumption, such as lower past or future prices of addictive goods, lead to an increase in current consumption, throughout an intertemporal substituting process, and past, present and future consumption are complements. Testing for rational addiction is testing for forward-looking behaviour. An addicted but myopic consumer is not farsighted, according to a simply backward-looking consumer decision, while a rational addicted consumer takes into account consequences of past, current and future information. The rational model implies that the coefficient on future consumption should have the same sign as the coefficient on lagged consumption (the sign differs only by the term δ). Only if $\theta_2 > 0$, a change in future events lead to an increase of current consumption.

APPENDIX 6.2 SOURCES OF DATA

Variables	Description	Source
viol	Rate of homicides per 100 000 inhabitants	DANE, Estadísticas Vitales
wgini	Weighted Gini (Gini index multiplied for the ratio between per capita income and national per capita income)	PNUD, Diez años de desarrollo humano en Colombia
turn	Voter turnout	
gdp	per capita income	DANE, Cuentas Regionales
young	Share of homicides of young people ($<$14 years) over total homicides	DANE, Estadísticas Vitales
extra	Amount of extra judiciary killings per 100 000 inhabitants	Policía nacional, Revista de Criminalidad
prop	Number of offences against property	Policía nacional, Revista de Criminalidad
urban	Share of urban homicides over total department homicides	DANE, Estadísticas Vitales

APPENDIX 6.3

Table 6.A1 Voter turnout in Colombia, 1990–2002

r	Total Vote	Registration	Vote/Reg (%)	VAP	Vote/VAP (%)	Invalid (%)	FH	Pop. Size
1990	7631691	13793566	55.3	19057000	40.0	0.2	7	32300000
1990	7631691	13793566	55.3	19057000	40.0	0.2	7	32300000
1991	4962383	15037526	33.0	19376190	25.6	n/a	6	32841000
1991	4962383	15037526	33.0	19376190	25.6	n/a	6	32841000
1994	6145436	17003195	36.1	21057200	29.2	7.8	7	34520000
1994	6145436	17003195	36.1	21057200	29.2	7.8	7	34520000
1998	9000000	20000000	45.0	22236403	40.5	n/a	7	36453120
1998	9000000	20000000	45.0	22236403	40.5	n/a	7	36453120
2002	10188929	24000636	42.5	0	46.4	18.6	n/a	n/a
2002	10188929	24000636	42.5	0	n/a	18.6	n/a	n/a

Definitions: www.idea.int/vt/country_view.cfm and Registraduria Nacional for the 2002 election.

Table 6.A2 Cultivation of coca leaves and poppies in Colombian Departments

	Cultivation of coca leaves 1991 hectares	Cultivation of coca leaves December 2003 hectares	Cultivation of poppies 2003 hectares
Amazonas		625	
Antioquia		4273	
Arauca		539	
Atlántico			
Bolívar	5300	4470	
Boyacá		594	
Caldas		54	
Caquetá	8600	7230	
Casanare			
Cauca		1443	600
César			651
Chocó		453	
Córdoba		838	
Cundinamarca		57	
Guainía		726	
Guaviare	21 400	16 163	
Huila			636
La Guajira		275	240
Magdalena		424	
Meta		12 814	
Nariño		17 628	540
Norte de Santander		4471	
Putumayo	2200	7559	
Quindío			
Risaralda			
San Andrés y Providencia			
Santander		632	
Sucre			
Tolima			1359
Valle del Cauca		37	
Vaupés		1157	
Vichada		3818	
Total	37 500	86 340	

Source: Gobierno de Colombia, Observatorio de Drogas. Censo de cultivos de coca.

PART 3

Democratic safeguards against illegitimate coercion

7. Language as platform: a theory of subsidiarity and the nation state

Leonard Dudley

La langue est le signe principal d'une nationalité.

Michelet (1875: 1)

INTRODUCTION

Consider the following political statement. A top international bureaucrat insists that because of scale economies, the supranational level of government is the one most appropriate for dealing with major social problems.

> The organization that I represent] intervenes directly on behalf of the poor, by setting on foot and maintaining many associations which it knows to be efficient for the relief of poverty.

At the same time, he criticizes national governments for appropriating powers best left to subordinate organizations.

> The foremost duty of the rulers of the State should be to make sure that the laws and institutions . . . shall be such as themselves to realize public well-being and private prosperity.[1] . . . The law must not undertake more, nor proceed further, than is required for the remedy of the evil or the removal of the mischief.[2]

It has been suggested that the latter quotation is one of the first explicit statements of the concept of subsidiarity, the principle that government functions should be assigned to the lowest possible level (Feketekuty, 2004). However, the person in question is neither the secretary-general of the United Nations nor the head of the European Commission. Rather, it is Pope Leo XII in his 1891 encyclical, *Rerum novarum*, using the criteria of scale economies and subsidiarity to justify a pyramid or power in which the Catholic Church and community groups associated with it are protected from the predation of sovereign states.

More recently, scale economies and subsidiarity have been used to justify the allocation of powers to the different levels of the European Union. Economies of scale were mentioned in Article 3b of the 1993 Treaty on European Union (the Maastricht Treaty):

> the *Community* shall take action . . . only if and in so far as the objectives of the proposed action cannot be sufficiently achieved by the *Member States* and can therefore, by reason of the *scale or effects* of the proposed action, be better achieved by the Community [italics added].

In addition, however, the concept of subsidiarity was invoked as a guide to the allocation of responsibilities. The Preamble to the same Maastricht Treaty resolves to:

> continue the process of creating an ever closer union among the peoples of Europe, in which decisions are taken as *closely as possible to the citizen* in accord with the principle of *subsidiarity* [italics added].

It is interesting to note that in these last two quotations, it is not supranational and local organizations that are being defended but rather the nation state. Representatives of the United Kingdom and some smaller states were worried about restrictions on their sovereignty if the powers of the economic union were extended into spheres of national jurisdiction.

Can economic theory justify the multi-level structures of observed political units such as the United Nations or the European Union? The above quotations suggest three aspects of such organizations that should be considered, namely, the pyramidal structure of power, the variations over time in the relative power of national governments and the possibility of overlap when the domains of different levels are not mutually exclusive. Let us consider each of these three dimensions in turn, inquiring to what extent observed institutions are compatible with economic theory.

To begin with the distribution of political power, the pyramidal structures that are implicit in the viewpoints of Leo XIII and the signatories of the Maastricht Treaty would seem to be incompatible with neoclassical economic theory. On the one hand, Samuelson's (1954) theory of public goods would suggest that whenever there are positive externalities in consumption and exclusion is not possible, the good in question should be financed by compulsory taxes. A public good should therefore be provided by the most comprehensive organism possible in order to minimize the per-capita fiscal cost. On the other hand, Tiebout's (1956) model of local jurisdictions and Buchanan's (1965) theory of clubs require that where exclusion is possible, individuals be allowed to associate freely for voluntary provision of the good. As Cameron and Ndhlovu (2001) have pointed out, the net result should be a single level of government with centralized but minimal powers that are just sufficient for maintaining the conditions favorable to voluntary association. We are far from the pyramidal structure with myriad forms of intervention observed in actual multi-state systems such as the European Union or the North American Free Trade Agreement.

Traditional economic theory also has trouble explaining the second aspect implicit in the above quotations, namely, the fluctuations over time in the relative power of the national government. The theory of public goods would predict that power would gravitate to the highest level when scale economies rise, and move away from that level when they decline. In practice, there does not even seem to have been any such tendency for power to shift in this way to and from the supranational level. Empirically, the reference point for political change seems rather to have been the intermediate level, that of the nation state. At the time of Leo XIII, movement of power was toward the nation state, away from local governments and supranational organisms like the Catholic Church. Between 1880 and 1905, for example, France introduced state-financed universal schooling and expelled both the Catholic Church and local authorities from participation in the educational system. However over the two most recent decades, movement has been in the opposite direction – away from the nation state. In the United Kingdom, France and Italy, formerly unitary states have been transferring legislative powers to regional governments and to the European level. In Canada, asymmetric transfer of power to the provinces, some acquiring more responsibilities than others, has been accompanied by a loss of control over commercial policy to the North American Free Trade Agreement.

Finally, there is yet a third aspect to subsidiarity that begs an explanation. An allocation of power based on scale economies would seem to imply sharp boundaries between the functions of each level of government. In reality, there is considerable overlap. In the European Union, as Alesina and Perotti (2004: 32–3) have observed, there is wide-ranging duplication in the areas of competence covered by the community and those covered by the national governments. For example, certain citizen protection and welfare policies are handled by both EU and national authorities. To take another case, the regional financing of banks and broadcasting by the German Länder may not be compatible with competition policy at the EU level.[3] In practice, then, the criterion of selection of the lowest level would seem often to conflict with the criterion of scale economies.

This chapter re-examines these three dimensions of the state in attempt to find a theoretical structure that supports both scale economies and subsidiarity. Why are observed public institutions so large and multi-layered, why has power shifted toward and then away from the central level rather than the upper level, and why is there so much overlap between jurisdictions? To explain the discrepancies between economic theory and observed practice, the chapter proposes a model in which the traditional concept of consumption scale economies in public goods is extended to take account of the more recently formalized notion of network externalities. In the theory of industrial organization, Katz and Shapiro (1985, 1986) modeled network externalities as a function of the number of users of a given type of 'hardware'. However, more recently, Church and Gandal (1996, 2004) have suggested that network effects may also depend on the availability of 'software' applications.

Translated into the realm of political economy, the hardware or 'platform' of the political unit might be considered to consist of a standardized culture. For simplicity, this culture might be called a 'language', although it could have religious, ethnic or historical components in addition to a linguistic dimension. As for the software or applications, it consists of various government services or programs that are not offered by competitive markets but that raise the returns to membership in the language network. Willingness to pay taxes to a given level of public administration will then depend on both the linguistic externalities from participating in a common culture and the 'program' externalities from having access to public goods that are complementary to that culture.

The chapter is divided into three sections. The first section describes a series of shocks that over the past two centuries have generated a need for explicit criteria to allocate power spatially through non-violent means. Universal literacy, increased mobility and multilingualism, it is argued, have created a demand for multiple layers of government. The second section then sets out a model of multi-level government in which each level has a dual function. It both provides a platform in the form of a language network, and supplies public programs that are specific to that platform. The relative importance of each language in private and public communication and the number of government programs provided in that language are determined simultaneously. The final section shows that the characteristics of the resulting equilibrium depend on the importance of both scale economies and network externalities.

The results of the chapter differ sharply from those of the standard model of public goods in which government powers are both modest and centralized. First, when a given territory is home to people of more than one culture or 'language', it is rational for its citizens to demand services from more than one level of government. Second, the number of public services offered by each level will depend not only on the extent of scale economies in supplying public services but also on the network externalities provided by each linguistic platform. Finally, when the aggregate public sector is large, there may be a discrepancy between the marginal benefit of a program to the citizen and its contribution to the revenues of the level of government offering it. In this case, there will be overlapping jurisdictions and duplication of services. The degree of overlap across levels of government will be inefficient only if each level determines the extent of its programs autonomously.

LITERACY, MIGRATION AND BILINGUALISM

If most Europeans and North Americans were illiterate and spent their lives within the boundaries of the region in which they were born, speaking only their mother tongues, there would probably be little need to discuss the concept of subsidiarity. Each state might struggle with its neighbors, but there would be little need to reconcile the interventions of different levels of government within a single political structure.

So it was in the West prior to the nineteenth century. With the exception of the Protestant regions of northern Europe, few people living outside the towns and cities were able to read and write. Moreover, almost all people spent their entire lives in the region in which they were born. Finally, although an elite group in each society was able to communicate in Latin, very few were able to read and write in a second vernacular language such as French, German or English. These three characteristics would change remarkably over the two centuries after 1800.

Fact 1: Literacy

At the beginning of the nineteenth century, only about half the population of England was able to read and write. In North America, the overall literacy rate, including slaves and Native Americans, was probably even lower. In France, less than 40 percent of the population was literate at that time.[4] In Spain and Italy, where literacy had declined since the Renaissance, fewer than two people in ten were able to read and write. The level of literacy was somewhat higher in Germany, but even there, one person in three was illiterate.[5]

This situation changed dramatically over the course of the nineteenth century. Innovations in the publishing industry reduced the cost of printing standardized information by an order of magnitude. With inexpensive textbooks for teaching and cheap novels and newspapers for reading, universal literacy became possible for the first time. By the eve of the First World War, government-financed compulsory primary education had been introduced into most countries of North America and Western Europe. Literacy levels were 90 percent or higher. Even in Spain and Italy, over half of the population was now able to read and write.[6]

Fact 2: Mobility

In the United States and Canada there has been net immigration since the beginning of colonization. However, in most Western European countries over the century and a half after 1800 there was net emigration. Millions of workers and their families left to settle in the New World and elsewhere. Then during the second half of the twentieth century, the direction of movement changed. The countries of Western Europe too began to receive net inflows of immigrants along with asylum seekers from outside the region. In addition, the degree of international mobility of workers within Europe greatly increased. By 2002, 7 percent of the population in the 15 EU member states were immigrants or citizens of foreign nations.[7] Among the economically active immigrants, roughly half were from Western Europe and North America, while the rest were from Eastern Europe, Turkey, Africa and elsewhere in Asia.[8] In short, labor mobility increased, bringing new challenges to workers and the governments of the states in which they settled.

Fact 3: Bilingualism

Until very recently, it has been expected that immigrants learn to function in the language of their host country. However, in Europe of the twenty-first century, this adaptation on the part of the immigrant is no longer considered essential. When ten additional member countries joined the European Union in 2004, the organization was obliged to recognize a total of 20 official languages. In practice, however, one of these languages was emerging as the successor of Latin to become the vehicular language for people speaking different vernacular languages. In 2003, only 16 percent of citizens in the EU 15 spoke English as a mother tongue, but an additional 31 percent were able to speak it well enough to hold a conversation. Roughly one European in two, then, was able to speak English. Next in importance was German which was spoken by 24 percent as a first language but only by 8 percent as a second language. French was the principal competitor to English as a vehicular language. It was spoken by only 14 percent of Europeans as a mother tongue, but an additional 14 percent had learned it as a second language.[9]

These three successive shocks – universal literacy, rising labor mobility and the emergence of a new vehicular language – have completely altered the demands upon Western governments over the past two centuries. The next section presents a theoretical model for analysing the impact of these shocks. We will see that in destroying the structure of states of the early modern period, they created a need for criteria to allocate functions to multiple levels of government by non-violent means.

THE MODEL

The model presented in this section explains how citizens determine the two components of the services they receive from public authorities. One component is made up of access to language networks administered by different levels of governments, each level operating in a different 'language', broadly defined. The second component is made up of services such as education, protection of property and regulation that are provided in a specific language by the governments in question. Externalities from the programs affect the utility derived from access to the respective language networks.

Messages

Suppose that in a given territory all citizens are identical. Assume that the representative citizen is served by two different levels of government, each using a different culture or 'language'. The representative citizen is bilingual, but her ability to read, write and speak is not necessarily the same for each language. Lazear (1999) and Shy (2001, ch. 11) have modeled the learning of languages that underlies this choice, but here the individual's degree of bilingualism is assumed to be predetermined.

Let the total number of messages that the citizen receives per period be normalized to one. Some of these messages will be from governments, others from private agents. Assume that the capacity of an individual to receive messages is limited, so that an additional message from one source will displace a message from another source. The fraction of messages in the national language, m_1, is measured from the left along the horizontal axis in Figure 7.1. The fraction in a second language (regional or international), m_2, is measured from the right. Figure 7.1 might therefore be applied to the distribution between a regional language such as Catalan in Spain or French in Canada and the predominant national language in each case. Alternatively, within the European Union, the distinction might be between a standardized national language and globish, the version of English used by international bureaucrats.[10]

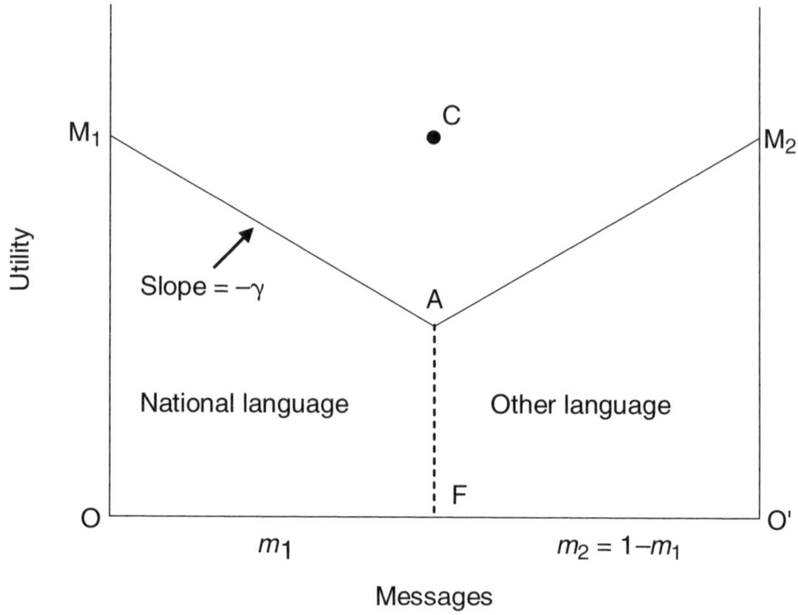

Figure 7.1 Equilibrium in message space

Programs

As mentioned, the citizen's utility depends not only on the messages she receives in each language but also on the number of government programs available in those languages. Let the total number of programs that governments are potentially able to offer be normalized to one, with n_i programs being offered in language *i*. These potential programs are then arrayed along the horizontal axis in Figure 7.2 from left to right in order of their intensity in the national language relative to their intensity in the other language. Assume that that the cost of a government program (for the representative citizen) is a constant, *c*, that is the same for both levels of government.

Suppose that the two levels are national and regional governments of a federal state. Then we might find defense at the extreme left, international relations more to the right and criminal law still farther right. At the right end of the scale, we might find primary and secondary education in a regional language, with regulation of municipal affairs more to the left. In the middle, would be areas such as health and social infrastructure that could potentially be in either of the two public sectors or not offered by governments at all.

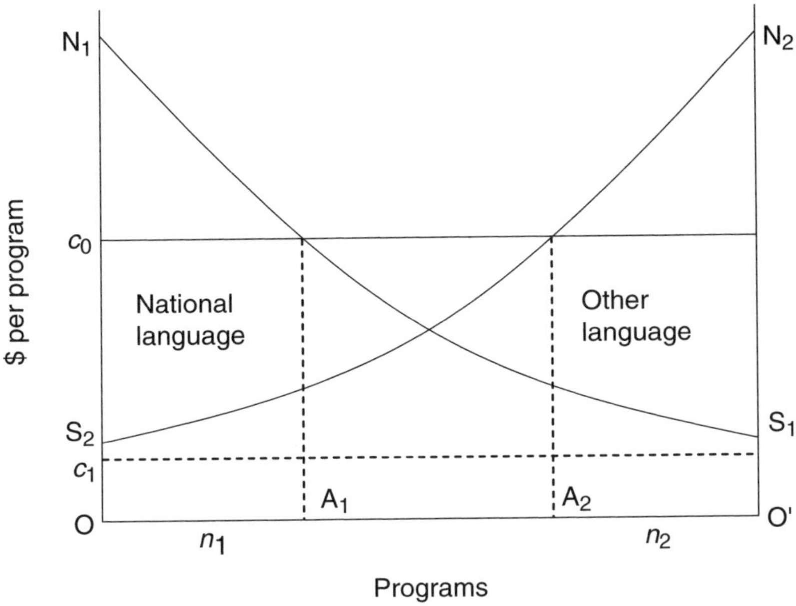

Figure 7.2 Equilibria in program space for low and high scale economies

Alternatively, one might imagine a similar graph distributing powers between individual states and the community of states to which they belong. In this second case, commercial policy might be at the far right, subsidies to agriculture more to the left. As before, defense and international relations would be on the left. In the middle might be environmental legislation, a program that could be offered by either level or neither. The important point to note is that in both cases, each level of government will have a distinct culture and/or language. Thus Figures 7.1 and 7.2 capture both dimensions of the public sector, namely, the traditional element of consumption scale economies and the newer concept of externalities from a language network.[11]

Welfare

If an additional government program is offered in language i, it will generate network externalities for those who participate in network i. Let the height of the intercepts M_i in Figure 7.1 be equal to n_i^{α}. The area under the willingness-to-pay schedules, MA and NA, indicates the utility the citizen derives from these messages and the programs to which they give access. The negative slopes of these lines indicate decreasing marginal utility of messages in the same language. Let the absolute value of the slopes be γ.

Then the total welfare of the representative citizen is equal to the sum of surfaces M_1AFO and $M_2O'FA$ less her share of the fixed costs, F_i, and variable costs, n_ic, of the government programs.[12]

$$W = \sum_{1=1}^{2} [m_i n_i^{\alpha} - \gamma m_i^2/2 - F_i - n_i c] \qquad m_2 = 1 - m_1 \qquad (7.1)$$

Differentiate Equation 7.1 with respect to m_1, recalling that $m_2 = 1 - m_1$. The first-order condition for a maximum is:

$$n_1^{\alpha} - \gamma m_1 = n_2^{\alpha} - \gamma(1 - m_1) \qquad (7.2)$$

The citizen's optimal position is represented by the point A, where the two marginal utility schedules in Figure 7.1 cross. There, she receives m_1 messages in her national language and $1 - m_1$ in another language. She will choose her optimal position such that the utility of the last message received in each language is equal.

How many programs should be offered in each language? Differentiate Equation 7.1 with respect to n_i:

$$\alpha m_i n_i^{\alpha - 1} + (n_i^{\alpha} - \gamma m_i)\frac{dm_i}{dn_i} = c \qquad (7.3)$$

This equation states that the marginal willingness to pay for an additional government program should be equal to the marginal cost of that program. The downward-sloping marginal-willingness-to-pay schedules expressed by the left side of Equation 7.3 are illustrated by the curves N_1S_1 and N_2S_2 in Figure 7.2.

Timing

The game takes place over four periods. In the first period, the national government decides the number of programs to offer in its language. Then in the second stage, the other level of government decides what programs to provide in its language. In the third stage, citizens choose the number of messages to receive in each language. Finally, in the fourth period, each government provides the promised programs and then taxes away the surplus the citizen receives from access to its network and from the programs it offers. The revenues obtained are then used to finance the cost of maintaining the network and providing the promised programs. Any surplus is either redistributed in the form of lump-sum transfers or retained by the government bureaucracy.

EQUILIBRIUM IN THE POLITICAL MARKET

Consider now how the shocks described in the first section might affect the multi-level political structure presented in the preceding section. We will begin with the case of low scale economies, then turn to the possibility of high scale economies. Finally, we will examine an intermediate case with moderate scale economies.

Accommodating Equilibrium

Suppose initially that scale economies in the provision of public services are low, so that the marginal cost, c_0, of providing an extra public service to the representative citizen is relatively high. Then we will have the situation illustrated in Figure 7.2. The national government will offer $OA_1 = n_1$ programs and the other government $O'A_2 = n_2$ programs. The availability of these programs determines the intercepts in Figure 7.1. Since in this case $n_1 + n_2 < 1$, the overall public sector is small and there is no overlap in services offered.

This simple model thus reproduces one of the features of observed governments, namely the pyramidal structure of power. When scale economies are moderate, it is rational for the citizen to choose an administrative structure in which there are multiple levels of government. Adopting the terminology that Church and Gandal (1996) apply to the firm, we can call this an accommodating equilibrium. The national government has no reason to attempt to block the entry of the other level of government.

The second level may be either a supranational institution or a regional government. An example of the former is the situation in France in 1801 after Napoleon's Concordat with the Catholic Church. Both the national government and the Church intervened moderately in French society. An example of the latter is the German Confederation of 1815 where power was divided between the confederation and 39 member states. The 1867 British North America Act that divided power between a central federal level and four Canadian provinces provides another example. In each case, there was a clear division of power with little overlap and considerable residual power as yet unallocated.

Monopoly

Suppose now that scale economies rise relative to the preceding equilibrium. If the scale economies are high, the marginal cost of an additional program for an additional citizen will fall. The dotted line c_1 in Figure 7.2 represents this situation. Since the national government has the first move, it will occupy all of the program space. Given this position, the second level of government has no role to play; that is, in equilibrium $n_1=1$ and $n_2=0$. Note, however, that this equilibrium depends on the order of play. If the other level of government had the first move, it would establish a monopoly.

As we saw in the first section, there was a substantial increase in literacy in most Western countries over the course of the nineteenth century. In addition the railroad and the telegraph greatly reduced the cost of communication over long distances. As a result, the marginal cost of providing standardized government services to large numbers of people fell sharply in each linguistic region. Accordingly, national governments were able to offer a complete range of government programs to their citizens. Tipping occurred, as the previous equilibrium in which local associations, international organizations and national governments played distinct roles was replaced by a monopoly on the part of the national state.

Consider some examples. In France, between 1872 and 1905, a series of laws expelled the Catholic Church from its established position within the educational system and other areas of French society. Over the following decades, the government of the Third Republic introduced the institutions of the welfare state. In Germany, the successive constitutions of the North German Confederation, the Second Reich and the Weimar Republic greatly increased the role of the central government. Finally in 1933, the *Ermächtigungsgesetz* granted the central cabinet a monopoly of power. An example of an equilibrium in which local languages obtained a monopoly is the splitting of Norway from its union with Sweden in 1905 and the subsequent expansion of government activity in each state. Even in Canada, a federal state, by the end of the Second World War, the central government played a dominant role. To finance its massive spending, it monopolized the collection of taxes on the income of individuals and corporations.

Overlapping Jurisdictions

Suppose now that scale economies are at an intermediate level between those of the first and second sub-sections above. The case of moderate scale economies is illustrated in Figure 7.3. With the marginal cost of a new program at the intermediate level c_2, the national government cannot afford to offer the complete range of programs. Yet costs are sufficiently low that the two levels together will offer all possible public programs.

Will there be some programs that are offered by both levels? Since the national government has the first move, it aligns marginal cost and marginal revenue offering OA_2 programs. The other level will then offer programs until its marginal revenue equals marginal cost, offering $O'A_1$. There will thus be an overlap between the two jurisdictions of A_1A_2.

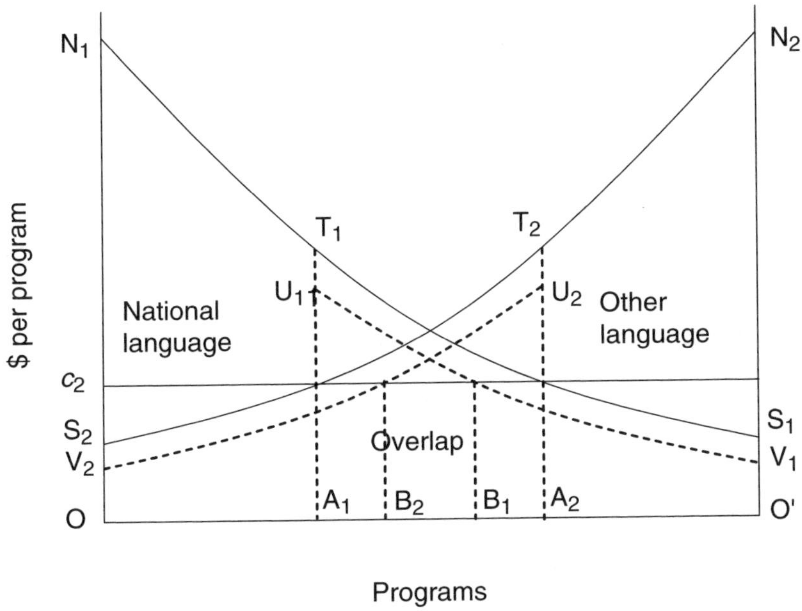

Figure 7.3 Equilibria in program space for intermediate scale economies

Is the duplication of programs by two levels of government efficient? Each level of government applies the right side of Equation 7.2 taking account of the effect of the second term on its share of message space in Figure 7.1. However, for the individual citizen, when a given program is already offered by one level of government, the additional messages from that level interfere with messages received from the other level of government. Although the citizen gains from having the extra program (an upward shift in M_1A or M_2A of Figure 7.1), she reaps little net benefit from the extension of the language network (a shift of *F*), since it comes at the expense of a contraction of the other network. In other words, for her, the second term on the right side of Equation 7.2 is close to zero. As a result, when there is duplication of services, the addition to social welfare of an extra program is given by U_1V_1 or U_2V_2 rather than by T_1S_1 or T_2S_2.

Not all duplication is necessarily inefficient. In Figure 7.3, the overlap B_2B_1 increases the citizen's utility. However, the amounts A_1B_2 and B_1A_2 reduce welfare since their cost, c_2, is greater than the utility the citizens obtain, as shown by the dotted lines.

During the last decades of the twentieth century, productivity in services lagged behind that in the rest of the economy. At the same time, increasing mobility, not only of labor, as described in the first section, but also of capital and goods and services meant that the optimal zone for many regulatory activities spilled over national boundaries. Consequently, the relative cost of providing government programs at the national level rose sharply. As national governments trimmed their activities, they privatized certain functions and transferred other powers to supranational institutions or to regional and local administrations.

Inevitably, jurisdictions overlapped, but not all duplication was inefficient. In the Canadian case, it was quite reasonable to have immigration and labor-training powers shared between Quebec and the federal government. Even Quebec diplomatic representatives in Paris and Washington might be justified. However, whether Quebec required a representative in Boston is open to question. Moreover, virtually all Canadians would agree that federal sponsorship of programs promoting Canadian federalism in Quebec between 1995 and 2000 was excessive.

In Europe, with the increased mobility and bilingualism described in the first section, a new language network has been formed that spills over national boundaries. In recent decades, the increasing numbers of European Union citizens able to speak English as a vehicular language have created a demand for standardized services at the Community level. Inevitably, these new areas of intervention overlap those of the member states and their regional governments.

We see then how the series of shocks described in the first section created the need for criteria to allocate responsibilities among multiple levels within a single political structure.

CONCLUSION

The traditional theory of public goods cannot explain the principal characteristics of multi-level political structures such as federal states in Switzerland and Canada or supranational organizations like the European Union and the United Nations. There are more levels of government, higher total levels of public spending and more overlap across jurisdictions than standard economic theory would predict. In addition, there would appear to be a contradiction between the two criteria of subsidiarity and scale economies used to assign responsibilities within such organizations. While the concept of scale economies suggests that government functions should be assigned to the highest level, the notion of subsidiarity recommends the lowest level able to perform a function effectively.[13]

This chapter has attempted to explain these contradictions between theory and fact by extending the theory of network externalities from the firm to the state. In the case of the firm, as Church and Gandal (2004) explained in a recent survey, one must distinguish between the hardware or platform and the software or applications. In the case of the state, the present chapter suggested, the equivalent of hardware or platform is a standardized language or culture used by a network of citizens. The counterpart to software or applications consists of government programs, that is, public goods and services whose availability increases the value of the linguistic platform to those who share it. The willingness to pay for access to a cultural network therefore depends not only on the number of other members but also on the programs that are offered within that network.

When two networks compete for the same taxpayers, the properties of uniqueness, stability, and optimality may fail to hold. The chapter showed that (a) there will be a demand for multiple levels of government, each functioning in a different 'language'; (b) there will be considerable variance in the resulting structure because of 'tipping', whereby one of the competing levels may be completely eliminated; and (c) there is likely to be considerable 'variety' in the form of duplicate programs, some of them inefficient, offered by overlapping levels of government.

ACKNOWLEDGEMENTS

The author wishes to thank Marc-Antoine Therrien for the preparation of information on the history of the concept of subsidiarity in an undergraduate term paper.

NOTES

1. Leo XIII, *Rerum Novarum*, 1891, article 32.
2. Leo XIII, *Rerum Novarum*, 1891, article 36.
3. Jeffery (2002).
4. Graff (1991; 195, 232, 252).
5. Author's calculations based on Cipolla (1969: 115).
6. Graff (1991: 374–6).
7. Münz (2004).
8. Münz (2004).
9. European Commission (2004).
10. Note that if both the regional and supranational levels are present simultaneously, the analysis must take place in three dimensions.
11. Once again, if both the regional and supranational levels are to be analysed simultaneously, we need a third dimension.
12. Note that the area under M_1A is equal to rectangle M_1CFO less triangle M_1CA; that is, for $i = 1$, the first term in the summation in Equation 7.1 less the second term.
13. Inman and Rubinfeld (1998).

REFERENCES

Alesina, A. and R. Perotti (2004), 'The European Union: a politically incorrect view', *Journal of Economic Perspectives*, **18** (4), 27–48.

Buchanan, J. M. (1965), 'An economic theory of clubs', *Economica*, **32**, 1–14.

Cameron, J. and T. P. Ndhlovu (2001), 'The comparative economics of EU "Subsidiarity": lessons from development/regional economic debates', *International Journal of Urban and Regional Research*, **25** (2), 327–45.

Cipolla, C. M. (1969), *Literacy and Development in the West*, Harmondworth: Penguin.

Church, J. and N. Gandal (1996), 'Strategic entry deterrence: complementary products as installed base', *European Journal of Political Economy*, **12**, 331–54.

Church, J. and N. Gandal (2004), 'Platform competition in telecommunications', in M. Cave, S. Majumdar and I. Vogelsang (eds), *The Handbook of Telecommunications*, New York: McGraw-Hill.

European Commission (2004), 'Languages of Europe', accessed at http://europa.eu.int/comm/education/policies/lang/languages/index_en.html

Feketekuty, G. (2004), 'Defining subsidiarity in the global system: legal and political criteria', Washington, DC: The International Commercial Diplomacy Project.

Graff, H. J. (1991), *The Legacies of Literacy: Continuities and Contradictions in Western Culture and Society*, Bloomington, IN: Indiana University Press.

Inman, R. P. and D. L. Rubinfeld (1998), 'Subsidiarity and the European Union', in P. Newman (ed.), *The New Palgrave Dictionary of Economics and Law*, Basingstoke, UK: Macmillan Reference Ltd, pp. 545–51.

Jeffery, C. (2002), 'The "Europe of the Regions" from Maastricht to Nice', University of Belfast, School of Politics and International Studies Queen's Papers on Europeanisation No. 7.

Katz, M. L. and C. Shapiro (1985), 'Network externalities, competition, and compatibility', *American Economic Review*, **75**, 424–40.

Katz, M. L. and C. Shapiro (1986), 'Technology adoption in the face of network externalities', *Journal of Political Economy*, **94** (4), 822–41.

Lazear, E. P. (1999), 'Culture and language', *Journal of Political Economy*, **107:6** (2), S95–S126.

Michelet, J. (1875), *Tableau de la France: géographie, physique, politique et morale*, Paris: A. Lacroix.

Münz, R. (2004), 'Migration, labour markets and migrants' integration in Europe: a comparison', Hamburg Institute of International Economics, Migration Research Group.

Samuelson, P. A. (1954), 'The pure theory of public expenditure', *Review of Economics and Statistics*, **36**, 387–9.

Shy, O. (2001), *The Economics of Network Industries*, Cambridge: Cambridge University Press.

Tiebout, C. M. (1956), 'A pure theory of local expenditures', *Journal of Political Economy*, **64**, 416–24.

8. *Leviathan* or *Geryon*? Power abuse in democratic societies

Louis M. Imbeau

> *Leviathan*: a sea monster, identified in different passages [of the Bible] with the whale and the crocodile and with the Devil; [. . .] an autocratic monarch or state.
>
> *Oxford Dictionary of English*

> *Geryon*: in Greek myth, a three-headed or three-bodied giant living in the far West on an island, Erytheia [. . .]; there he pastured a herd of magnificent cattle [. . .]. It was one of the labours of Heracles to steal the cattle and drive them back to Greece.
>
> *The Concise Oxford Companion to Classical Literature*

INTRODUCTION

In the wake of Hobbes' famous book, political philosophy has traditionally considered a single manifestation of power concentration in society: the autocratic monarch, or State, represented by the biblical monster *Leviathan*. Classical students of power in political science have followed this tradition. Dahl, for example, limited the extension of the term 'power' to the coercive influence exercised by the State (1963: 50–1). For Lasswell and Kaplan (1950: 74) 'it is the threat of sanctions [by the State] which differentiates power from influence in general'. But more recently political sociology has considered a social organization in which multiple forms of power concentration coexist. *Geryon*, the mythological three-headed giant, is a more valid representation of power structures in society than Leviathan, the dragon-like monster of the Bible.

The point I want to make in this chapter is that if, relaxing the classical assumption of a single form, we assume that power concentration takes on multiple forms, we find that power abuses vary with forms of power concentration and that mechanisms aimed at preventing power abuse are no less varied. I will proceed in three steps. First I will provide a definition of power and I will discuss why it is necessary to look at multiple forms of power concentration in order to get a better picture. Second, I will describe the three main forms of power concentration in democratic societies, political, economic and preceptorial powers. Third, I will propose a typology of power abuses and of the mechanisms designed to prevent them.

DEFINING POWER AND ITS MANIFESTATIONS

The literature on power generally distinguishes two types of power: power-to and power-over. Power-to, or outcome power, is 'the ability of an actor to bring about or help bring about outcomes'. Power-over, or social power, is 'the ability of an actor deliberately to change the incentive structure of another actor or actors to bring about, or help bring about outcomes' (Dowding, 1991: 48). Social power therefore implies outcome power but the reverse is not true. Outcome power may exist without any social power. I may have the power to turn around the furniture in my living room but this ability to bring about a new allocation of space in my interior is not related to any 'power over' another person. Here I will focus on social power. Each time I use the word 'power', I will mean 'social power', unless otherwise specified.[1]

These definitions are 'dispositional' in the sense that they focus on a dispositional property of an actor, that is, the ability or the capacity to do certain things. From this point of view, saying that *A* has the capacity to influence *B* does not imply that *A* actually influences *B*. *A* might decide not to use her power in which case social power remains potential.[2] The alternative to a dispositional definition is a 'causal', or operational, one which focuses on behaviour and which is often formulated in terms of control. For example, Dahl proposed a dispositional definition of power as the capacity for one person to influence another, that is to make another person do (or not do) what she would not do (or would do) otherwise (Dahl, 1963: 40). However, when writing with Lindblom, he proposed a causal definition of power as control:

> In loose language, *A* controls the responses of *B* if *A*'s acts cause *B* to respond in a definite way. To put it in stricter but more cumbersome language: *B is controlled by A to the extent that B's responses are dependent of A's acts in an immediate and direct functional relationship*. (Dahl and Lindblom, 1976: 94)

I concur with Dowding to say that 'the simple problem with the causal definition is that it is false' (1991: 4). If *A* decides not to use her resources to influence *B* or if *A*'s attempt to influence *B* fails, then we would have to declare that *A* has no power over *B*, according to the causal definition. Yet *A* could be powerful and decide not to use her power.

The basic issue then for one who wants to understand power relationships in society is to know who has power. But how? Basically by observing one's capacity to influence, that is one's control over resources that give such capacity. I see three sources of power, or three resources that the powerful may use to influence another one: positions of authority (or force), wealth and knowledge; hence my metaphor of the *Geryon*. Like this three-headed monster, power concentration presents itself in a triad.

Is there a 'fashion of triads' (Marquand, 1988)? Social scientists and philosophers seem to like to add to government and markets as organizing principles of societies a third principle.

> They . . . sense that alongside the familiar exchange and command modes of coordinating the actions of people in society, there is a third, more elusive, 'fuzzier' mode, which is in some sense more fraternal or communitarian; that we collaborate with our fellows, not only because we have been ordered to or because we calculate that it is worth our while to, but because we have learned to, because we believe that it is our duty to, because the ties of loyalty and mutual obligation which derive from membership of a community impel us to; and that, in practice, we cannot understand the real workings of real societies unless we appreciate how important this third mode is, and tease out its secrets. (Marquand, 1988: 262)

To illustrate his point, Marquand quotes several authors who proposed their own triads: Charles Lindblom (1977) looked at three types of social relations in society – exchange relations in markets, authority relations in governments and 'preceptoral' relations between advertisers and consumers or between indoctrinators and indoctrinated; Brian Barry (1973) presented three models of social collaboration – the liberal, the hierarchical, and the altruistic collaboration models; Streeck and Schmitter (1985) distinguished three models of social order – the 'market', the 'state', the 'community' – to which they suggested adding a fourth one the 'association'; Pieore and Sabel (1984) talked about 'markets', 'hierarchy', and 'flexible specialisation'.[3]

But are triads only a fashion? Is their use only aesthetic or is there some substance to them? Another way to set the issue is to ask the question why rational choice political economy generally limits itself to government and market relationships and why we need a third way. Let's try to answer this question.

Liberalism and its heir, rational choice political economy, have kept the pre-liberal idea that preferences are exogenous. Indeed, in pre-liberal thinking, individual preferences emanated either from God or from the Devil and telling the difference between the two was the exclusive domain of the Church. Liberal thinking replaced this mediated relationship with a direct one. God spoke directly to individuals. In both these traditions, individual preferences came from outside society. As the heir of this evolution, rational choice political economy naturally considers individual preferences as exogenous. They need not be explained. Rational choice political economy is interested in explaining outcomes ensuing from the preferences of individuals who 'are said to have moral sovereignty over their own desires or privileged access to their own best interests' (Dowding, 1991: 31). Thus the explanation starts with individuals fully aware of their interest.

Now bounded rational explanations consider preferences as endogenous as they are in part defined by social interactions. Of course there is no need to believe in God to adopt the point of view of exogenous preferences. No more than one needs to be an agnostic to consider a feedback loop between the individual and society and to assume that preferences are endogenous! So, adopting a bounded rational approach we may consider that society influences the formation of an individual's conception of his interest and that individuals may be wrong as to what their interests are. Dowding identifies two ways in which an individual may be wrong in believing that his choices are in his interests.

> First, I may be right in believing that I need *u* in order to get the wanted *x*, but be unaware that *u* also leads to the consequence *y* which is feared more than *x* is wanted. Second, I may want *x* yet be unaware that I need *u* in order to get it and so oppose *u* despite my want for *x* outweighing my opposition to *u*. (1991: 36)

Preferences are endogenous.

What does that tell us about power relationships? Several things. First, power is about the ability to act on one's evaluation of costs and benefits. If *A*'s power is *A*'s ability deliberately to change *B*'s incentive structure then *A* uses her power when she applies her resources to modify *B*'s calculus of costs and benefits so as to make him choose a new course of action that is susceptible to make *A*'s desired outcome more likely. Second, there are several resources that can be put to use to change another's incentive structure. Three of them have far ranging effects in society and may be said to have a structural impact on social relationships: force ensuing from positions of authority, wealth, and knowledge. If you want to convince me to do *a* knowing that I would not do it by myself, you can either force me, bribe me into doing it, or simply persuade me that *a* is needed for realizing something that I strongly desire. Third, the influenced need not be powerless for power to be effective. *B* rationally chooses what he does according to his preferences. In a sense, he is 'powerful' as he has outcome power, or power-to. *A*'s power lies in her capacity to make *B* feel that he actually prefers what she wants him to. And she will be all the more powerful that she has control over more resources. Therefore, studying safeguards against power abuse in democratic societies implies looking at a triad of power resources that may be used by the influencer to modify the calculus of costs and benefits made by the influenced. In the next section, I turn to describing these manifestations of power concentration.

FORMS OF POWER RELATIONSHIP: THE THREE FACES OF POWER

Several characteristics define power relationships: the resource that the influencer uses to exercise power, the method through which the influencer actualizes her power resource, and the type of modification to the incentive structure of the influenced that a power relationship produces. These characteristics allow us to identify at least three encompassing forms of power relationship in society, as depicted in Table 8.1.

Political Power or Power in Force and Coercion

The most obvious form of power relationship is political power, or power through coercion and force. It has received an extended treatment in the literature so it does not need much development here. Political power is the influence capacity that actors draw from the positions they occupy in an authority structure, the typical one in modern society being the State. As Max Weber put it, governments have a monopoly over the legitimate use of violence.[4] Thus government officials may make someone do what she would not do otherwise by using force on her. The method for actualizing power is threat of punishment and punishment, considering that, for threat to be credible, it must sometimes be applied.[5]

Threat of punishment mainly acts on one side of the benefit-cost structure: it increases the cost of doing what is prohibited or of not doing what

Table 8.1 Characteristics of power relationships

	Type of power relationship		
	Political	Economic	Preceptorial
Resource	Force/coercion	Wealth	Knowledge
Method	Threat/punishment	Exchange	Persuasion
Modification of incentive structure	Impacts on costs	Impacts on benefits	Impacts on beliefs about costs and benefits

is prohibited or of not doing what is mandatory. Through this modification of an actor's incentive structure the threat changes her preferences so as to make her choose a course of action that is different from what she would have chosen had only her original preferences prevailed. For example, the benefit-cost analysis a car driver implicitly makes when she decides to exceed the speed limit on the expressway includes the fine that the police would impose on her if she were caught. The higher the fine and the higher the number of police cars on the road (that is the higher the probability of being caught), the higher her expected cost. When this cost gets higher than the expected benefit of fast driving, she decides to comply with the rule. The threat of punishment may make her modify her choice through increasing the cost of not complying.

Economic Power or Power in Wealth

Economic power is quite different from political power as it is based on wealth. Indeed, wealth conveys power. Adam Smith, and, prior to him, Hobbes, once drew our attention to this fact. Here is how he stated the issue:

> Wealth, as Mr. Hobbes says, is power. But the person who either acquires, or succeeds to a great fortune, does not necessarily acquire or succeed to any political power, either civil or military. His fortune may, perhaps, afford him the means of acquiring both, but the mere possession of that fortune does not necessarily convey to him either. The power which that possession immediately and directly conveys to him, is the power of purchasing; a certain command over all the labour, or over all the produce of labour which is then in the market. His fortune is greater or less, precisely in proportion to the extent of this power; or to the quantity either of other men's labour, or, what is the same thing, of the produce of other men's labour, which it enables him to purchase or command. The exchangeable value of every thing must always be precisely equal to the extent of this power which it conveys to its owner. (*Wealth of Nations*, I, 5.3)

Once again Smith had it right. Wealth conveys power because it gives the person who controls it the capacity to make others do what they would not do otherwise or, equivalently, the capacity to change the incentive structure of another person so as to help produce a desired outcome.

Economic power is also different from political power in that it is actualized through exchange rather than force. Indeed, wealth gives one the capacity to offer compensation in exchange for the desired behaviour. Thus the leverage on the incentive structure applies to the benefit rather than to the cost side. To see this, it suffices to look at the fundamental market relationship between a supplier and a demander. Each wants the other to forgo his property rights over a given good and, in order to realize this desired outcome, each one is willing to give the other a benefit as compensation.

You want my fish, I want your potatoes. If you give me some of your potatoes, I will give you some of my fish. We influence each other. We both have power. But our capacity to influence stops when we run out of power resource. If you run out of potatoes, you will not be able to make me forgo any more of my fish. And, as long as I have fish, I still have the capacity to influence other people. The wealthier I am, the higher the number of persons I can influence through giving a portion of my wealth; the more economically powerful I am.

Economic power is the capacity for a party to a market exchange, through compensation, to make the other party forgo his property rights over some desired good or service. The main source of economic power is wealth, as Smith had it, that is, money but also factors of production.[6] The wealthier an individual or a firm is, the higher its control over the terms of exchange and, consequently, over the outcome of this exchange. Economic power is actualized through exchange. Whereas in the political realm, one uses threat to influence another, here, exchange is used. The buyer offers something of value to a seller who agrees to forgo his property right over a good or service. No violence, only mutual agreement to an exchange of values.

Preceptorial Power or Power in Knowledge

Preceptorial power is the capacity an actor has of influencing another actor through persuasion. The resource on which preceptorial power is based is knowledge, that is, information and understanding: information about facts, understanding about relationships among facts. Those who have control over both information and understanding can make others do what they would not do otherwise. This can go from making a man buy a bigger car than needed to making a young adult detonate a bomb carried in her bag while riding a bus. The method through which preceptorial power is actualized is persuasion, that is, suggestion supported by rhetoric.

The term 'preceptorial' refers to the relationship between a teacher and her student. The good preceptor does not need to use either punishment or bribery to convince her student to work hard and to assimilate (that is, to make his) what she is teaching him. She rather motivates or persuades her student through speech and action. Preceptorial power differs from the preceding two forms of power not only in the resource on which it is based – knowledge rather than position of authority or wealth – or in its actualization method – persuasion rather than threat or exchange – but also in the mechanism through which influence works. Whereas threat and exchange directly act on costs and benefits, persuasion plays on beliefs about costs and benefits.

The costs and the benefits of an action are its consequences. When consequences are believed to be favourable, they are benefits; when they are believed to be unfavourable, they are costs. Persuasion consists in using facts and theories (or information and understanding) to modify an actor's evaluation of his benefits and costs. Thus, by making him believe that some fundamental desire – like being loved, being safe, or even reaching heaven after death! – is linked to a specific action, the influencer can make the influenced do what he would not do otherwise. When the persuasion succeeds, the person under influence 'rationally' chooses the behaviour wanted by the influencer as the new evaluation he makes of the costs and benefits of this behaviour makes this choice advantageous. Without violence or compensation, the preceptor can bring one to believe that a specific behaviour is necessarily linked to the outcome he wants to reach. Thus he thinks that he is empowered (that is, he has power-to) as he is brought to believe that he can make the outcome happen.

Preceptorial power pervades all societies. It is recognizable in democracies under many forms including commercial advertising and religious proselytism, but also, in the policy process, under capture relationships, expert consultation, agency relationships, and political propaganda.

It is easy to see how the control over knowledge may help one influence another through commercial advertising. Commercial advertising seeks to make a consumer buy a product that he would not buy either because it is too expensive or because he does not want it. Through advertising the seller tries to persuade the consumer that he needs the product and that its price is right. Commercial advertising works essentially for two reasons: information asymmetry (the seller knows more about her product than the buyer) and buyer's credulity, that is, his vulnerability to suggestion. Knowledge about her product allows the seller credibly to boost its quality and to downplay its flaws. The potential buyer's credulity makes him believe that what he is told about the product and its contribution to his happiness is true and, therefore, needs not be questioned. The same logic applies to religious proselytism where the use of preceptorial power can make one accept the authority of a moral code (or of an interpretation of a moral code) that he would not spontaneously accept. Thus knowledge of a religious tradition gives credibility to the discourse of a religious official whereas the credulity of the faithful makes him believe what the religious official says is the truth, even the most fantastic stories about mankind and its relationship to the world like, for example, the fights opposing gods on Mount Olympus that ancient Greeks believed to be true, or the vision of an almighty God sitting on a throne with his Son and the Holy Spirit that Christianity describes, or the paradise promised to the 'believers' if they behave themselves that we find in many religions. Preceptorial power may even lead to the ultimate sacrifice of one's own life, like in holy wars or even in suicide bombing. A normally unbearable cost, death, is presented as bringing in immeasurable benefit, paradise. A short painful moment for an eternity of happiness. For the believer, the choice is clear!

Preceptorial power is also present in the policy process. It may happen, for example, in a sector where there is a natural monopoly, that the dominating firm controls most of the knowledge about issues pertaining to its product or service. Who knows better about communications than the only telecommunication company around which has been gathering information and making experiments for decades before? It seems normal that a government that wants to regulate that sector looks for information where it is, that is with the dominating firm. In fact, the need itself for regulation may first come from the firm as it may want to limit the access to its sector so as to protect its dominating position. Thus, using its knowledge as a resource, the firm can persuade the government of the necessity of regulation and of its content. George Stigler first described this phenomenon, later called 'capture': 'as a rule, regulation is acquired by the industry and is designed and operated primarily for its benefits' (Stigler, 1971: 3).

Another form of preceptorial power in the policy process is when experts intervene to influence decisions at the stages of elaboration or implementation. These experts use their knowledge in order to influence policymakers. This is a power relationship. The type of expertise or knowledge used varies widely, going from the scientific knowledge of many consultants to the simple personal experience of users asking for policy changes on the basis of a negative experience. But the pattern is the same. An actor uses his knowledge to persuade another to act in a way that she would not have chosen otherwise.

Still another manifestation of preceptorial power in the policy process is the principal–agent relationship. The subordinate in a government bureaucracy, the agent, controls information that his superior, the principal, ignores. This information could be limited to the agent's performance but it often also includes important information about public problems and public policies. Ministers are often ignorant of their ministry, at least in the first months in office, and therefore must depend on the knowledge-experience bureaucrats have accumulated over the years. In this context, the agent may want to influence his superior and make her adopt measures that she would not adopt if she had all the information. This situation frequently occurs when an agent disagrees with his superior as to the policy line to follow or when an agent would like to get a private benefit without his superior knowing. Thus the agent exercises preceptorial power over the principal.

One can think of a fourth important manifestation of preceptorial power in the policy process, political propaganda. Government officials spend a large amount of their time and energy communicating with the public. In the perspective of power relationship, we may say that they are using their knowledge about policy problems and about government activity to persuade voters to support a certain line of action. In a democratic context, voters supporting a policy programme means voters supporting the person or the party that promotes it. Therefore much of the public policy discourse is aimed at persuading voters to do what they would not do otherwise, that is, to go to the voting booth in the first place, and to vote for a given party. By modifying voters' incentive structure, politicians and bureaucrats, through their preceptorial activity, persuade them that their power over the choice of policy-makers and of policies is greater than it really is. As a consequence, voters do vote even though their individual votes have no effect on the outcome. Persuasion modifies voters' beliefs about their own power over decisions. It empowers them.

When preceptorial power succeeds, the outcome is often positive. Consumers may get higher utility through buying a product whose characteristics were brought to their attention. Voters may choose between contending visions of society thus making the will of the majority prevail. Believers are led to choose what is morally better for them and for the community. But the outcome of preceptorial power may also be negative. Consumers may buy products that they do not need or at a higher price than their opportunity cost. Voters may elect an incompetent candidate, or fail to sanction an undeserving incumbent. Believers may be led to choose a line of action that is detrimental to themselves and to the community.[7]

As it is the case for the other two types of power resource, knowledge may be more or less concentrated. When knowledge is highly concentrated, the ideas of a few individuals prevail. This could happen, for example, when a single hierarchy has a monopoly over religious beliefs in a society. Then an inattentive observer may have the impression that some ideas prevail, but in effect, it is people who prevail over others, people who successfully position themselves as knowing, and who want to use that position to influence others. Actually, it is when one is deemed to be right that one has preceptorial power. Then one is in a position to influence another through persuasion; one has the capacity persuasively to tell others what to do or not to do. Preceptorial power is also concentrated when there is no opposition to a government's discourse or when only one producer on a market can advertise her product.

At this point, it may be useful to summarize the argument and to see where it leads us. Social interactions boil down to power relationships between influencers and influenced. The influencer tries to produce a desired outcome through using a resource that she controls – authority, wealth or knowledge – in order to modify the incentive structure of the influenced so that he does something that he would not do otherwise thus promoting the influencer's objective. It is time to look at the abuses influencers often make of their power and at the mechanisms societies have devised to prevent them.

A TYPOLOGY OF POWER ABUSES AND OF THE MECHANISMS DEVISED TO PREVENT THEM

Power Abuses

When is there power abuse? The *Oxford Dictionary of English* defines abuse as the 'use (of something) to bad effect or for a bad purpose' (2003: 7). For there to be an abuse, there must be a use. Power is not always actualized. It is a potential for action and we can talk about power use and power abuse only when this potential is actualized. An actor uses and perhaps abuses her power whenever she does try to influence another actor. In general, the literature does not bother much about defining power abuse. We often content ourselves with assuming that 'power monopolized is power abused' (Kirwan, 1995: 77), and to devise ways of limiting its concentration. I will deviate from this tendency and propose a typology of power abuse.

The basic form of a power relationship is '*A* influences *B*' which means, according to our definition, that *A* uses a power resource she controls to make *B* do what he would otherwise not do. This is not to mean that *B* is powerless. Quite the contrary! Why would *A* bother about influencing *B* if *B* is completely powerless and has no authority, no wealth, and no knowledge at all? *A* influences *B* because *B* has some degree of force, wealth, or knowledge that he can put to *A*'s service in order to realize *A*'s wishes or that he can refrain from using so as not to interfere with *A*'s endeavour. *B* doing something that he would not do otherwise means either not opposing resistance to *A*'s project or using his own power to further *A*'s goals. Therefore, it is safe to say that *B*, the influenced, always has control over some power resource.

Isolating dyadic power relationships and cross-tabulating the main resource controlled by the influencer and the influenced, we find nine types of power abuses, as depicted in Table 8.2. Looking at these nine types, we have an extended, if not exhaustive, list of power abuses.

Types **A**, **B** and **C** are the main abuses that holder of authority positions can make themselves culprit of. Type **A** corresponds to the bad effect that may ensue from an influencer using force against an influenced who also has some control over force. Most force–force relationships entail neutral effect. *A* demands and *B* complies. The judge tells the police to put a person in jail, the police executes the mandate. The police imposes a fine on a driver who pays it.[8] There is no bad effect in these power relationships. However

Table 8.2 Types of power abuses

Main resource of the influencer	Main resource of the influenced		
	Force	Wealth	Knowledge
Force	**A** Tyranny or oppression	**B** Extortion	**C** Censorship Repression
Wealth	**D** Corruption	**E** Monopolistic and monopsonic behaviour	**F** Economic espionage
Knowledge	**G** Blackmail/defamation Deception (through capture behaviour, agency relationship, or political propaganda)	**H** Blackmail/ defamation Deception (leading to abusive advertising) Fraud	**I** Blackmail/ defamation Deception (leading to manipulation)

the use of authority may end up in cruel, unreasonable, or arbitrary effects on the influenced. Then power abuse takes the form of tyranny or, when these effects are prolonged, oppression. Type **B** (force–wealth) power abuse happens when the influencer is in a position of authority and uses this resource to extort money or other things of value from wealthy individuals. Type **C** (force–knowledge) power abuse happens when the position of authority is used to influence a person with preceptorial power. This type of abuse mainly takes two forms, censorship and repression.

When the main resource of the influencer is wealth, three types of power abuses are possible, types **D**, **E** and **F**. They are cases of abuse of economic power. Type **D** (wealth–force), often takes the form of corruption when wealthy individuals influence persons in positions of authority through bribery. It may be difficult empirically to differentiate type **B** and type **D** abuses (extortion and corruption) as it is not always clear who is the influencer in those two cases. This is why the line of defence of those who are accused of corruption often consists in pretending that they actually were the influenced, not the influencers, or that it was in fact extortion. But the theoretical difference between the two types is quite clear. Corruption implies that the wealthy influences the forceful whereas extortion implies the opposite. Type **E** (wealth–wealth) abuses are related to monopolistic/monopsonic behaviour resulting in non-competitive pricing. Here, the power relationship is between two actors, the supplier and the demander, both of whom have control over some wealth. By definition, of course, the influencer (the party in a dominating position) has more control than the influenced. Through his dominating position in a market, the influencer may indulge in monopolistic (monopsonic) activity that may lead the influenced to pay (receive) a higher (lower) price than a competitive market would produce. Monopolistic abuses more often happen in relationships among firms and between a firm and consumers. Monopsonic abuses are frequent in labour markets where a dominant employer faces unorganized workers in large numbers. Buyers of labour often have a greater capacity to influence the outcome of an exchange than sellers as each exchange decision weighs more in the welfare function of the latter than the former. A no-deal outcome has much harder consequences on a poor worker's life than on a big entrepreneur's. No deal for a poor worker means no revenue and therefore a more difficult life in an environment where shelter and food is generally exchanged for money. No deal for a big entrepreneur means lower production and lower profit, but rarely constitutes a threat to his own survival or that of his family. We have all heard of entrepreneurs taking vacations in a Caribbean resort after a bankruptcy! So buyers of labour may make workers accept a lower wage than they would if the exchange were less unequal. Finally, type **F** (wealth–knowledge) power abuse is the possible result of a power relationship between a wealthy influencer and a knowledgeable influenced. Typical of this power relationship is the firm using its economic capacity to gather intelligence in the form of economic espionage, including industrial spying or the theft of trade secrets.

Power abuses ensuing from the use of knowledge by the influencer may result in three types of power abuses, types **G**, **H** and **I**. All three types are characterized by blackmail and defamation, and by deception. One way an influencer can use knowledge in order to make another do what he would not do otherwise is through blackmail, that is, through the threat of revealing compromising information. The resistance of the influenced often leads to defamation. Deception of type **G** (knowledge–power) may be the outcome of several uses of knowledge as a power resource: a firm's capture behaviour, an agent's detrimental use of information asymmetry, or a politician's political propaganda. In type **H** (knowledge–wealth), deception leads to abusive advertising. Type **H** power relationship also leads to commercial fraud when one uses one's knowledge to obtain an undue advantage from another. Deception in type **I** (knowledge–knowledge) happens when a knowledgeable influencer wants to persuade another who has neither force nor wealth. The intellectual resistance of the influenced to the persuasion effort of the influencer can be

Table 8.3 Types of mechanisms to prevent power abuse

Main resource of the influencer	Main resource of the influenced		
	Force	Wealth	Knowledge
Force	**A** Division of powers Decentralization Federalism Competitive elections Competition	**B** Protection of property rights	**C** Transparency Freedom of the Press Subsidized official opposition
Wealth	**D** Anti-corruption laws	**E** Anti-trust laws Minimum wage laws Income maintenance programmes	**F** Protection of intellectual property rights Laws against economic espionage
Knowledge	**G** Laws against libel and defamation Transparency Public consultation Monitoring	**H** Laws against libel and defamation Laws against deceptive and abusive advertising	**I** Laws against libel and defamation Laws against sectarian behaviour Mass education

paralleled with the possibly violent resistance of the influenced to the force imposed by the influencer in the force–force relationship. The eventual deception resulting from this relationship may lead to manipulation.

This typology shows the variety of power abuses that pervade social interactions. In effect, almost every aspect of social life is plagued with this pathology. It is not surprising that a large number of mostly legal measures have been devised to cope with these abuses. These measures can also be usefully classified in a similar 3 × 3 matrix as the one depicted in Table 8.3.

Safeguards Against Power Abuses

We find nine types of mechanisms aimed at preventing power abuses. Type **A** mechanisms are those to which the literature most often refers. They are mechanisms that disperse power within governments (internal-dispersion mechanisms) or between governments and other actors (external-dispersion mechanisms). There are three main internal-dispersion mechanisms to limit power abuses: the division of powers, decentralization and federalism. The division of powers is a horizontal dispersion that developed from the legal tradition which, after Montesquieu, has taught us that one important way power could be dispersed, thus bringing some protection against tyranny and oppression, was through an institutional device that separates the responsibility to make laws (legislative), the responsibility to apply the law (executive), and the responsibility to sanction lawlessness (judiciary). The basic argument is that if these responsibilities are assigned to different persons, or group of persons, everybody would be better protected against abuses. Decentralization is a vertical form of dispersion that comes from the administrative tradition of delegating authority from the top to the bottom of a hierarchy. Superiors and subordinates exercise control on each other through information asymmetry and monitoring thus dispersing power. Finally, federalism further scatters power by separating competencies between central and territorial authorities. Moreover, this territorial dispersion implies some sort of multiplicative dispersion as the division of powers and decentralization are reproduced in lower governments. In each case, the argument is the same: society is better protected from power abuse if some of the power held by a person in position of authority passes to someone else: from the monarch separately to legislators and to judges through the separation of powers; within each branch, from the top of the hierarchy to subordinates through decentralization; and from central authorities to territorial authorities through federalism. External-dispersion mechanisms have traditionally been limited to the choice of governors. Thus the authoritarian method of appointment was superseded by democratic institutions that dispersed the power to choose governors to a large number of persons: universal suffrage, regular and competitive elections, limited term of office, and possibility for most citizens to run for office. More recently, the political-economy tradition has added a new external-dispersion mechanism for curbing potential power abuse: competition among government organizations. Competition shifts the power from suppliers of government services to the consumers who can choose which service to 'buy'. In other words, users decide which organization will provide a given service and which will not. Thus they are empowered as they can make government officials change their offer of policy.

Type **B** mechanisms are those that protect property rights thus limiting extortion. Type **C** mechanisms limit censorship and repression through transparency obligations, freedom of the press and subsidized official opposition. These measures contribute to shift power from government officials to critiques outside government. Indeed, to the extent that they must give up their control over information through transparency, government officials expose themselves to the influence of people outside government who disapprove of their choices. A free press and a subsidized official opposition give the holders of knowledge more possibility to use their power and to resist censorship and repression.

Among the mechanisms aimed at preventing power abuses by the wealthier are anti-corruption laws (type **D**) that protect the authority from undue influence from the wealthier but also from the collusion between some forceful and some wealthy actors. Type **E** mechanisms limit monopolist and monopsonic behaviour. From a legal standpoint, the issue of stating whether a firm is in a dominating position is separated from the issue of there being an abuse of this position. Depending on the legal system, anti-trust laws prohibit monopolies and cartels, or the abuse of a market-dominating position, or both. Concerning monopsonic behaviour, it is interesting to note that, like in the political realm there are special provisions aimed at giving political power to a large number of individuals through elections, there are, in the economic realm, provisions aimed at protecting unqualified and unorganized workers from abuses of power ensuing from the dominating position of employers directly affecting them. Among these provisions we could cite minimum wage laws that protect workers from abusive labour prices and income maintenance programmes which provide a substitute for the salary offered by the entrepreneur. Thus the negotiating power of workers is increased and the possibility of power abuse by the entrepreneur is decreased. Type **F** mechanisms protects from economic espionage through protecting intellectual property rights and criminalizing industrial spying and the theft of trade secrets.

Finally a last set of mechanisms prevents power abuses from influencers using their control over knowledge to influence others. Laws against libel and defamation are intended to limit defamatory behaviour and fall into types **G**, **H** and **I**. Protections against deception include, in type **G**, transparency obligations and public consultation to limit capture behaviour, and monitoring to limit the problems of adverse selection and moral hazard ensuing from an agent's abuse of information asymmetry. Deception in advertising (type **H**) is limited through laws against deceptive and abusive advertising. Finally, deception leading to manipulation is limited through laws against sectarian behaviour and through mass education (type **I**). Note here that mass education has the same function as elections in type **A** mechanisms and minimum wage laws and income maintenance programmes in type **E** mechanisms that is, to empower a large number of individuals so as further to disperse power. Mass education gives individuals intellectual and rhetorical tools to resist attempts by knowledge holders at abusively influencing them.

Safeguards against power abuse are either negative or positive. Negative measures identify abusive behaviour and provide for appropriate punishment aimed at dissuading power abuse. This is what first comes to mind when considering how power abuse is discouraged in a society. Positive measures act on the conditions that lead to power abuse by limiting power concentration and by increasing power diffusion. The most well known positive measures are the traditional division of powers in government. But many other institutional provisions do promote power dispersion even though we do not usually think of them in those terms. Any institution granting political, economic or preceptorial power to a large number of individuals contribute to dispersing power. Such measures include universal suffrage, minimum wage laws and income maintenance programmes, mass education, transparency and public-consultation obligations imposed on government officials, protection of property rights and of fundamental freedoms.

In the last analysis, we realize that the adoption and application of institutional mechanisms aimed at limiting power abuses resulted from the workings of power relationships. Potential or actual victims of power abuse used their resources to influence holders of authority positions in such a way that more stringent measures were gradually adopted and implemented. This process is likely to continue.

CONCLUSION

Social interactions are characterized by power relationships. Individuals use their control over power resources – force, wealth, and knowledge – to influence others, thus possibly concentrating more power into their hands. Power concentration leads to various types of power abuse that have brought about the development of important sets of institutional safeguards aimed at protecting individual freedom either through dissuading from certain abusive behaviour or through preventing power concentration and diffusing power among social agents.

According to Greek mythology, the giant *Geryon* had three upper bodies over a single pair of legs. We may conjecture that each one of his three heads commanded over one pair of arms. Thus he could fight three different enemies at the same time. But could he strike three simultaneous blows over a single target? Was there enough coordination among its three heads for coordinated action to be possible? Mythology says nothing about *Geryon*'s capacity to concentrate the will of his three heads and the power of his three pairs of arms. Could it be that this very lack of concentration made it possible for Heracles eventually to kill the giant? What teaching can we draw from this myth for our understanding of power concentration in society?

The highest form of power concentration and therefore the worst case for defenders of individual freedom appears when force, wealth and knowledge are controlled by the same individuals. When the influencer can use all three types of resource to pursue his objectives, then the potential for power abuse is at its apex. Recent history provides us with several examples of such concentration. Stalin had a high control over his government apparatus, economic resources as well as the tools of propaganda and he provided an image of the extremes that power concentration could reach. Similar situations could be observed in Mao's China and in Pol Pot's Cambodia where authority, wealth and knowledge were also highly concentrated. But Hitler could reach the same level of abuse through his control of only political and preceptorial powers. Is it possible then that power resources do not have the same potential for evil?

If we were to rank order power resources in terms of their potential for evil, we would conclude from a look at history that political power comes first. People in position of authority often abuse their power and these abuses have dramatic impacts on the lives of members of a population. Oppression clearly does not breed happiness. Therefore we would focus our efforts on limiting the concentration of authority. But we would soon find that political power almost always needs some form of preceptorial power to persuade the masses 'voluntarily' to submit to authority since complete control over a population through coercion alone is too costly if at all possible. Therefore we would also make sure that some island of public dissidence is maintained. And we would conclude that concentration of economic power in itself seems to lead to more benign forms of power abuse. This last conclusion would hold as long as we would limit our observation to contemporary developed societies. But things would appear in a different light if we were to look at other types of societies where wealth concentration is typically much greater. Looking at Ethiopia or Eritrea, for example, we would find that thousands of people starve to death each year as a consequence of an extreme level of economic power concentration. In light of this fact, we would have to conclude that concentration of economic power has the highest potential for evil!

Because they see a *Leviathan*, libertarian anarchists contend that the problem rests with a monopoly State: 'protecting property and upholding contracts sometimes requires force. But [anarchists] deny that such force must emanate from a coercive monopoly. Competing private agencies will suffice' (Hummel, 2005: 200). This may be true if we assume that private security agencies in a stateless society would limit themselves to protecting property and upholding contracts. But when we broaden the picture and consider the *Geryon*, we realize that these private agencies would be likely to try to take advantage of their power in order to increase it by submitting more people to their will, by extorting wealth from rich individuals or by forcing knowledgeable individuals to put their persuasion capacity to their service. The problem is not with a monopoly by the state but with a concentration of authority in the hands of the few within the state. Likewise, the problem with economic power is not the possibility of accumulation through property rights but with the concentration of wealth in the hands of the few. And the problem with preceptorial power is not the normative cohesion created through persuasion in a society but with the concentration of truth in the hands of the few. The best protection against power abuse is the playing of the power of one against the power of another: division and competition within each type of power relationship and between them.

ACKNOWLEDGEMENTS

I developed the main thrust of the argument presented here in the winter of 2006 while on sabbatical leave at the Istituto di Economia e Finanza at 'La Sapienza' University in Rome. I am grateful to Gianluigi Galeotti and to the members of his research team Domenico da Empoli, Emma Galli and Fabio Padovado for generously welcoming me in their seminar on fiscal federalism. I am also grateful to Nicole Dubé for reading and commenting on my text. I gratefully acknowledge the support of the Facultá di Giurisprudenza at 'La Sapienza' University and of the Social Science and Humanities Research Council of Canada. Of course, I take full responsibility for any shortcoming my text might have.

NOTES

1. It is the absence of this distinction between these two types of power (outcome and social power) that is responsible for much of the confusion one finds in Boulding's *Three Faces of Power* (Boulding, 1989).
2. Bachrach and Baratz coined the phrase 'nondecision' to refer to this possibility in the policy process:

   > A nondecision . . . is a decision that results in the suppression or thwarting of a latent or manifest challenge to the values and interest of the decision-maker. To be more nearly explicit, nondecision-making is a means by which demands for change on the existing allocation of benefits and privileges in the community can be suffocated before they are even voiced; or kept covert; or killed before they gain access to the relevant decision-making arena; or, failing all these things, maimed or destroyed in the decision-implementing stage of the policy process. (1970: 44)

3. It is easy to add to Marquand's list: McLean (1987) proposed three cooperative modes of resource allocation, 'government', 'market' and 'persuasion'; Kenneth E. Boulding (1989) suggested three types of power relationships – 'threat', 'economic' and 'integrative'; John Kenneth Galbraith (1983) identified three forms of power – 'condign', 'compensatory' and 'conditioned' – about which Boulding remarked that this typology 'roughly' corresponded to his own (Boulding, 1989: 11). Not only is the triad fashion widespread but it goes back

a long way in history. Jean-Louis Corriéras (1998: 25) cited Adalbéron dit Ascelin, bishop of Laon, France, for writing in 977: 'Triple is God's house that we believe to be one: here below some pray (*orant*), others fight (*pugnant*), still others work (*laborant*).' Even Confucius proposed his own triad when asked about good government: 'Enough food, enough weapons and the confidence of the people' (*Analects of Confucius*, Book XII, paragraph 7). And this list of quotations is not closed. There are a myriad of authors who see a three-headed monster where most others see a two- or a one-headed creature.

4. Weber postulated that an association should be called political 'if and in so far as the enforcement of its order is carried out continually within a given territorial area by the application and threat of physical force on the part of the administrative staff' (Weber, 1947: 154).
5. Another setting where physical violence is an important instrument of power is organized crime. We will not consider it here.
6. Smith's notion of 'power of purchasing' is to be distinguished from the notion of 'purchasing power'. The first is related to persons or firms who have, or do not have, power; the second refers to money, which gives its owner the capacity to buy goods and services according to the exchange rate and to the prices set in a given market.
7. One may argue that communication media play an important role in preceptorial power as they produce and distribute information. In fact, they are mainly involved in exchange relationships. Their role is to produce audiences (that is to gather a large number of people ready to listen to what their medium has to say) and to sell these audiences to firms for commercial advertising or to governments and political parties for political propaganda. In doing so, the media do not try to persuade except following the requests of their clients. And then, they do not care much about coherence. Thus they can state on page 1 that product *X* is better than product *Y*, and say exactly the opposite on the next page. Media produce information to gather readers/auditors/viewers rather than use information to persuade them in doing what they would not otherwise do. When they have power, it is rather economic power. Preceptorial power stands with those who use the media to spread their message.
8. The power relationship between the policeman and the driver is a force–force relationship because both have control over the use of authority: the policeman may make the driver comply with the regulation through force or through the threat of the use of force. The driver also has force power as he can resist and refuse to pay the fine or he can enter another relationship where he would act as the influencer, as a voter for example in an election or as a fighter in a revolution.

REFERENCES

Bachrach, P. and M. Baratz (1970), *Power and Poverty: Theory and Practice*, New York: Oxford University Press.

Barry, B. (1973), *The Liberal Theory of Justice*, Oxford: Clarendon Press.

Boulding, K. E. (1989), *Three Faces of Power*, Newbury Park, CA: Sage Publications.

Confucius (2006), *Analects of Confucius*. Book XII – Yen Yuan, paragraph 7, accessed 27 April at http://secretgovernmentlabs.com/page/bookconfuciusanalects.

Corriéras, J.-L. (1998), *Les fondements cachés de la théorie économique: La science économique à l'épreuve des sciences sociales*, Paris: L'Harmattan.

Dahl, R. A. (1963), *Modern Political Analysis*, Englewood Cliffs, NJ: Prentice-Hall Inc.

Dahl, R. A. and C. E. Lindblom (1976), *Politics, Economics and Welfare. Planning and Politico-economic Systems Resolved into Basic Social Processes*, Chicago, IL: University of Chicago Press.

Dowding, K. M. (1991), *Rational Choice and Political Power*, Aldershot, UK: Edward Elgar.
Galbraith, J. K. (1983), *The Anatomy of Power*, Boston, MA: Houghton Mifflin.
Hummel, J. R. (2005), 'Tullock on anarchy', in E. Stringham (ed.), *Anarchy, State and Public Choice*, Cheltenham, UK and Northampton, MA, USA: Edward Elgar, pp. 200–5.
Kirwan, K. A. (1995), 'The use and abuse of power: the Supreme Court and separation of powers', *Annals of the American Academy of Political and Social Science*, **537**, 76–84.
Lasswell, H. D. and A. Kaplan (1950), *Power and Society*, New Haven, CT: Yale University Press.
Lindblom, C. E. (1977), *Politics and Markets. The World's Political-Economic Systems*, New York: Basic Books.
Marquand, D. (1988), 'Preceptoral politics, yeoman democracy and the enabling state', *Government and Opposition*, **23** (3), 261–75.
McLean, I. (1987), *Public Choice, An Introduction*, Oxford: Basil Blackwell.
Piore, M. J. and C. Sabel (1984), *The Second Industrial Divide: Possibilities for Prosperity*, New York: Basic Books.
Smith, A. (1776), *Wealth of Nations*, reprinted 1998, Oxford: Oxford University Press.
Stigler, G. J. (1971), 'The theory of economic regulation', *Bell Journal of Economics and Management Science*, **2** (1), 3–21.
Streeck, W. and P. Schmitter (1985), 'Community, market, state – and associations? The prospective contribution of interest governance to social order', in W. Streeck and P. Schmitter (eds), *Private Interest Government*, London: Sage.
Weber, M. (1947), *The Theory of Social and Economic Organization*, New York: Oxford University Press.

9. Political institutions and policy innovations: theoretical thoughts and evidence on labor market regulation

Lars P. Feld and Jan Schnellenbach

INTRODUCTION

Economists often perceive themselves as being in a classical liberal tradition that proposes checks and balances as constitutional means to protect individuals from state intervention, exploitation or even violence. When it comes to discussions about political reform and innovation, the same people however put much trust in political leadership. Glorified examples of how fundamental economic reform was enforced by charismatic characters are Margaret Thatcher in the UK (Kavanagh and Seldon, 1989; Siebert, 1997; Klodt, 1999) and Ronald Reagan in the US (Buchanan, 2000). In Germany, Ludwig Erhard is given almost exclusively the credit for the German economic miracle after World War II (Reichel, 2002). Consequently, the role of political leadership figures prominently in debates about how to start the necessary economic reforms in countries like Germany or Switzerland (Heiniger *et al.*, 2004). In addition, the quest for political leadership is often accompanied by emphasizing particular countries as role models for reforms intended by certain parties or groups. Depending on party affiliation, countries as diverse as New Zealand (Wallis, 1998), the Netherlands (Becker, 1998; Den Butter and Mosch, 2003) or Denmark (Döhrn *et al.*, 1998; Green-Pedersen, 2001) and of course the UK and the US have been praised as examples for successful economic reform.

Based on both lines of thought, ways are explored that supposedly help to achieve fundamental economic reforms. Frequently, this leads to the proposal to revise constitutional provisions in order to enable political entrepreneurs to start their surge of policy innovations without the intervention of veto players. There are many critical arguments against such a research and policy strategy starting with the statistical problems for drawing causal inferences that are implied by a case study. A successful reform in one country, be it the Netherlands or the UK, provides only one observation (each) for investigating the impact of particular economic or political conditions on implementing economic reform. Very often, proponents of political leadership additionally overemphasize the role of historical figures in that process without making an attempt to quantitatively assess the relative importance of the different factors shaping successful reforms *ceteris paribus*. It is the very nature of these case studies that they are vulnerable to selection problems however useful they may be to get an idea of the details of reform processes. Fortunately, several studies exist that provide useful syntheses and a careful weighing up of existing case studies (Sturzenegger and Tommasi, 1998; Williamson, 1994). There are however counter-examples as well (Heiniger *et al.*, 2004).

The methodological problems are nonetheless not the most important criticisms. Relying on political leadership as key for economic reform is inappropriate for at least two fundamental reasons. First, as pointed to above, constitutions are designed in order to prevent (bad or incompetent) politicians from doing too much harm to citizens. From a classical liberal perspective in political philosophy, constitutional provisions are supposed to provide safeguards against state interventions into private affairs of individuals. In Feld (2005), this tradition is summarized in the context of the European Constitutional Project. Abolishing constitutional restraints in order to prevent veto players from restricting political entrepreneurs to conduct successful policy reforms may well improve the well-being of citizens in a polity if such a government is benevolent. However, there is also the danger that politicians abuse their additional powers such that the (economic) conditions of a country deteriorate. Dictators are seldom benevolent although quite a few economists still use the benevolent dictator assumption to develop their arguments for certain reform proposals.

Second, the possibilities as well as the reality of political leadership in Western democracies are wrongly assessed. A good example is the leadership attributed to Ronald Reagan who is widely credited for being instrumental to the economic recovery of the US 25 years ago. The American president is strongly restrained by checks and balances laid out in the constitution. Despite all media acknowledgments of being the most powerful person in office, the US constitution establishes a constitutionally weak presidency (Filippov *et al.*, 2004: 239). Considering American political reality, it is evident that Reagan could not have conducted far-reaching economic reform without the consent of the American people. In a careful analysis of the California tax revolt and its perception in other states, Matsusaka (2004: Chapter 7) underlines that Reagan took the opportunity to continue a policy of rolling back the state at the federal level that he had perceived as the newly emerging majority preferences in California while he governed the Golden

State. He was political entrepreneur enough to take up that mood. After opposing the first tax-cutting initiative in 1968, he proposed property tax limits in Proposition 1 in 1973, one year before he left office, written with the help of Milton Friedman and defeated by a small margin.

Hence, the political leadership by Ronald Reagan did not involve any relaxation of constitutional checks and balances. Reagan's political leadership consisted in transforming voters' feelings of being betrayed by politicians and bureaucrats in a new wave of classical liberal economic policy. The assessment of other successful reforms basically does not deviate from the US example. Fundamental economic reform in the Netherlands could only take place with a broad-based public support negotiated in the Wasenaar Accord in 1982. Again, the number of veto players was actually not reduced by any constitutional means, but interventions by powerful groups were prevented by politically binding agreements such that a broad support by the public could be secured. It appears that political support by the electorate is at least as important as political leadership to conduct fundamental economic reform, perhaps the only exception being the Thatcher reforms in the UK.

Given this cursory discussion of key conditions for successful reform, the question emerges as to whether constitutional provisions, as the rules of the political game, actually shape policy innovation. In this chapter, we take a more systematic look on the impact of constitutions on economic policy reform. Starting from a skeptical view on the role of political leadership, we sketch a framework of the economics of policy innovation in the third section by focusing on crucial ingredients that induce reforms such as the timing of policy innovation and punctuated equilibrium. Our main theoretical focus, however, is on a comparative analysis of policy reform under different constitutional regimes such as presidential and parliamentary systems, direct and representative democracy, or centralized and decentralized decision-making in the fourth section. Drawing on arguments by Tsebelis (1995, 2002), we provide preliminary thoughts on how the different provision of veto positions in different constitutional systems shapes policy innovations. In addition, we discuss how far the theory of veto players can be used in the analysis of policy reform.

In addition, empirical evidence on the impact of these different regime types on labor market regulation is provided by using a new data set on employment protection legislation (Feld, 2001, 2002). The econometric model is developed in the fifth section while the empirical results follow in the sixth section. Labor market regulation is chosen because it is perceived to be a key policy area in European economic reform (Blanchard and Wolfers, 2000). For empirical purposes, policy innovation is defined in these sections according to the most widely accepted definition in political science literature (Walker, 1969; Smith, 2001): political innovations are programs or policies which are new to the jurisdiction that introduces them, independent of the number of other jurisdictions that have already implemented them.[1] The final section offers some concluding remarks.

SCHUMPETERIAN APPROACHES TO POLITICAL INNOVATION AND REFORM

The theory of innovation in the tradition of Schumpeter relies to a great extent on personal characteristics of individuals who turn out to act as entrepreneurs (Schumpeter, 1912). At its core lies a surprisingly uneconomic, rather psychological theory of entrepreneurship concerned with an extraordinary intrinsic motivation of some individuals to build a legacy, with their risk-defying attitudes and with their exceptional creativity. External restrictions such as market structure do also exert an influence on the quantity and quality of innovation in this framework, but the personal characteristics remain the *conditio sine qua non*. In contrast, the more recent (neoclassical) economics of innovation describes entrepreneurship as a routine activity of businesses and focuses on the optimal amount of investment into R&D activities under various conditions (see the pioneering work of Dasgupta and Stiglitz, 1980, or Dasgupta, 1986). Personal characteristics such as risk-aversion (Kihlstrom and Laffont, 1979) or entrepreneurial skills (Lucas, 1978) are also incorporated into neoclassical models of entrepreneurial activity, but are not as fundamental as in Schumpeter's framework.

Given this development in the theory of private sector entrepreneurship, it appears to be rather surprising that Schumpeterian approaches still feature prominently in the theory of public sector entrepreneurship, reaching back to the assertion in Schumpeter (1942) that politicians are not to be understood as agents maximizing voters' preferences. Rather, they are conceived as specialists with a comparative advantage in finding solutions to public problems, and in using their leadership qualities in order to convince voters of the superiority of the proposed solutions. From such a perspective, one can easily arrive at the conclusion that public entrepreneurship can *ceteris paribus* be augmented by increasing the protection enjoyed by the incumbent (Wohlgemuth, 2000). In her approach to self-regulation of small-scale common pool problems, Ostrom (1990) also utilizes the notion of the public entrepreneur as an individual who invests into changing the rules of the common pool game. Occasionally, economists involved in political counseling call for political leadership in manufacturing fundamental economic reform (Heiniger *et al.*, 2004). Harberger (1993) does not hesitate to honor politicians who, from his perspective, have displayed such leadership as 'heroes'. There are also some contributions committed to define conditions under which political leadership is particularly needed, such as Hall (1993) who states that a situation in which an old paradigm has failed and is discredited creates a demand for a new paradigm which, in our context, has to be supplied by political entrepreneurs.

While bold entrepreneurial leadership may be appealing within private sector innovation economics, it is paradoxical within the framework of collective decision-making. If one believes in the relevance of the assumption of benevolent governments, leadership is superfluous. The incumbent is simply doing what is expected of him routinely, rather than performing any extraordinary or even heroic task (Kirchgässner, 2002). If, on the other hand, one adheres to the assumption of self-interested governments, then strong leadership is a cause of uneasiness rather than comfort – after all, there is no reason to presume that an exceptionally talented and gifted incumbent uses her skills to maximize citizens' welfare (Murphy *et al.*, 1991). Advocates of political leadership appear to take a position between these two approaches: they are aware of the imperfections of collective decision-making and the self-interested motivation of average decision-makers in political processes, but at the same time hope for the occasional appearance of a benevolent political hero who is willing and able to overcome these obstacles. Wallis (1998) coins the term 'coherent policy leader' for such political entrepreneurs.

Such an approach can be criticized by referring to the simple economic fact that rules (or 'institutions') backed by suitable incentives have an influence on the decisions made by individuals. If drawn from a population of heterogeneous individuals, politicians and bureaucrats are certainly likely to differ with regard to their political skills, their degree of benevolence or their risk-aversion with regard to the introduction of new, untested policies. But given the inescapable ex ante uncertainty about the true qualities of a candidate, instead of waiting for benevolent leadership to accidentally come by, it appears to be much more reasonable to search for rules that systematically encourage even risk-averse incumbents to attempt welfare-enhancing reforms and that systematically contain their self-interested propensities. The analysis in this chapter is therefore focused primarily on the impact of formal institutions on the likelihood of political reform and of policy innovations.

THE ECONOMICS OF POLITICAL INNOVATION: A FRAMEWORK

From the perspective of a pure welfare economist, the problem of timing policy innovations is a non-issue. Taking an efficient equilibrium as a point of departure, a change of policy is due whenever a (usually exogenous) change has occurred in the restrictions of the benevolent planner's maximizing exercise. Even from a naive political economy point of view, a delayed efficiency-enhancing reform would be puzzling as long as there are mechanisms to compensate possible losers out of these gains. Nevertheless, the empirical fact that reforms usually occur with substantial time lags is by now commonplace in the literature (Drazen, 1996).

There are some sophisticated approaches to explain delayed implementation of reforms. Drazen (1996) presents a dynamic war of attrition-game in which different groups know a superior policy, but have to incur costs of implementation. Knowing only their own costs for certain, they calculate a reservation cost depending on the probability distribution of the other groups' implementation costs, and free ride as long as their suspected probability that the other group carries the burden is high enough. Every unit of time that goes by without a concession by another group signals that the net benefit of reform and, correspondingly, willingness to pay is relatively low for these other groups. Inaction therefore leads to a gradual rise of reservation cost levels through updating the assumed probability distributions so that, given sufficient time, reform will eventually occur (see also Alesina and Drazen, 1991). A related approach to the problem also sketched by Drazen shows that a group expecting a loss of utility under reform does not favor reform if this loss is sufficiently large, so that it overcompensates an assumed rise of the costs of reforming in the next period. A necessary prerequisite for reform in this framework is a sufficient decline of the utility associated with the status quo policy over time in order to render the expected outcome of the reform policy more attractive than a perpetuated status quo.

As Saint-Paul (2000; Chapter 7) shows in a labor market context, uncertainty concerning the individual costs and benefits of reform also generates a status quo bias. This point can be generalized to other policy issues. A different model based on individual uncertainty about the benefits of reform from Fernandez and Rodrik (1991) is based upon the assumption that there may be post-reform mobility from the sector that is experiencing a loss of welfare to the winning sector. In this case, larger reform measures which credibly signal irreversibility have a greater chance to succeed if mobility between sectors is costly. This result can be contrasted with approaches from Dewatripont and Roland (1995) as well as Wei (1997) who argue in favor of incremental reforms because the option of reversal is kept in gradual reform measures, and therefore trial and error experiments are perceived to be less costly ex ante.

A common theme in the literature is the role of crisis as a trigger of implementing reform policies. An obvious impact of economic crisis is the depreciation of the value of the status quo policy, which is accompanied by a perceived rise of the benefit of change. A less obvious implication of introducing crisis is that a deteriorating value of the status quo policy may decrease the relevance of distributive quarrels over who is supposed to carry the burden of changing the status quo (Drazen and Grilli, 1993). Rodrik (1994) argues that a macroeconomic crisis makes the status quo policy unattractive for the vast majority of individuals, which allows reformers to bundle efficient, but redistributive microeconomic reforms with macroeconomic stabilization policies. If the theory market on which the median voter's conjectures about the relative efficiency of policies are determined is modeled endogenously, then a crisis can be instrumental in destabilizing a given equilibrium on the theory market and induce collective learning (Schnellenbach, 2004). Finally, Krueger (1993) argues that acute crises are instrumental in generating an opportunity to break out of a vicious cycle of rent-seeking and slow economic decay and Bates and Krueger (1993) argue that the total absence of reform in times of satisfactory growth rates is an empirical fact.

Even if crisis is commonly understood as a trigger for reform, this does not help us understand why the responsiveness of economies to crises varies substantially (Rodrik, 1996). Answering this question makes it necessary to peek into the black box of the institutions of collective decision-making, which the bulk of the contributions sketched above does not. An example is the war of attrition game in which it is simply presupposed that the groups playing this game have a *de facto* veto power that allows them to obstruct policy reforms. Another constraint of the literature surveyed here is the limited range of policies that it is applied to: its main interest is the implementation of efficient policies by developing economies or post-socialist transition countries. The set of efficient policies is usually assumed to be well defined and roughly in line with what is known as the Washington Consensus. As a result, the models allow for uncertainty on the individual level, but on the aggregate level there is little to learn about the relative efficiency of different policies (Krueger, 1992) – this feature of existing models may be challenged for its lack of realism.

A common, although not always explicitly stated theme of the contributions sketched in the above subsection is that policy reforms or innovations are essentially a non-marginal phenomenon. Changes in economic policy are not rational, marginal adjustments to changing restrictions, but much rather substantial leaps from one distinctive equilibrium set of policies to another. This statement is true even for reforms that follow a gradualist concept and are enacted as a sequence of piecemeal reforms, as a simple thought experiment shows: consider a sclerotic economy that, at time t_0 and as a result of successful rent-seeking activities in the past, suffers from inefficient labor market institutions that generate involuntary unemployment. At the same time, a neighboring economy cuts public spending and profit taxes, which leads to a reallocation of capital and a further rise of involuntary unemployment in the sclerotic economy. The literature discussed above would then lead us to believe that no reform will be successfully implemented in the sclerotic economy until the conditions on its labor market have deteriorated to a level that is sufficiently bad in order to lead at least some of the rent-seeking groups to tolerate reform, which may happen at some later time t_n. The crucial point is that in the time span between t_0 and t_n we expect no marginal adjustments of the sclerotic institutions to the slowly changing restrictions of policy-making (the outflow of capital to the neighboring economy). For this characteristic of non-marginal adjustments in delayed reform processes, it does not matter if the reform that is eventually enforced at t_n follows a gradualist concept or is implemented all at once. The appropriate theoretical metaphor then appears to be that of a punctuated equilibrium (see Gould and Eldredge, 1993 or Gersick, 1991 for surveys), which distinguishes between equilibrium periods, in which the underlying system is stable and changes either not at all or very little, and periods of transition leading the system towards a new equilibrium.

If such reasoning is applied to the problem posed here, the distinction between routine and reform politics has to be further clarified. If we talk about policy reforms or policy innovations, then this is to imply a conceptual change of policy, or put differently: a change of paradigm. Examples are a change from import substitution to a regime of export-led growth in the context of development economics, or a refurbishment of labor market institutions from pure employment protection toward enhancing efficiency. Preceding such a change of paradigm, however, an understanding of the suboptimal properties of the status quo is necessary. Suppose, for example, that in a tightly controlled democracy the government has an informational advantage relative to the electorate and is convinced that an alternative policy would yield superior results to the status quo policy. The median voter, however, is still convinced of the relative superiority of the status quo. In this setting, the approaches committed to the concept of political entrepreneurship would hope for strong and honest political leadership that either convinces the median voter of the relative superiority of an alternative policy, or that simply enacts such a policy against the preferences of the median voter.

An example is Harberger (1993), who even attributes Chilean reforms implemented during the Pinochet dictatorship to political heroism. There are plenty of normative problems associated with such a position. One is that individuals prefer certain institutions or policies not only due to efficiency considerations, but also because they are in line with other values that individuals may hold. Another one is that usually, the public entrepreneur also has no secure knowledge, but attaches some positive probability to the outcome that an alternative policy is superior. If she is willing to take this risk, it nevertheless cannot simply be presumed that the median voter has the same degree of risk-aversion or decides under similar additional restrictions. Political leadership that circumvents democratic control would then force the median voter into a policy experiment that she would not be willing to risk herself. In both cases, fundamental normative criteria to evaluate collective decision-making processes would be violated.

What is more important, though, in our (generally positive) approach to reform is the fact that bold political leadership in the Schumpeterian sense is highly improbable. If the market for theories about the relative efficiency of policy proposals is modeled as a frequency-dependent communication process, then reasonable assumptions about the conformism of individuals lead to a self-stabilizing majority whose opinion is, in normal non-critical periods, very difficult to influence externally (see Schnellenbach, 2004). Only if skepticism about a majority-backed status quo is already widespread can a change of the median voter's theories and preferences be expected. In such a situation, however, no bold political leadership is necessary, but only the supply of an alternative policy proposal. This restriction further substantiates the punctuated equilibrium view of policy reform. Without widespread uneasiness with the status quo, policy reform is improbable to occur in a democracy. Nevertheless, formal institutions play a pivotal role in shaping collective responses to situations where economic reform is indicated. In the following section, we will elaborate on this influence.

INSTITUTIONS OF COLLECTIVE DECISION-MAKING AND THE PROPENSITY TO REFORM

A delay of reform with deteriorating benefits of the status quo policy is associated with substantial costs if an alternative policy is available that produces a more beneficial outcome with a reasonably high probability. In other words, timing matters. Therefore, political institutions that strongly respond to available information *ceteris paribus* ought to be preferred over institutions where information is not utilized or where an increased willingness to reform in the electorate does not lead to corresponding actions by the legislature. The following subsections discuss the relative responsiveness of different institutions of collective decision-making.

Presidential versus Parliamentary Regimes

Persson and Tabellini (1999, 2003) provide empirical evidence that presidential systems induce less public spending than parliamentary regimes. This is attributed to the checks and balances between different agents in government, that is between a president and a parliament who are elected in separate elections. The effect is reinforced if there are two chambers of parliament who again are elected in separate elections. It also turns out that in presidential regimes, there is less redistribution toward the majority and relatively more redistribution toward small, but powerful constituencies (see Persson *et al.*, 2000). This latter fact is explained by referring to a lack of legislative cohesion in a presidential system, which follows from the missing need for a president to maintain a stable legislative majority. This enables the executive to negotiate on an issue-to-issue basis with parliamentary committees that prepare legislative decision-making. In a parliamentary democracy, the powers of government usually rest upon a stable parliamentary majority which is attempted to be held intact over the entire legislative term. This, in turn, creates greater incentives to conduct a broad redistribution toward the stable majority that is backing government.

At first sight, one is tempted to conclude from these results that political innovations are more likely to occur under a presidential regime, simply due to the reduced necessity to consider the interests of the members of a stable majority in parliament (Alesina *et al.*, 2006). The opportunity of the executive to negotiate directly with experts in the committees and to do so on an issue-to-issue basis can be seen as an avenue to engineer a change of policies more rapidly compared to a parliamentary system with its uniform majority and pressures toward a coherent bundle of policies. Such a view, however, ignores the role of veto players in the legislative process. Presidential systems are frequently associated with strong checks and balances between branches of government. The problem is particularly obvious in a scenario of divided politics in which veto powers can be exploited for strategic party purposes. Even if the president's party also has a majority in parliament, the separate electoral accountability of both powers may lead one branch of government to veto the other if a risky policy experiment is expected to produce results during a campaign for re-election. Similarly, a political response to a growing approval to reform in the electorate can be delayed if the votes for the two branches of government are cast at different dates and only one of the veto players ran on a reform-friendly platform.

Indeed, a parliamentary democracy in which the executive branch can work with a stable corresponding majority in the legislature can be expected to implement reforms with lesser frictions. In parliamentary regimes, the government depends on a majority of representatives such that a confidence requirement is imposed (Persson and Tabellini, 2003). In order to achieve political stability, the government has incentives to secure the support of MPs by two different instruments that are simultaneously used: the whipping system and the career opportunities for individual MPs force them to stick with the position of their own party majority in parliamentary votes. On the one hand, a representative who does not follow the majority proposal of her party is threatened by being neglected in the next round of promotions in government to even bringing an end to her political career when she is not considered on a secure position on a party list. On the other hand, promotion to leading positions in a party or (federal or state) government serves as a positive incentive. This argument is reinforced if the executive can bundle reforms with a confidence vote and thereby threaten to dissolve parliament and hold new elections. These political structures prevent the representatives in parliament from opposing the proposed reform of their government too strongly unless the re-election prospects of the government and the affiliated party members do not deteriorate that strongly that the parliamentary seat of individual MPs is at risk. In this latter case, representatives start to care for their own constituencies instead of their party.

A more comprehensive theory of veto powers has been formulated by Tsebelis (1995), who shows that adding a veto power never decreases, but usually increases the Pareto set in a model of spatial voting. Over the entire policy space, this implies that the set of status quo policies which cannot be replaced by an alternative is strictly non-decreasing in the number of veto players. This argument is in line with empirical evidence available on this problem (see Feigenbaum *et al.*, 1993). The number of veto players does, however, vary not only between presidential and parliamentary systems, but also between different institutional designs of the latter. For example, a majoritarian system that yields a two-party parliament is characterized by a smaller number of veto players than a system of proportional representation which produces coalition governments.

The relevance of veto players for reform policies can also be illustrated with anecdotal evidence concerning labor market reform in Denmark (see Green-Pedersen, 2001). There, the 1970s have brought both a sharp increase of the number of parties in parliament, leading to often unstable minority governments, and a deterioration of labor market conditions with a steady rise of involuntary unemployment following the exogenous shocks of two oil crises. While the 1980s have seen a slight improvement, they also saw a number of proposed comprehensive reform programs including tax and structural reforms that could not be passed through parliament by minority governments. In 1993, however, a social-democratic government used a short window of opportunity (one year of majority rule) to pass comprehensive reform legislation. From 1994 on, the social democrats remained in power, but again as a minority government. At this time, however, the conservative opposition chose to act cooperatively, so that further reform measures could be passed. The reason was that by now, the minority government was able to choose from different opposition groups, both conservative and left-wing, to cooperate with on an issue-to-issue basis. This factual reduction of veto powers of any single opposition group has facilitated the implementation of fiscal and labor market reforms that eventually reduced the number of unemployed by over one-third relative to its peak in 1993. To sum the discussion in this subsection up, we can state:

Hypothesis 1: Reform more likely occurs under regimes with less veto players, such that a presidential system can be expected to be less reform-friendly than a parliamentary system *ceteris paribus*, and a majoritarian system can be expected to be more reform-friendly than a system of proportional representation.

Direct versus Representative Democracy

The reason for veto players to exist is not to obstruct reforms, but to provide checks and balances and thereby avoid excessive power at the disposition of a single branch of government. A different mechanism to provide incentives for representatives to act according to the preferences of voters when no election looms, is to provide veto power to the electorate by allowing voters to organize an optional referendum or by introducing a mandatory referendum. In the framework of Moser (1996) and Heiniger *et al.* (2004), such an institutional provision simply works as an introduction of an additional veto player to the reform game, and the obvious implication is that direct democracy obstructs political leadership and thereby reduces the prospects of successful reform policies.

When the referendum allows the electorate to act as veto player, it is important to note that it can be expected to work very differently compared to political parties forming the opposition in a purely representative system. In a representative system with divided government, the party that is not participating in government can easily be seen to have an incentive to deny approval of reform measures that have a high probability of improving welfare, simply to improve its chances of being elected into government at the next elections. The median voter in a referendum is obviously not plagued by such strategic considerations. Since political parties and interest groups are less influential in direct than in representative democracy, the effect of adding the citizens as another veto player in the political game is ambiguous.

An example shows how direct democracy can be even used by the executive branch to weaken interest groups and threaten the legislature into approving reform measures that it would otherwise obstruct. In 2004, the newly elected governor of California, Arnold Schwarzenegger, proposed a reform of workers' compensation for work-related accidents in California. The old scheme was characterized by higher costs and lower compensation than comparable systems in other states, and thus was perceived to be inefficient. Nevertheless, the Californian legislature has been very reluctant to approve a reform of this system, in part because its two chambers are controlled by different partisan majorities. Governor Schwarzenegger decided to organize an initiative which threatened to implement policies that, from the perspective of the legislature, were even more unfavorable than the proposal it had hitherto rejected. When it became evident that the initiative had a good chance to be successful, the legislature finally agreed to approve the governor's reform of workers' compensation.[2] This example shows how the initiative as an instrument complementary to the referendum can be used to dissolve political lock-ins and reduce the power of representative veto players (although it does not necessarily lead to such an outcome as Schwarzenegger's 2005 experience shows).[3] The evidence collected by Matsusaka (2004) and referred to above corroborates this view. To sum up, we can state:

Hypothesis 2: While the impact of referendums on policy reforms is theoretically uncertain and a referendum may unambiguously slow down reform processes only relative to the purely representative Westminster system but not necessarily relative to other purely representative systems, the instrument of an initiative can be expected to speed up reform processes.

Centralized versus Decentralized Decision-Making

As our final theoretical point, a distinction between centralized and decentralized collective decision-making has to be made. On the one hand, decentralized provision and financing of public goods or fiscal federalism can be regarded as a type of vertical checks and balances (Besley and Coate, 2003). In that sense, federalism adds a veto player to the political game such that less policy innovation can be expected. On the other hand, federalism may increase policy innovation because horizontal competition between jurisdictions forces them to offer citizens new solutions to collective problems in order to increase the efficiency of public good provision (Oates, 1999). Decentralized experimentation provides opportunities to test new policies at lower cost than centralized policy experiments might involve. Thus, federalism offers the potential of vertical spillovers and more efficient policy reform. Indeed, welfare reform in the US followed along these lines of thought (Feld and Schnellenbach, 2004).

How political innovations diffuse from one jurisdiction to the other is much debated in the literature. The point that voters may gather information from the policies conducted in neighboring jurisdictions and use it in their voting decisions has been prominently made by Besley and Case (1995), although it has featured already in earlier contributions such as Salmon (1987). Indeed, Besley and Case have managed to provide evidence for American states that voters tend to punish incumbents for raising taxes if neighboring jurisdictions did not do the same. Thus, voters appear to use information from other jurisdictions to judge the relative efficiency (or ability) of their own incumbent. But they do so selectively: information on taxes is used, while other available information, for example on unemployment rates, has no significant impact on voting decisions. Nevertheless, this empirical result has important implications in the sense that information crossing the borders between jurisdictions has been shown to trigger political change.

Voting an incumbent out of her office because of her perceived inefficiency is one thing, but actively pursuing a reform policy is something very different. Under uncertainty, such an experiment with a previously unknown policy measure may be interpreted as the political equivalent to R&D expenditures. Any policy experiment carries the risk of failure and therefore the risk of being associated with high costs affecting both aggregate welfare and the popularity of the incumbent. It may therefore be tempting to free-ride on the policy experiments conducted in other jurisdictions, so that an under-supply of such experiments results in a decentralized setting, where the positive knowledge externalities of experimentation are not part of the decentralized maximization problems (see Rose-Ackerman, 1980). Strumpf (2002), however, shows that this is only a serious problem when jurisdictions are very similar. Kollman *et al.* (2000) argue that decentralized experimentation is superior to centralized experimentation if the problems for which solutions are to be found in the experiments are not too complex and if there are no scale economies in experimentation.

If factor migration between jurisdictions is considered as an additional externality-generating mechanism on top of the informational externalities, then these factor migrations between efficient and less efficient jurisdictions can be interpreted as an endogenous source of crisis, which in turn triggers demand for policy reform (Schnellenbach, 2004). Even if this demand does not necessarily arise in the correct (the relatively inefficient) region, the general point still holds that decentralized settings produce additional incentives to experiment with new policies than centralized settings. Summing up, we can therefore state:

Hypothesis 3: Given sufficient heterogeneity of jurisdictions, a polity with centralized decision-making is characterized by less policy experimentation and reform measures than a polity comprised of independent decentralized units.

AN ECONOMETRIC MODEL FOR LABOR MARKET REGULATION

The Data

In order to test the impact of institutions on reform processes, we have chosen to have a closer look at labor market regulation. Some authors view strict labor market regulations in Europe as the key factor leading to high unemployment and to persistence of unemployment, particularly emphasizing employment protection legislation (EPL) (Siebert, 1997). Although arguments against this view are also made (Addison and Teixeira, 2001), Blanchard and Wolfers (2000) and Blanchard (2006) provide convincing evidence that EPL contributes to the worse economic situation in continental Europe compared to the Anglo-Saxon countries. It appears that strict EPL increases the cost of firing in economic downturns so that fewer workers are initially laid off. If the recession lasts sufficiently long, employees are nevertheless eventually laid off in order to reduce production. When it comes to economic recovery, firms in countries with strict EPL hesitate to hire employees because they are uncertain about the magnitude of the economic upturn and face rigid EPL. Unemployed people remain unemployed longer so that their human capital further depreciates. When labor demand finally increases, some of these workers do lack adequate skills. The result is structural unemployment.

Aside the impact of EPL on unemployment, the determinants of EPL are investigated to a lesser extent, with institutional influences receiving little attention. Saint-Paul (2000) provides an argument based on insider–outsider theory and concludes that reforms of the labor market may be blocked if rent-seeking insiders succeed in gaining legislative support. This is more probable the higher the number of veto players. Agell (1999, 2000) explains EPL and other labor market institutions as an insurance for employees against adverse economic shocks or structural shifts in labor demand. This is fully in line with the arguments by Rodrik (1998) that citizens in more open economies demand insurance for the risk to be laid-off.

One of the difficulties in conducting an empirical study on EPL consists in the availability of feasible data sets. The EPL indicators provided by the OECD (1994, 1999) used in most studies vary insufficiently over time. They cover an average of the late 1980s and of the late 1990s, respectively. These indicators measure regulation on individual and collective dismissals, fixed-term contracts, and temporary work. Lazear's (1990) data are on a yearly basis from 1956 to 1984, but they cover only two aspects of individual dismissals in regular labor contracts, the legal notice period and severance pay and do not distinguish between individual dismissal in regular contracts and collective dismissals, temporary work and fixed-term contracts. Blanchard and Wolfers (2000) consider variation over time, but to the costs of having Lazear's imperfect indicator for the 1970s. Nicoletti *et al.* (2001) have constructed a time-varying indicator of EPL for 19 OECD countries by taking the 1990 and 1998 OECD summary indicators of EPL and combining it with information on the timing of EPL reforms. However, this is also not providing sufficient time variation for an empirical study in which EPL is considered as being an indicator of political innovation.

The data used in this chapter cover regulation on individual and collective dismissals, fixed-term contracts, part-time work, temporary work and working time in 12 EU member countries, Belgium, Denmark, France, Germany, Greece, Ireland, Italy, Luxembourg, the Netherlands, Portugal, Spain and the United Kingdom during the period 1970 to 1996 on an annual basis.[4] About 600 laws and legal notices enter the indexes, with a restriction to written statutes provided in the labor code, the private code or other laws. Courts' rulings and contractual self-regulations by unions and employer organizations are not considered. The written statutes can thus be understood as minimum standards only. However, the advantages of these data lie in the fact that they are generally binding for all employers and employees.

These indicators measure strictness of EPL on an ordinal scale from 0 to 9. They take on the value of '0' when there is no legal restriction in a country at a given point in time, '9' when a regulation precludes certain actions and the medium scale value '5' when regulations correspond to EU directives or ILO conventions. Table 9.1 indicates that the UK, Ireland and Denmark possess relatively liberal labor market regulations while Germany, France and Belgium have more restrictive EPL. The strictest EPL are observed in Greece, Italy and Spain.

This order of countries is not too different from the ranking obtained from the data of Lazear (1990) and the OECD (1994, 1999). This holds despite the fact that in contrast to the indicators used here, those authors provide rankings of countries with '1' for the country with the lowest strictness of labor market regulations and higher values for lower ranks. No number occurs twice. The message of both kinds of measurement is the

Table 9.1 Comparison of indexes of employment protection legislation, 12 EU-member countries

	Lazear (1990)	OECD (1999)			Own indexes		
	1956–84	Late 1980s	Late 1990s	Weighted late 1990s	Average 1970–84	Average 1985–91	Average 1992–7
Belgium	10	13	13	16	6.27	10.75	11
Germany	11	14	18	20	8.91	10.54	10.78
Denmark	14	7	8	8	8.27	7.5	6.22
France	15	10	21	21	8.8	11.25	12.28
Greece	16	16	24	24	11.56	12.17	12.33
Italy	19	18	23	23	12.91	13	12.5
Ireland	1	4	4	5	4.84	7	7.78
Luxembourg	–	–	–	–	3.82	4.5	9.28
Netherlands	9	11	14	13	11.91	11.29	11.44
Portugal	13	19	25	26	4.22	7.71	9.56
Spain	17	17	22	22	5	13.46	10.94
UK	7	2	2	2	4.47	6	5.56
Mean	12.14	10.71	14.14	14.71	8.79	10.05	9.97
Median	11	11	14	16	8.80	10.75	11
Maximum	19	18	23	23	12.91	13	12.50
Minimum	7	2	2	2	4.47	6	5.56
Standard Dev.	4.10	5.15	7.38	7.61	2.95	2.43	2.86

Notes: '–': Not available.

Source: OECD (1999), p. 67. Lazear's index is based on the average of 1956 to 1984. The own indexes are the rank sums of regulations for individual and collective dismissal, fixed-term contracts and temporary work averaged over the respective periods for comparability.

same: higher values reflect stricter EPL. The differences between the existing data and those used in this paper mainly occur with respect to the time dimension. The 1970s were a time period of increasing strictness of EPL for the original EC member countries. The deregulation discussion in the 1980s and 1990s influenced regulation outcomes as well. There is deregulation of the laws on individual dismissals in Portugal in 1983, 1988 to 1990 and in France in 1986. Regulations of collective dismissals and temporary work were relaxed in the Netherlands in 1985 and 1990. There is deregulation of fixed-term contracts in Italy, of part-time work in Belgium and Spain and of working time in France. Many of them were only moderate, however, and were compensated by an additional tightening of these provisions later. Examples are the re-regulation of working time in France in recent years or the regulation of individual dismissals in Germany after the government change to the coalition of social democrats and greens in 1999.

The Model

Despite the fact that fundamental labor market reforms cannot be observed in these 12 EU countries, it still offers an opportunity to study the political economy of incremental reform steps that have often been perceived by trade unions as the first steps for an attack on labor rights in most continental European countries. Because of this political perception, the data do not necessarily contradict the notion of punctuated equilibrium postulated above. Based on these considerations, we propose the following model:

$$EPL_{it} = \alpha_1 + \beta_1 HVP_{it} + \gamma_1 VVP_{it} + \delta_1 X_{it} + \varepsilon_{1it} \quad (9.1)$$

where EPL_{it} denotes the index of strictness of employment protection legislation. HVP_{it} is a vector of variables capturing the importance of veto players on the horizontal level, VVP_{it} is a vector of variables capturing the importance of veto players from a vertical perspective, and X_{it} is a vector of economic, demographic and political control variables. α, β, γ, δ are vector valued coefficients to be estimated while ϵ represents the error term. We estimate the model using annual data over the period 1970 to 1996. The subscript i=1, . . . , 12 indicates EU member countries and t=1970, . . . , 1996 index years.

The importance of veto players either at the horizontal or vertical level is measured by variables obtained from the data sets by Beck *et al.* (2001) and Keefer and Stasavage (2003). Following the theoretical arguments above, we expect presidential systems or systems with proportional representation to entail stricter EPL. Having a closer look at the data reveals however that among the 12 EU member states in the sample neither presidential nor majoritarian systems are widespread. Only France could be considered presidential under some conditions, while only France (until 1985) and the UK hold majoritarian elections. Thus, these variables are only dummies for these two countries. We therefore choose to include an additional variable that measures the degree of checks and balances prevailing in a country. This variable ranges from 1 to 10 measuring stronger checks and balances with higher numbers. As suggested by the theory of veto players, stronger checks and balances increase the number of veto players and hence of trade unions' positions to defend strict EPL. We thus expect this variable to exert a positive impact on the strictness of EPL.

The existence of veto players from a vertical perspective is measured by the fiscal autonomy of sub-central jurisdictions in particular in taxation.

The theoretical arguments with respect to the impact of federalism on policy reform are ambiguous. While it may increase the number of veto players, in particular when a second chamber of parliament exists, it may increase the propensity to innovate if systems competition between sub-central jurisdictions prevails. The latter argument mainly holds with respect to taxation whenever tax competition between jurisdictions forces them to experiment with new solutions. In order to check this argument sub-central tax autonomy is included as a measure for competitive federalism. Hypothesis 3 states that this should particularly hold in heterogeneous jurisdictions. A country's heterogeneity is measured by ethnic and linguistic fractionalization of a country. Since both are not expected to be tremendously high in EU countries, we additionally control for the political fragmentation of a government as a measure for heterogeneity.

Unfortunately, direct democracy does not play a big role in EU member countries. Only Ireland and partly Italy can be considered as using referendums on a statutory level. In addition, Denmark regularly holds referendums at the constitutional level. We are thus not able to test Hypothesis 2. However, it is possible to control for the periods in which Greece, Portugal and Spain were governed by dictators. If political leadership were key for policy reform, it would at least have been possible in these days to use it for the best of their countries. As control variables, real GDP per capita and the unemployment rate are used as indicators for economic crises. Openness and the lagged average index of EPL of neighboring countries are included as measures for the intensity of international competition. Following Rodrik (1998), openness is measured as the sum of exports and imports in percentage of GDP. If his hypothesis is correct that citizens in more open economies demand a better insurance against the risks of opening their markets, openness should lead to higher EPL. The rationale for including the average strictness of EPL in neighboring countries originates from the literature on tax competition (Feld and Reulier, 2005). The lower the strictness of EPL in competing states, the stronger is the pressure from regulatory competition in a country to reduce its regulatory strictness as well. A positive relationship is thus expected between a country's own strictness of EPL and that of its competitors, in our case the neighbors. Finally, the size of a country is controlled for by including population size.

As Ashworth *et al.* (2003) argue, the correct estimation method for an analysis of policy innovation is a discrete hazard model estimated by maximum likelihood techniques. Using this method, an observation is included in the sample until the policy innovation, in our case the change in labor market regulation, occurs and drops afterwards. This method thus requires a large number of observations. Since we can only look at 12 EU member countries over time, this method is not useful for our sample. A traditional ordered logit model using a maximum likelihood estimator comes closest to the discrete hazard model which is why it is used here. Another econometric problem consists in the simultaneous relationship between the strictness of EPL in country *i* and time *t* and that of its neighbors at the same point in time. With an ordered logit model, and a discrete hazard model likewise, this endogeneity problem cannot be resolved in the usual fashion. Thus, the lagged values of the neighbors' regulations are included in the model. Finally, our estimation strategy is to focus on individual and collective dismissal only. The subsidiary regulations, like that on fixed term contracts or temporary work, do not change the picture very much. These results can be obtained from the authors upon request. This estimation strategy is followed by first calculating an overall index of dismissal regulation and then analysing both individual regulation components.

EMPIRICAL RESULTS

The estimation results are presented in Table 9.2. In general, the model explains the EPL indicators relatively well according to the Pseudo R^2 and the LR statistics. This holds although the index of collective dismissal regulation is considerably less well explained by the model. In addition, the variables included in the model have a consistent impact across the equations.

The most important results can be found with respect to the horizontal and vertical impact of veto players. While we find no significant impact of parliamentary systems or systems of proportional representation on the strictness of (individual or collective) dismissal, stronger checks and balances exert a positive influence that is at least marginally significant. The stronger the checks and balances, the stronger the potential for veto players to have an impact on policy outcomes. In the case of EPL, higher checks and balances obviously mean less deregulation of the labor market. Thus, Hypothesis 1 cannot be rejected. Still, we are not able to find any results with respect to parliamentary systems or systems with proportional representation, which should not be too much of a problem because of the low variance of these characteristics in the sample of 12 EU countries. The checks and balances variable appears to capture the potential for veto players on a horizontal level much more precisely.

Contrary to veto positions on a horizontal level, the results on decentralized decision-making measured by sub-central tax autonomy indicate that federalism need not lead to a political stalemate on the labor market. According to the estimates in Table 9.2, sub-central tax autonomy does not have any impact on the overall index of dismissal regulation and the index

Table 9.2 Ordered logit model of employment protection legislation, 12 EU-member countries, 1971–1996, pooled estimates

Independent Variables	Index of Dismissal Regulation	Index of Dismissal Regulation	Index of Individual Dismissal Regulation	Index of Individual Dismissal Regulation	Index of Collective Dismissal Regulation	Index of Collective Dismissal Regulation
Parliamentary systems	0.387	0.384	−0.397	−0.391	0.070	0.101
	(1.48)	(1.47)	(1.58)	(1.55)	(0.26)	(0.38)
Proportional representation	−1.072	−1.070	−0.102	−0.106	0.116	0.126
	(1.35)	(1.34)	(0.15)	(0.16)	(0.15)	(0.16)
Checks and balances	0.284**	0.282**	0.242*	0.246*	0.157	0.173(*)
	(2.85)	(2.79)	(2.52)	(2.52)	(1.59)	(1.72)
Sub-central tax autonomy	0.004	0.011	0.326	0.317	−0.639(*)	−0.705(*)
	(0.01)	(0.02)	(0.86)	(0.84)	(1.72)	(1.87)
Dictatorship	2.161**	2.166**	1.712*	1.714*	0.743	0.723
	(3.29)	(3.29)	(2.35)	(2.36)	(0.96)	(0.96)
Ethnic fractionalization	−3.335**	−3.358**	−7.769**	−7.726**	−4.533**	−4.198**
	(3.25)	(3.24)	(6.93)	(6.80)	(4.75)	(4.22)
Political fragmentation of the government	–	0.028	–	−0.049	–	−0.234
		(0.16)		(0.26)		(1.29)
Lagged index of individual dismissal regulation of neighboring countries	−1.599**	−1.602**	−0.001	−0.002	–	–
	(8.60)	(8.55)	(0.02)	(0.03)		
Lagged index of collective dismissal regulation of neighboring countries	1.480**	1.483**	–	–	0.165**	0.159*
	(9.28)	(9.21)			(2.69)	(2.57)

Real GDP per capita	−0.002	−0.003	−0.092**	−0.090**	0.028	0.030
	(0.06)	(0.07)	(2.84)	(2.83)	(0.93)	(0.96)
Openness (in % of GDP)	1.294**	1.282**	3.899**	3.920**	−0.293	−0.191
	(2.67)	(2.62)	(7.23)	(7.19)	(0.59)	(0.38)
Government consumption (in % of GDP)	−0.069	−0.071	−0.055	−0.054	−0.146**	−0.132*
	(1.34)	(1.35)	(1.05)	(1.00)	(2.88)	(2.53)
Unemployment rate (in %)	0.106**	0.106**	0.301**	0.300**	0.181**	0.177**
	(2.78)	(2.78)	(7.32)	(7.29)	(4.90)	(4.74)
Population (in millions)	0.046**	0.046**	0.056**	0.056**	0.006	0.006
	(5.69)	(5.69)	(6.61)	(6.62)	(0.77)	(0.86)
Pseudo-R^2	0.146	0.146	0.148	0.148	0.079	0.080
Log-likelihood	−607.91	−607.90	−464.67	−464.63	−485.15	−484.30
LR statistics	207.91**	207.94**	161.21**	161.27**	82.76**	84.46**

Notes: The figures in parentheses are the **z**-statistics. '**', '*' and '(*)' indicate significance at the 1, 5 or 10 percent level. The Pseudo-R^2 and the LR-statistic indicate the overall performance of the models.

of individual dismissal regulation. The estimated coefficient is far from any significance level. Collective dismissal regulation is however negatively affected by sub-central tax autonomy. This effect is significant at the 10 percent level only. The effect makes particular sense for collective dismissal regulation because social plans are often bundled with contributions from employers, regional authorities and the central authority. In Germany, for example, social plans for declining industries have been financed with subsidies from the state governments and special deals from the unemployment insurance scheme administered by the Federal Labor Agency. If states had the power to tax and set tax rates, but in addition also had less implicit entitlements for federal transfers to bail them out, it would have been more difficult to bundle binding agreements with employers, trade unions, state and federal authorities.

In addition to sub-central tax autonomy, the heterogeneity of a country plays a role for labor market regulation. Ethnic fractionalization exerts a significantly negative impact on dismissal regulation in all estimated equations. The higher ethnic fractionalization, the lower is the strictness of dismissal regulation. This result is robust in all robustness tests performed. However, political fractionalization does not play any role and is not statistically significant. All in all, Hypothesis 3 cannot be rejected on the basis of these results.

The control variables reveal an interesting pattern of results. First, it appears that the European experience with dictators is not only uncomfortable for human rights reasons, but also with respect to labor market outcomes. During the periods of dictatorship in Greece, Portugal and Spain in the 1970s, dismissal regulation is *ceteris paribus* significantly higher. This mainly holds with respect to individual dismissals, while collective dismissal regulation is not affected by dictatorship. The impact of regulatory competition on dismissal regulation is a bit puzzling. While it appears that there are two countervailing influences in the overall index, it turns out that only collective dismissal regulation is significantly affected by the strictness of collective dismissal regulation in the neighboring countries. This relationship is positive as expected from the theory of systems competition. If a neighboring country reduces (increases) the strictness of collective dismissal regulation, the country under consideration responds strategically by reducing (increasing) its regulatory strictness as well. Openness has the expected positive sign in the models explaining the overall index of dismissal regulation as well as the index of individual dismissal regulation. These effects are significantly different from zero at the 1 percent level, while the effect of openness on the index of collective dismissal regulation is far from any significance level. These results partially support the hypotheses by Rodrik (1998) and Agell (2002). The remaining results are clear-cut: higher income countries have significantly less strict individual dismissal regulation, but income does not affect the other equations. Government consumption is significantly negatively associated with collective dismissal regulation, which indicates a substitutive relationship between public employment and strong requirements for social plans in the case of structural changes. The sign of the unemployment rate is significantly positive in all equations while smaller countries have significantly stricter overall and individual dismissal regulation.

CONCLUDING REMARKS

In this chapter, we have argued that a simplistic reliance on political leadership in order to achieve fundamental economic reform is misplaced. Such a view neglects the fact that checks and balances are introduced in constitutional political economy as a restriction on governments in order to protect citizens. Furthermore, the advocacy of political leadership is based on a wrong assessment of the situation in countries providing the role model. Perhaps with the only exception of the UK under Margaret Thatcher, successful economic reform has been based on popular concern with and awareness of economic crisis. Successful political leaders defended this concern throughout the reform process against partial interests.

More interesting than these general considerations are discussions about comparative reform capabilities of different political regimes. Based on the theory of veto players, we have developed empirically testable hypotheses on the differential potential of veto positions in presidential (high checks and balances) versus parliamentarian systems (low checks and balances), direct versus representative democracy, and centralized versus decentralized decision-making. The theoretical considerations show that merely counting veto players is not sufficient to understand the propensity for political innovation. In particular fiscal competition between sub-central jurisdictions accompanied by lower fiscal transfers from the center or a less egalitarian horizontal fiscal equalization system entails an additional potential for higher political innovation. Similarly, direct democracy must be differentiated in the two instruments of referendums and initiatives. While the second is attributed to higher political innovation, the referendum cannot simply be interpreted as a reform brake. Although citizens are becoming a powerful veto player in a referendum, it also reduces the impact of interest groups and of parties, hence of ideology, on policy outcomes. Reforms might be more easily accepted by the electorate than by the parliament which is much more prone to interest group influence.

Two of the three hypotheses are tested empirically using new data on employment protection legislation, in particular dismissal regulation, in 12 EU countries from 1970 to 1996. It turns out that higher checks and balances are associated with stricter dismissal regulation, while subcentral tax autonomy does in general not prevent labor market reform, but even decreases the strictness of collective dismissal regulation. In addition, regulatory competition has the expected dampening effect only in the case of collective dismissal regulation while openness appears to trigger higher regulation in the case of individual dismissal regulation. Unfortunately, *Hypothesis 2* could not be tested due to the lack of data. Still, we don't know whether direct democracy prevents reforms. Given the fact that most successful reforms needed the support by a majority of citizens in order to be successful, direct democracy does not appear to be overly restrictive. Further analysis is however needed to support that view.

NOTES

1. A policy innovation is hence a program, policy, law or regulation that is new to the jurisdiction implementing it, while it is not necessary that it is new to the whole sample of jurisdictions. From a bird's eye view, an act may then be both an imitation and an innovation. It has to be pointed out, however, that perfect imitation seldom occurs: usually, a policy that is imitated is at the same time accommodated to the specific conditions of the imitating jurisdiction. This fits nicely with Schumpeter's distinction of invention and innovation, where only 'invention' describes the actual creation of novelty.
2. See 'Schwarzeneggers neuer Streich', *Neue Zürcher Zeitung*, 20 April 2004, p. 5.
3. See 'The Arnold and Mike show', *The Economist* 377, No. 8452, 12 November 2005, pp. 54–5.
4. See Feld (2001, 2002) for details as to how the variables are coded and computed. An appendix providing an example for the coding is available upon request from the authors.

REFERENCES

Addison, J. T. and P. Teixeira (2001), 'The economics of employment protection', Institute for the study of labor discussion paper no. 381, October.

Agell, J. (1999), 'On the benefits from rigid labour markets: norms, market failures, and social insurance', *Economic Journal*, **109**, F143–F164.

Agell, J. (2002), 'On the determinants of labour market institutions: rent-sharing vs. social insurance', *German Economic Review*, **3**, 107–35.

Alesina, A. and A. Drazen (1991), 'Why are stabilizations delayed?', *American Economic Review*, **81**, 1170–88.

Alesina, A., S. Ardagna and F. Trebbi (2006), 'Who adjusts and when? On the political economy of reforms', mimeo, Harvard University.

Ashworth, J., B. Geys and B. Heyndels (2003), 'Political fragmentation and tax innovations: the case of environmental taxes in Flemish municipalities', mimeo, Vrije Universiteit Brussel.

Bates, R. and A. O. Krueger (1993), 'Generalizations arising from the country studies', in R. Bates and A. O. Krueger (eds), *Political and Economic Interactions in Economic Policy Reform*, Oxford: Basil Blackwell.
Beck, T., G. Clarke, A. Groff, P. Keefer and P. Walsh (2001), 'New tools in comparative political economy: the database of political institutions', *World Bank Economic Review*, **15**, 165–76.
Becker, U. (1998), 'Beschäftigungswunderland Niederlande?', *Aus Politik und Zeitgeschichte*, B11/98, 12–21.
Besley, T. and A. C. Case (1995), 'Incumbent behaviour, vote-seeking, tax-setting and yardstick competition', *American Economic Review*, **84**, 394–414.
Besley, T. and S. Coate (2003), 'Centralized versus decentralized provision of local public goods: a political economy analysis', *Journal of Public Economics*, **87**, 2611–37.
Blanchard, O. (2006), 'European unemployment: the evolution of facts and ideas', *Economic Policy*, **45**, 5–59.
Blanchard, O. and J. Wolfers (2000), 'The role of shocks and institutions in the rise of European unemployment: the aggregate evidence', *Economic Journal*, **110**, C1–C33.
Buchanan, J. M. (2000), 'The soul of classical liberalism', *Aussenwirtschaft*, **55**, 7–17.
Dasgupta, P. (1986), 'The theory of technological competition', in K. Binmore and P. Dasgupta (eds), *Economic Organizations as Games*, Oxford: Blackwell.
Dasgupta, P. and J. Stiglitz (1980), 'Industrial structure and the nature of economic activity', *Economic Journal*, **90**, 266–93.
Den Butter, F. A. G. and R. H. J. Mosch (2003), 'The Dutch miracle: institutions, networks, and trust', *Journal of Institutional and Theoretical Economics (JITE)*, **159**, 362–91.
Dewatripont, M. and G. Roland (1995), 'The design of reform packages under uncertainty', *American Economic Review*, **85**, 1207–23.
Döhrn, R., U. Heilemann and G. Schäfer (1998), 'Ein dänisches "Beschäftigungswunder"?', *Mitteilungen der Arbeitsmarkt- und Berufsforschung*, 2/98, 312–23.
Drazen, A. (1996), 'The political economy of delayed reform', *Policy Reform*, **1**, 25–46.
Drazen, A. and V. Grilli (1993), 'The benefit of crises for economic reform', *American Economic Review (Papers & Proceedings)*, **83**, 598–607.
Feigenbaum, H., R. Samuels and R. K. Weaver (1993), 'Innovation, coordination and implementation in energy policy', in R. K. Weaver and B. Rockman (eds), *Do Institutions Matter? Government Capabilities in the US and Abroad*, Washington, DC: The Brookings Institution.
Feld, L. P. (2001), 'Institutioneller Wettbewerb und Arbeitsmarktinstitutionen in Europa', in T. Apolte and U. Vollmer (eds), *Arbeitsmärkte und soziale Sicherungssysteme unter Reformdruck*, Stuttgart: Lucius & Lucius, pp. 289–317.
Feld, L. P. (2002), 'Growth, unemployment, investment, and employment protection legislation: panel evidence for the EU-12 from 1970 to 1996', University of St. Gallen working paper.
Feld, L. P. (2005), 'The European Constitution project from the perspective of constitutional political economy', *Public Choice*, **122**, 417–48.
Feld, L. P. and E. Reulier (2005), 'Strategic tax competition in Switzerland: evidence from a panel of the Swiss cantons', CESifo working paper series no. 1516, accessed at http: //sstn.com/abstract = 796704.

Feld, L. P. and J. Schnellenbach (2004), 'Begünstigt fiskalischer Wettbewerb die Politikinnovation und -diffusion? Theoretische Anmerkungen und erste Befunde aus Fallstudien', in C. A. Schaltegger and S. Schaltegger (eds), *Perspektiven der Schweizer Wirtschaftspolitik*, Zürich: vdf, pp. 259–77.

Fernandez, R. and D. Rodrik (1991), 'Resistance to reform: status quo bias in the presence of individual-specific uncertainty', *American Economic Review*, **81**, 1146–55.

Filippov, M., P. C. Ordeshook and O. Shvetsova (2004), *Designing Federalism: A Theory of Self-Sustainable Federal Institutions*, Cambridge: Cambridge University Press.

Gersick, C. (1991), 'Revolutionary change theories: a multilevel exploration of the punctuated equilibrium paradigm', *Academy of Management Review*, **16**, 10–36.

Gould, S. J. and N. Eldredge (1993), 'Punctuated equilibrium comes of age', *Nature*, **366**, 223–7.

Green-Pedersen, C. (2001), 'Minority governments and party politics: the political and institutional background to the Danish miracle', Max-Planck-Institut für Gesellschaftsforschung discussion paper 01-1, Köln.

Hall, P. (1993), 'Policy paradigms, social learning and the state: the case of economic policymaking in Britain', *Comparative Politics*, **25**, 275–96.

Harberger, A. (1993), 'Secrets of success: a handful of heroes', *American Economic Review (Papers & Proceedings)*, **83**, 343–50.

Heiniger, Y., T. Straubhaar, H. Rentsch, S. Flückiger and Thomas Held (2004), *Ökonomik der Reform. Wege zu mehr Wachstum in Deutschland (in der Schweiz)*, Zürich: Orell Füssli.

Kavanagh, D. and A. Seldon (eds) (1989), *The Thatcher Effect: A Decade of Change*, Oxford: Oxford University Press.

Keefer, P. and D. Stasavage (2003), 'The limits of delegation: veto players, central bank independence and the credibility of monetary policy', *American Political Science Review*, **93**, 407–23.

Kihlstrom, R. E. and J.-J. Laffont (1979), 'A general equilibrium theory of firm formation based on risk aversion', *Journal of Political Economy*, **87**, 719–48.

Kirchgässner, G. (2002), 'On the role of heroes in political and economic processes', *Kyklos*, **55**, 179–96.

Klodt, H. (1999), 'Arbeitsmarkterfolge in Großbritannien: Die marktwirtschaftliche Strategie', *WiSt*, **8**, 394–9.

Kollman, K., J. H. Miller and S. E. Page (2000), 'Decentralization and the search for policy solutions', *Journal of Law, Economics and Organization*, **16**, 102–28.

Krueger, A. O. (1992), *Economic Policy Reform in Developing Countries*, Oxford: Blackwell.

Krueger, A. O. (1993), 'Virtuous and vicious cycles in economic development', *American Economic Review (Papers & Proceedings)*, **83**, 351–5.

Lazear, E. P. (1990), 'Job security provisions and employment', *Quarterly Journal of Economics*, **105**, 699–726.

Lucas, R. E. (1978), 'On the size distribution of business firms', *Bell Journal of Economics*, **9**, 508–23.

Matsusaka, J. (2004), *For the Many or the Few: The Initiative Process, Public Policy and American Democracy*, Chicago, IL: University of Chicago Press.

Moser, P. (1996), 'Why is Swiss politics so stable?', *Schweizerische Zeitschrift für Volkswirtschaft und Statistik*, **132**, 31–60.

Murphy, K. M., A. Shleifer and R. W. Vishny (1991), 'The allocation of talent: implications for growth', *Quarterly Journal of Economics*, **106**, 503–30.

Nicoletti, G., R. C. G. Haffner, S. Nickell, S. Scarpetta and G. Zoega (2001), 'European integration, liberalization, and labor-market performance', in G. Bertola, T. Boeri and G. Nicoletti (eds), *Welfare and Employment in a United Europe*, Cambridge, MA: MIT Press, pp. 147–235.

Oates, W. E. (1999), 'An essay on fiscal federalism', *Journal of Economic Literature*, **37**, 1120–49.

Organization for Economic Co-operation and Development (OECD) (1994), *The OECD Jobs Study: Facts, Analysis, Strategies*, Paris: OECD.

Organization for Economic Co-operation and Development (OECD) (1999), *Employment Outlook, June 1999*, Paris: OECD.

Ostrom, E. (1990), *Governing the Commons. The Evolution of Institutions for Collective Action*, Cambridge: Cambridge University Press.

Persson, T. and G. Tabellini (1999), 'The size and scope of government. Comparative politics with rational politicians', *European Economic Review*, **43**, 699–735.

Persson, T. and G. Tabellini (2003), *The Economic Effects of Constitutions*, Cambridge, MA: MIT Press.

Persson, T., G. Tabellini and G. Roland (2000), 'Comparative politics and public finance', *Journal of Political Economy*, **108**, 1121–61.

Reichel, R. (2002), 'Germany's postwar growth: economic miracle or reconstruction boom?', *Cato Journal*, **21**, 427–42.

Rodrik, D. (1994), 'The rush to free trade in the developing world: why so late? Why now? Will it last?', in S. Haggard and S. B. Webb (eds), *Voting for Reform: Democracy, Political Liberalization and Economic Adjustment*, New York: Oxford University Press.

Rodrik, D. (1996), 'Understanding economic policy reform', *Journal of Economic Literature*, **34**, 9–41.

Rodrik, D. (1998), 'Why do more open economies have bigger governments?', *Journal of Political Economy*, **106**, 997–1032.

Rose-Ackerman, S. (1980), 'Risk-taking and re-election: does federalism promote innovation?', *Journal of Legal Studies*, **9**, 593–616.

Saint-Paul, G. (2000), *The Political Economy of Labour Market Institutions*, Oxford: Oxford University Press.

Salmon, P. (1987), 'Decentralization as an incentive scheme', *Oxford Review of Economic Policy*, **3**, 24–43.

Schnellenbach, J. (2004), 'Learning from decentralised policy: the demand side', paper presented at the Royal Economic Society 2004 annual conference at Swansea, UK.

Schumpeter, J. A. (1912), *Theorie der wirtschaftlichen Entwicklung*, Leipzig: Duncker & Humblot.

Schumpeter, J. A. (1942), *Capitalism, Socialism and Democracy*, 4th edn, 9th impression, London: Allen & Unwin, 1961.

Siebert, H. (1997), 'Labor market rigidities: at the root of unemployment in Europe', *Journal of Economic Perspectives*, **11**, 37–54.

Smith, J. D. (2001), 'Horizontal and vertical federalism: the diffusion of legislative policy innovations in the American states', University of North Texas working paper.

Strumpf, K. (2002), 'Does government centralization increase policy innovation?', *Journal of Public Economic Theory*, **4**, 207–41.

Sturzenegger, F. and M. Tommasi (eds) (1998), *The Political Economy of Reform*, Cambridge, MA: MIT Press.

Tsebelis, G. (1995), 'Decision making in political systems: veto players in presidentialism, parliamentarism, multicameralism and multipartyism', *British Journal of Political Science*, **25**, 289–325.
Tsebelis, G. (2002), *Veto Players: How Political Institutions Work*, Princeton, NJ: Princeton University Press.
Walker, J. L. (1969), 'The diffusion of innovation among the American states', *American Political Science Review*, **63**, 880–99.
Wallis, J. (1998), 'Understanding the role of leadership in economic policy reform', *World Development*, **27**, 39–53.
Wei, S.-J. (1997), 'Gradualism versus Big Bang: speed and sustainability of reforms', *Canadian Journal of Economics*, **30**, 1234–47.
Williamson, J. (ed.) (1994), *The Political Economy of Policy Reform*, Washington, DC: Institute for International Economics.
Wohlgemuth, M. (2000), 'Political entrepreneurship and bidding for political monopoly', *Journal of Evolutionary Economics*, **10**, 273–95.

10. Compliance in the EU enlargement process: institutional reform and the limits of conditionality

Bernard Steunenberg and Antoaneta Dimitrova

INTRODUCTION

From a limited occurrence in the past, in the last decade, enlarging the European Union has become almost a continuous process. One enlargement barely over, a whole row of candidates waits at the door. The latest enlargement, to include the post-communist countries of Central and Eastern Europe and Cyprus and Malta, started with applications from Bulgaria, the Czech Republic, Estonia, Hungary, Latvia, Lithuania, Poland, Slovakia, Slovenia and Romania to join the EU in the first half of the 1990s. In 1998, the EU started negotiations for membership with the first group, the Czech Republic, Hungary, Poland, Estonia and Slovenia, named the Luxembourg group after the European Council which took the decision to start negotiations. At the European Council in Helsinki in 1999 a decision was taken that the next group of candidates (deemed not ready in 1997), could start negotiations in February 2000 after additional adjustment and preparations. These were: Slovakia, Latvia, Lithuania, Bulgaria and Romania. In April 2003, the EU signed a Treaty of Accession with all of the above candidates except Bulgaria and Romania. The eight post-communist states acceded in May 2004 together with Cyprus and Malta; while Bulgaria and Romania signed their Accession treaty in 2005 and joined the Union on 1 January, 2007. With one enlargement barely complete and despite signs of enlargement fatigue, the success of the European project seems to exert a magnetic pull on the Union's neighbours. Croatia has been driven by hopes that its economic performance and overall transformation would allow it to accede in 2007 with Bulgaria and Romania, but its 2003 bid for membership was delayed (but not cancelled) by problems with the country's cooperation with the ICC in The Hague. Turkey started negotiations in October 2005 but they were bogged down by crisis and disagreement over Cyprus in 2006. Under its new President Yushchenko, the Ukraine has been pushing, albeit still unsuccessfully, for similar candidate status. The Republic of Macedonia is leading a group of Western Balkan states hoping to join the Union in the foreseeable future. Moldova and Georgia have also been harbouring hopes to strengthen their modernization by moving towards accession to the EU.

If it manages to put its internal divisions and doubts about enlargement aside, the European Union has a unique chance to induce reform in the hopeful candidate states waiting outside its door. The most important instrument for reform, which has gained prominence during the last enlargement to date, is conditionality.[1] Conditionality has been used in development assistance by international organizations such as the World Bank since the 1980s and has been defined as the practice of allocating aid resources to be used consistently with a set of previously agreed objectives. If the recipient country does not follow these objectives or the conditions linked to them, the donor can stop the flow of resources (World Bank, 2005). Conditionality came later on the EU agenda and evolved differently from the international financial organizations' loans system. In the European Union, conditionality developed from a minor policy tool used in a limited way in agreements with third countries and development assistance, to become the main pillar of EU enlargement governance and a successful tool of EU foreign policy (Smith, 2003). It is quite distinct from the financial conditionality employed by the World Bank and the IMF, as the benefits which countries receive are not only financial, but are linked to EU membership (see Dimitrova, 2005; Dimitrova and Pridham, 2004; Schimmelfennig and Sedelmeier, 2005a, b). These benefits may involve direct transfers under the EU's polices such as the CAP, but also symbolic gains in stature or increases in FDI in anticipation of a country's improvement of economic stability upon joining the Union.

Following from this, it is important to distinguish between EU conditionality applied in the context of enlargement and the same policy applied when enlargement is only a distant notion or not on the table at all (for example in relations with a country such as Belarus). When conditionality is applied in the context of enlargement, we can assume that actors have much more to lose than direct monetary benefits. When benefits are anticipated in the context of EU assistance programs, actors may not perceive their losses in any other but monetary terms and may be likely to respond as much to EU demands as to any other donor (for example the World Bank, IMF and so on). By contrast, in this chapter we aim to explain the effectiveness of European Union enlargement conditionality with its multiple reform and *acquis* related goals. We define EU enlargement conditionality as an exchange between the EU and a candidate country in which the EU offers the candidate a (realistic) prospect of

EU membership, if the candidate implements a wide range of (EU driven) domestic reforms. Conditionality involves the withdrawal of the benefits of accession if the governments of the candidate states fail to comply with the requested reforms. On the EU side, these reforms are motivated by anticipating a new member of a club, which needs to adapt to key features of the existing membership: a stable democratic regime obeying the rule of law and supporting a well-functioning market economy, capable of implementing the rules of the club, that is, the *acquis communautaire*. If and when EU enlargement is to continue, the Union will need conditionality as a way to get new candidates to reach a level of preparation so that their joining would not disturb the functioning of the internal market, the system of multi-level governance and the democratic norms of the Union. But does EU conditionality always work? Can the EU induce reforms in all potential candidates for membership; create an endless push for modernization, liberalization of economies and democratization? This chapter argues that EU conditionality has an expiration date, in other words that it works only when certain conditions are satisfied.

In the process leading to the opening of the accession negotiations and subsequently the period in which these negotiations take place, the EU creates the expectation that the applicant country will at some yet unknown moment join the Union when it has satisfied the conditions of membership. The perceived benefits of EU membership, whether they concern economic development, national recognition, or freedom and political stability, form the driving force behind substantial domestic reforms in the applicant countries. At the same time, the candidate country in the face of its governing elites needs to be convinced that, at some point in time, it will be admitted to the Union, otherwise there is little reason to continue making hard and difficult domestic changes.[2]

In this bargaining process over EU membership, there are incentives for cheating. The government of the candidate country, on the one hand, faced with domestic opposition and declining popularity, might be tempted to postpone some of the reforms and comply in a symbolic way with the conditions set out by the EU. This may decrease domestic costs for the government in the candidate country. Once this deviation from the agreement is detected, the Union may decide to postpone further negotiations and stop enlargement.

On the other hand, the EU may prefer to have a stable and democratic neighbouring country, but may not be inclined to grant it full membership. It may therefore stimulate the candidate to introduce various reforms without granting it the 'reward' of EU membership. A decision on entry could, in principle, be delayed or even postponed for many years. In this context, the risk of breaking off the negotiations is high, while the prospect of EU membership or substantial domestic reform is low (see also Steunenberg, 2002).

In order to secure enlargement, the EU could commit itself by setting the date of accession of the candidate country. The question is what effect such an action will have on the reform efforts of the candidate. In this chapter we analyze the conditions under which the accession negotiations will be able to support conditionality, that is, the introduction of reforms based on the prospect of EU membership. These negotiations are taken as a game with an infinite number of rounds in which both parties assess the commitment of the other in terms of their actions. Based on our analysis, we show that conditionality is most effective when the one-time benefits of deviating from the agreement are relatively small and EU membership provides substantial benefits to both the EU and the candidate. In addition, the effectiveness of conditionality is eroded the moment the EU announces the date of accession. From that moment on compliance has to be based on other mechanisms than conditionality.

The chapter is structured as follows: we first discuss the current literature on conditionality with regard to EU enlargement. The next section presents our theoretical arguments. The last part of the chapter explores empirical evidence of how conditionality has been employed and develops potential indicators for measuring the scope of effectiveness of EU conditionality in the last enlargement.

CONDITIONALITY AND THE EUROPEAN UNION

The remarkable increase in the use of conditionality by the European Union has been matched by a explosion of studies discussing its features and measuring the impact of EU conditionality on a variety of countries, policy areas and institutional settings (Schmitter, 1995; Grabbe, 1999, 2001, 2003; Mattli and Plümper, 2002; Plümper *et al.*, 2003; Schimmelfennig and Sedelmeier, 2004, 2005a, b; Vachudova, 2002, 2005). This interest is due to the fact that EU conditionality is extremely broad and ever expanding. The scope of EU conditionality in the last enlargement has been remarkable, given that in previous enlargements taking on the EU's rules and regulations, the *acquis*, has been considered sufficient. By contrast, in the process of enlarging to the East, the EU has moved from the *acquis* towards a wider set of transformation targets, outlined first in the well known Copenhagen criteria (Dimitrova, 2004: 8–9).[3]

An additional administrative criterion was introduced by the Madrid European Council in December 1995 and led to considerable administrative reforms in the candidates (Dimitrova, 2002). Increasing further the scope of conditions, the European Commission added a number of areas such as human rights or nuclear safety in which the Union itself does not have competences or common rules made by its member states. In fact these were so numerous that it is possible to claim that a new enlargement method has been developed (Maniokas, 2004) and a separate 'enlargement *acquis*' has arisen including requirements for horizontal administrative reform, regionalization, reform of the judiciary, improvement the plight of certain minorities, border treaties (friendship and cooperation treaties), safety of nuclear power plants and so on.

Having established the unprecedented scale and breadth of EU conditionality and its central part in enlargement governance (Grabbe, 1999, 2001; Dimitrova, 2002), research in this area has moved on to trying to understand how conditionality operates.

A number of proposed explanations for the mechanism underlying the apparent success of conditionality are based on rationalistic concepts and frameworks. Vachudova (2001) and Moravcsik and Vachudova (2003: 44) have referred to Keohane and Nye's 'asymmetrical interdependence' concept to explain the working of conditionality as a form of concession in bargaining during enlargement negotiations. The applicant countries have, according to them, accepted the costs of adaptation because they were lower than the costs of exclusion from the EU club and its benefits. For that reason, these countries engage in further negotiations for membership. As Plümper *et al.* (2003) indicate, it also means that only national governments that clearly perceive benefits from enlargement, will apply for membership and engage in negotiations with the EU.

Schimmelfennig *et al.* (2003) develop further a bargaining framework focused on the idea of 'reinforcement by reward'. They suggest that the strategy of reinforcement by reward makes the EU withhold rewards in the form of institutional ties and financial assistance if a target government fails to comply with democratic conditions. Political actors calculate the rewards are higher than the costs of adoption and therefore they comply (2003: 297). They test this material incentives framework against an alternative explanation, a social influence mechanism, on the cases of non-compliant states in the area of human rights: Slovakia under Meciar, Turkey and Latvia. They find that domestic governments' cost benefit calculations were crucial for compliance. In Latvia adaptation to the EU conditions did not endanger the government's power base and the fear of losing membership rewards provided sufficient impetus for change (2003: 514). In Slovakia, costs outweighed the benefits of institutional ties for the Meciar government (2003: 505). In Turkey, progress started only when a concrete membership perspective appeared on the horizon in 1999, but significant change was limited to areas where the core of state power had not been affected (2003: 509).

Schimmelfennig, Engert and Knobel's framework is a step forward from the generalized explanation offered by Moravcsik and Vachudova, but it does not distinguish any features of conditionality that might influence bargaining outcomes. More efforts to elaborate these features are made in a number of studies. Mattli and Plümper (2002) and Plümper *et al.* (2003) focus on the incentives within the national political arena of the applicant country to understand the effectiveness of conditionality. Mattli and Plümper (2002) show that the 'demand' for EU membership is related to a country's regime type and its willingness to implement economic reforms. With regard to regime types, they claim that if a country has a more democratic regime, the national political leaders have a greater incentive to push for reforms which would align their country with the rules and institutions of the EU.

Plümper *et al.* (2003) focus on the interactions between the applicant country and the EU. They argue that the EU has difficulty in assessing the 'real' progress made in these countries in introducing market reforms, which could lead to the entry of candidates with half-way reforms. In their view, the time taken to agree on domestic reforms could be taken as an indicator of existing domestic market distortions and thus insufficient compliance to the *acquis*. Using this information, the EU is expected to select only those candidates that are able to implement the *acquis* at short notice. Although this model may illuminate some of the features of the choice of future EU members, it does not provide much insight into conditionality.

Schimmelfennig and Sedelmeier (2005) propose an external incentives model explaining the effects of conditionality by suggesting that governments would adopt EU rules if the benefits of EU rewards exceed the domestic adoption costs. Further they expect the cost benefit balance to depend on four sets of factors. These are the determinacy of conditions, the size and speed of rewards, the credibility of threats and promises and the size of adoption costs (2005: 12–13). The test of this model on comparative cases from the new EU member states suggests that the success of the external incentives model differs depending on the type of conditionality, *acquis* conditionality working better than democratic conditionality (2005: 212–15). The empirical analyses in Schimmelfennig and Sedelmeier's edited volume found credibility of conditionality and the size of adoption costs to be the key variables influencing compliance. In its conclusions, the volume singles out credibility and, size of EU rewards versus domestic adoption costs as key determinants of conditionality. In terms of credibility the opening of negotiations with some states increases the credibility of rewards for all the candidates, as it demonstrates the EU is willing to conclude negotiations (2005: 215). The credibility of the threat of exclusion from membership also decreases as accession progresses (Dimitrova, 2005).

Schimmelfennig and Sedelmeier's study also finds that credibility is linked to the consistency of allocation of rewards, in other words the level of priority the EU accords to the fulfillment of its conditions in comparison with other considerations, for example security. Internal EU conflict about conditionality and cross-conditionality may also damage the credibility of conditionality awards (2005: 13–14).

While these efforts have increased considerably our understanding of how conditionality might achieve its goals, they can be pushed further by returning to the game theoretical roots of the bargaining frameworks applied by all of these authors. A systematic and formal model of conditionality will be offered in this chapter as a way to predict how conditionality would affect future candidates for accession.

THE COMPLIANCE GAME

In order to understand conditionality, we need to focus on both the potential applicant country and the EU. In this way, we differ from Plümper *et al.* (2003) who focus on the various groups within the applicant state's domestic political arena to explain whether this state will pursue domestic reforms.

The negotiations between the EU and the government of the country interested in membership can be represented by a two-person game in which both players have the option to continue pursuing cooperation or to give up the idea of EU enlargement. The option of giving up is realistic as the EU may not want to allow in yet another member state, while the possible applicant may find it important to maintain its sovereignty. The 'game form' reflecting this interaction, which includes the events resulting from strategy pairs, but without an evaluation of these events, is presented in Table 10.1.

The strategies available to both players are as follows. The EU may aim to expand its jurisdiction and to widen the internal market, stimulate and stabilize further democratic transformations, or increase its international influence. It is willing to accept membership under the condition that an applicant introduces sufficient domestic changes so that it can reasonably expect that it would be capable of implementing the *acquis communautaire*. Depending on the efforts made by the applicant, the behavioral options to the EU are either support or oppose EU membership of the applicant.

Table 10.1 The compliance game

		Applicant	
		Continue with EU imposed reforms	Halt EU imposed reforms
EU	Support process toward EU membership	(*c*, *c*) Reformed membership	(*s*, *b*) Unreformed membership
	Delay process toward EU membership	(*b*, *s*) Reformed satellite	(*d*, *d*) No enlargement

Key: $(x, y) =$ (payoff EU, payoff applicant).

The applicant strives for EU membership since it perceives a range of benefits from it. These benefits could be economic, related to the internal market, or political, related to national stability and freedom. In addition, the applicant may also use the EU to implement a 'reform' strategy domestically in order to make modernization and reform of domestic institutions possible. Based on the conditions set out by the EU, the government of the applicant country has two options, either to implement institutional reforms as proposed by the EU or to focus on other, domestically determined changes which are not related to the demands of the EU. Whether conditionality works and enlargement will take place thus critically depends on the efforts made in both the applicant country and the EU.

Based on these available strategies, the interactions between the EU and the applicant may lead to four distinct outcomes. First, when both the applicant and the EU work together, the government in the applicant country will implement reforms sufficient to become a member of the Union. This situation is labeled 'reformed membership' and leads to enlargement. The second possibility is that the applicant is not prepared to carry out the reforms demanded by the EU, and the EU is not really willing to support the candidate in its reform process. This outcome will lead to no enlargement. The third outcome is that the EU supports the applicant and maintains the applicant's prospect of EU membership although the applicant does not carry out the required domestic reforms. This is the situation of 'unreformed' membership. The fourth and last outcome is based on the EU's refusal to support the applicant, while the applicant introduces various reforms. In this case, the applicant changes its domestic institutions and policy in a way that is favorable to the EU and becomes a 'reformed satellite' of the Union.

The question is how the EU and the applicant rank these outcomes in terms of payoffs. With regard to the gains of EU membership and enlargement, it seems reasonable to assume that they are of variable sum. Both players may gain from cooperation, otherwise none would be interested in pursuing these negotiations and ultimately enlargement. The net-benefits of enlargement to the EU and the applicant will be denoted as *c*. We realize that there will be costs involved as well, stemming from the introduction of potentially unpopular measures in the applicant country. Similarly, the heads of state and government within the EU might be faced with domestic opposition against further enlargement and the possibility of deadlock or watering down of European integration, which may reduce the overall benefits of negotiation. Taken together with the perceived benefits of membership, the net-result will be some payoff equal to *c*. If the EU does not support the applicant's reform process and accession, or the applicant no longer wants to pursue EU membership, the payoff will be equal to *d*. The most beneficial outcome to the applicant would be a situation of unreformed membership, since it does not need to introduce reforms while, at the same time, it obtains EU membership. Similarly, the EU may benefit most from the situation in which the applicant introduces domestic reforms without acceding to the EU such as for example, adjusting customs tariffs or aligning its regulatory framework with the Union. The other side of each of these outcomes is that the other player does not prefer it: unreformed membership is not an option to the EU, while the position of a reformed satellite is not preferred by the government of the applicant. Although the magnitude of the payoffs may differ between the applicant and the EU, the payoffs to both players rank in the same way, that is, b ('bonanza') $>$ c ('cooperation') $>$ d ('defection') $>$ s ('sitting duck').

Based on this payoff structure, the game is a Prisoners' Dilemma game. Assuming both players know that the game will only be played once, an agreement between the EU and the applicant about the conditions that could lead to EU membership is not self-enforcing. Both players have a dominant strategy: while the EU prefers 'delaying' to 'supporting', the applicant prefers 'halting' to 'continuing' the EU imposed reforms. As a consequence, the one-shot Nash equilibrium consists of delaying the process towards EU membership and halting the EU imposed reforms leading to no enlargement. At the same time, having 'no enlargement' make both players worse off than if they had both worked along as part of the accession process.

A one-shot game, however, does not reflect the negotiations between the EU and the applicant in the period before a date of accession is determined. The applicant needs to negotiate becoming a candidate first and then continue negotiating on the various aspects of the *acquis communautaire* and the enlargement *acquis* built around the Copenhagen criteria. For instance, in the case of Turkey, while the country submitted its application for membership in June 1987 it took more than ten years before the EU granted it the status of candidate in December 1999 (see Table 3).[4] The negotiations between the EU and the candidate could be indefinite as there is no firm date of accession. Such a date may not be set at all. We therefore focus on repeated games with an indeterminate time horizon to explore further the effectiveness of conditionality.

THE ACCESSION NEGOTIATIONS: CANDIDACY WITHOUT A FIXED DATE

The bargaining between the EU and the applicant country is better characterized as a series of negotiations in which the players exchange their views on the accession agreement in terms of the extent to which the applicant satisfies the conditions set by the Union and the extent to which the Union is willing to support the applicant's candidacy. At any round of the game, there is a positive and constant probability that the game will be played for a next round. This probability, the structure of the game and the payoffs to players are common knowledge. The stream of payoffs, when both players collaborate and do not deviate from their agreement to prepare for enlargement, is

$$C = c + cw + cw^2 + \ldots + cw^n + \ldots = \frac{c}{1-w} \qquad (10.1)$$

with w as the discount factor, $0<w<1$.

The discount factor, which we see as independent from the accession dynamics, reflects the way in which players perceive future payoffs. A large discount factor means that future payoffs would remain highly valued by players, thus representing an important share of the total flow of payoffs. Conversely, a small discount factor means that the total flow of payoffs is mainly affected by benefits received by players at present.

The question is whether one of the players has an incentive to deviate from this strategy? If, for instance, the EU maintains its support for the applicant, while the applicant does not introduce the required reforms at period n, it will get

$$D = c + cw + cw^2 + \ldots + cw^{n-1} + bw^n + dw^{n+1} + dw^{n+2} + \ldots$$

with b as the one-time bonus the applicant enjoys since it keeps its prospect on membership while does not introduce the domestic reforms. In the subsequent rounds of the game, the applicant will be punished by the EU and receives payoff d, which is based on the one-shot Nash equilibrium strategy. We assume that once defection is detected, the player will be punished by the other in the subsequent rounds (the so-called grim strategy). We will discuss relaxing this assumption later, since there may be alternative strategies able to support cooperation.

It would be unprofitable for a player to cheat on the agreement if the benefits of working together along the path of accession exceed those of cheating. Once discovered by the other party, cheating will be punished by a defection leading to a breakdown of the agreement. In other words, as long as $C \geq D$ a player does not have an incentive to defect. This makes the agreement between the EU and the applicant *incentive compatible*. An incentive compatible agreement secures the mutual cooperation during the accession phase, which makes conditionality effective. The EU is willing to support the applicant's candidacy, while the applicant is prepared to introduce various reforms in order to satisfy the demands to the Union.

What are the determining factors of an incentive compatible agreement? Consider that one of the players decides to cheat. The moment a player decides to deviate, his or her stream of remaining payoffs is:

$$D = b + dw + dw^2 + \ldots + dw^n + \ldots = b + d\frac{w}{1-w} \qquad (10.2)$$

The agreement is incentive compatible if $C \geq D$. Combining Equations (10.1) and (10.2), we get:

$$\frac{c}{1-w} \geq b + d\frac{w}{1-w}$$

which equals (see, for instance, Binmore, 1992: 357–60):

$$w \geq \frac{b-c}{b-d} \qquad (10.3)$$

The numerator $(b-c)$ is the additional payoff for breaking the agreement. The denominator $(b-d)$ is the difference between the payoff of breaking and the remaining payoff of the one-shot Nash equilibrium strategy. Since $(b-d) = (b-c) + (c-d)$, it can also be interpreted as the sum of the net-payoff of breaking and the net-payoff of keeping the agreement (Hovi, 1998: 95).

Equation (10.3) sheds more light on the conditions for the success of conditionality, which are related to the discount factor (left hand side) and the distribution of the relative or net benefits to the players (right hand side).

First, the discount factor, w, in the left hand side of the equation, needs to be sufficiently large in order to have collaboration. A large discount factor means that both players evaluate the continuing collaboration rather positively, which is reflected by a relatively long time horizon. In other words, both players must be rather patient. Impatience on the side of one of the players would translate in a rather low discount factor, which makes an incentive compatible agreement unlikely. Impatience may lead to defection and the halting of the negotiations, which makes conditionality ineffective.

Second, and given a certain value of the discount factor, the right hand side of the equation becomes smaller increasing the likelihood of stable cooperation if the one-time benefits of breaking the agreement by either the applicant or the EU – that is, the value of b – are relatively small compared to the benefits of collaboration – that is, the values of c for both players. It might be particularly relevant for the EU to monitor the magnitude of b in the applicant country. Especially in case of a domestic crisis or forthcoming national elections, the one-time benefits of defection may increase for the government of the applicant country thus decreasing the prospects for long term cooperation and conditionality.

Third, the right hand side of the equation also becomes smaller if the benefits of collaboration between the applicant and the EU – the values of c for both players – are substantially larger than those of giving up the possibility of enlargement and EU membership of the applicant – that is, the value of d.[5]

The relationships between various payoffs to the players, that is, the values of b, c, and d, can be presented in a different way by rearranging the terms in Equation (10.3). As shown by Hovi (1998: 95), equation (10.3) can be rewritten as:

$$(c - d) \geq \frac{1 - w}{w}(b - c) \qquad (10.4)$$

which, in addition to our earlier observations, shows that the difference between the payoffs of collaboration and defection – that is, the difference between c and d – should be sufficiently large. For conditionality to work, the EU has to make sure that, compared to the costs of domestic reform, the applicant has sufficient net benefits to maintain its relationship with the Union. In this respect, the creation of special EU support programs for applicant countries, such as PHARE, later ISPA and SAPARD, has helped to keep the candidate countries interested in EU membership and, more importantly, to maintain conditionality. These programs and other forms of EU support to the candidates are related to the magnitude of $(c - d)$.

The analysis so far is based on the strategy of endless punishment of a deviating player (the grim strategy). This is a rather severe way of punishing the other player, which may be unnecessary to induce cooperation. The Union or the applicant does not need to give up the prospect of enlargement when a defection of the initial agreement is detected. Other strategies might lead to cooperation as well. The critical condition is that the discounted stream of payoffs resulting from playing the game cooperatively should be equal or higher than the payoffs from defection, that is, $C \geq D$. In other words, if the defecting player is punished in a sufficient number of rounds to eliminate his or her gain from breaking the agreement, both players have an incentive to keep to their cooperative strategy (Shubik, 1970: 189; Osborne and Rubinstein, 1994: 146). This means that many alternative strategies may exist that hold a credible threat to the other player and can support cooperation.

FIXING THE DATE OF ACCESSION

Returning to the reality of enlargement, we can claim that the moment the EU announces a date for accession, this act converts the accession negotiations from an infinite into a finite game. The number of times the game will be played becomes common knowledge, and both players know exactly how many rounds there will be.

The outcome of such a repeated game is the same as the one-shot game if information is complete. While one may expect that the EU will build a reputation as 'supportive' to enlargement and the candidate is 'reformist' in order to profit from the benefits of enlargement, this intuition is not supported by the logic of backward induction. Once the players have reached the last round of the game, the situation is exactly the same as in the one-shot compliance game in Table 10.1. At the last round, the EU will no longer support the candidate's process toward membership while the candidate will halt its domestic reforms. Based on this decision, which can be foreseen in the previous rounds, both players will defect from the cooperative solution of enlargement in preceding rounds. The uncooperative solution of 'delaying the process toward EU membership' and 'halting reform', which cannot be punished by either player in the last period of the game, is, in fact, rolled back to the first period. It causes both players to defect in all periods of this finite repeated game.[6]

One way of 'dealing' with this situation would be for the EU to give up its goal of reforms in the candidate country and accept the candidate's current domestic situation as sufficient for EU membership. The EU's strategy of supporting the candidate turns into a dominant strategy from which it will not deviate. In terms of the payoffs in Table 10.1, it means that for the EU $c > b$ and $s > d$. The payoff structure to the candidate may remain the same, that is, $b > c > d > s$. In equilibrium, the candidate halts its reforms, while the EU supports the candidate's last step towards membership. This behavior has two implications. First, conditionality loses its effectiveness the moment a date of accession is set. The candidate will anticipate its membership and its government will no longer be willing to introduce various domestic reforms. Second, announcing the date of accession only makes sense at the very last moment when the EU is confident that the candidate has introduced sufficient reforms. At this stage, unless other mechanisms are used, the candidate may no longer work on transposing not yet adopted parts of the *acquis communautaire*.

The next question is whether there are possibilities to compensate for the vanishing effectiveness of conditionality in the last stage of the accession negotiations. Any kind of safeguard clause used by the EU will provide for the possibility of excluding a state from the benefits of membership in case the state has not completed the agreed domestic reforms. In the case of the eight new members from Central and Eastern Europe, the EU kept the possibility of temporarily excluding the candidate from the *acquis communautaire* – and thus from full membership – if the candidate did not fully comply.[7] For Bulgaria and Romania, the EU has included safeguard clauses in the Accession treaty allowing accession to be deferred in case of failed reforms.[8] These clauses are frequently referred to as a way to keep the candidate's momentum. In May 2005, for example, the European Commission required fast and decisive improvements in Romania's competition and state aids policy. The EU Commissioner on competition policy, Nelly Kroes, indicated that without further changes Romania 'may leave the Commission with no other choice than to propose postponing its EU membership'.[9]

The use of such safeguards expands the strategies available to the EU and the candidate. The compliance game as presented Table 10.1 has to be expanded with at least one additional strategy which involves punishing a defecting player. The EU may withhold membership to the candidate, while the candidate reverses some of the EU favored reforms. The new game, which includes such additional 'punishment' strategies, is presented in Table 10.2. These changes make a difference, as the introduction of 'punishment' strategies may lead to 'partial' compliance in a finite game (Powell, 1991: 1306–8; Hovi, 1998: 98–9). Compliance is 'partial' since it does not apply to all rounds of the game.

Assume that this game is played only for two rounds, which is known to both players. Playing the cooperative strategy of implementing reforms while the EU supports the candidate in its process toward membership is not a Nash equilibrium. The game has two equilibriums: the first consists of both players defecting, which means that the EU delays the candidate's membership, while the candidate does not introduce the reforms proposed by the EU. The second equilibrium is that both play their punishment strategy. These equilibriums indicate that additional safeguards cannot impose compliance in the last round of the game, since this round is equivalent to

Table 10.2 The extended compliance game

		Candidate		
		Continue with EU imposed reforms (*C*)	Halt EU imposed reforms (*D*)	Reverse EU imposed reforms (*P*)
EU	Support process toward EU membership (*C*)	(2, 2)	(0, 3)	(−2, 0)
	Delay process toward EU membership (*D*)	(3, 0)	(1, 1)	(−1, 0)
	Halt EU membership (*P*)	(0, −2)	(0, −1)	(−1, −1)

Key: (x, y) = (payoff EU, payoff applicant).

a one-shot game. However, it is possible to have cooperation between the EU and the candidate in the preceding round using the following strategy: play *C* in the first round and if the other player also does, play *D* in the second round. In all other circumstances play *P*.

Playing *CC* in the first round and *DD* in the second is an equilibrium: if the EU follows this strategy it obtains a payoff of 2 in the first round and 1 in the second adding together to a payoff of 3. If it defects, it will receive a payoff of 3 in the first round and −1 in the second, leading to a total payoff of 2. In other words, cooperating in the first round and defecting in the second is the best reply of the EU if the candidate is using the same strategy. Based on the symmetry of the payoffs, a similar result can be established for the candidate. Moreover, since playing *DD* in the second round is a Nash equilibrium, the proposed strategy is also subgame perfect.

A crucial condition for the emergence of partial compliance is that the one-time benefits of defecting are sufficiently reduced by the punishment strategy. As the example in Table 10.2 shows, the overall payoffs of playing *DP* or any of the other combinations must be smaller than those of playing *CD*. Only if one player is capable of imposing substantial costs on the other party, will the 'punishment' strategy help in securing compliance. Although the possibility of punishment may postpone the unwanted behavior of halting reforms, it cannot fully prevent it. In the last round, the EU and the candidate will deviate from the 'cooperative solution'. The EU will delay its support to the candidate and the candidate will slow down its reforms. With the end of the negotiations in sight, the EU enlargement conditionality becomes ineffective.

THE LIMITS OF CONDITIONALITY

The analysis points to a number of hypotheses on whether an applicant country will comply with the EU's conditions for membership. We make a distinction between the period in which the date of accession has not yet been set and the period after this date is set.

In the context of an indeterminate time horizon, the effectiveness of conditionality (through maintaining an incentive compatible agreement) depends on three determining factors. First, it is particularly important that the perceived gains to the candidate of the cooperation with the EU are substantially larger than the benefits of maintaining an 'independent' state outside the EU. These benefits should become apparent during the process of extensive domestic reform so that the applicant still has an incentive to be interested in EU membership. Second, the relative magnitude of one-time benefits of breaking the negotiations must be small. This requires a continuous awareness especially on the side of the EU to monitor these benefits in periods of domestic crisis or forthcoming national elections. If the benefits of breaking negotiations have somehow substantially increased,[10] it makes sense to offer additional and temporary benefits to an applicant state to prevent the difference between these gains and the gains of cooperation with the EU growing too much. A difference that is too large may make the agreement no longer self-enforcing. Third, both parties should be patient, that is, have a rather long time horizon in which they expect to receive mutually positive benefits. Impatience may erode the self-enforcing nature of the agreement and make conditionality ineffective.

The moment the date of entry is set, the assumption of an indeterminate time horizon no longer holds. The infinite game between the EU and the candidate converts into a finite or perhaps a one-shot game in which cooperation is difficult to maintain. Conditionality, which has been associated with the mutual cooperation between the EU and the applicant country, will no longer be an effective tool of reform. One implication is that a candidate's performance with regard to implementing the *acquis communautaire* will be negatively affected by the intervening period between signing the accession treaty and the moment of actual membership. Another implication is that the EU needs to use another mechanism to induce compliance with remaining conditions and reforms, for example regarding the transposition of directives, as cooperation resulting from infinitely repeated play is no longer effective.

Following our analysis, we can formulate, in a rather informal way, a number of hypotheses on the effectiveness of conditionality and the extent to which candidate countries absorb the conditions laid down by the EU.[11] These hypotheses are:

1. if the date of accession is not fixed, EU conditionality will be effective if membership brings relatively substantial positive gains, the one-time benefits of breaking with the EU are relatively small, and the applicant is patient with regard to the progress of the negotiations;
2. when the date of accession is set, the EU will no longer focus on conditionality, and the candidate will slow down the implementation of domestic reforms required by the EU; and
3. the EU will keep the period between announcing the date of accession and the actual accession as short as possible.

In next section, we will explore whether empirical evidence exists supporting these hypotheses. More specifically, we will focus on the limits of conditionality related to the changes between infinite and finite games. As the negotiations progress, the announcement of the accession date is expected to have a substantial impact on conditionality, turning it from an effective into an ineffective tool to the EU. We hope to illustrate this and some related points with evidence of use of conditionality by the European Commission and the performance of countries in Central and Eastern Europe which recently became EU members.

In the empirical part we will not discuss further the conditions supporting conditionality in negotiations with an indeterminate time horizon. As indicated, conditionality is expected to be effective as long as applicants perceive sufficient positive gains from further negotiations relative to the benefits of defection or breaking with the EU. With regard to the ten countries in Central and Eastern Europe, which applied for EU membership in the mid-1990s, these benefits are clearly positive so that negotiations started and conditionality could play a role. For other neighboring countries, which did not apply, this is not the case. At the same time, it is also not clear whether a country's negative assessment of benefits and perceived costs, the EU's unwillingness to accept an application, or both have led to this outcome.[12] This opaque (self) selection process, which leads to the making of an application, makes researching the first hypothesis tricky.

DEVELOPMENTS IN EU CONDITIONALITY

In the course of the last EU enlargement to include the post-communist countries of Central and Eastern Europe and Cyprus and Malta, the Union for the first time introduced a set of explicit criteria (the Copenhagen criteria) applied during the negotiations. The various stages in this process are summarized in Table 10.3.

Table 10.3 Stages of the enlargement process

States	Association Agreements	Application	Commission opinion	Start of negotiations	End of negotiations	Signing of Accession Treaty	Accession
Bulgaria	March 1993; 1 February 1995 (into force)	December 1995	July 1997	February 2000	17 December 2004	25 April 2005	1 January 2007
Croatia	October 2001*	21 February 2003	20 April 2004	N/A**	N/A	N/A	N/A
Cyprus	December 1972; Protocol 1987	3 July 1990	30 June 1993	30 March 1998	December 2002	16 April 2003	1 May 2004
Czech Republic	December 1991 with Czechoslovakia; October 1993	January 1996	July 1997	March 1998	December 2002	16 April 2003	1 May 2004
Estonia	12 June 1995; 1 February 1998 (into force)	November 1995	15 July 1997	March 1998	December 2002	16 April 2003	1 May 2004
Hungary	December 1991; 1 February 1994 (into force)	March 1994	July 1997	30 March 1998	December 2002	16 April 2003	1 May 2004

Latvia	June 1995; February 1998	October 1995	July 1997	February 2000	December 2002	16 April 2003	1 May 2004
Lithuania	12 June 1995; 1 February 1998 (into force)	8 December 1995	July 1997	15 February 2000	13 December 2002	16 April 2003	1 May 2004
Malta	1971 (into force)	16 July 1990; October 1996 freezes application; re-activated 1998	July 1997	February 2000	December 2002	16 April 2003	1 May 2004
Poland	December 1991	April 1994	July 1997	March 1998	December 2002	16 April 2003	1 May 2004
Romania	February 1993; February 1995 (into force)	22 June 1995	July 1997	15 February 2000	14 December 2004	25 April 2005	1 January 2007
Slovakia	December 1991 with Czechoslovakia; October 1993	June 1995	July 1997	February 2000	December 2002	16 April 2003	1 May 2004
Slovenia	June 1996	January 1996	July 1997	March 1998	December 2002	16 April 2003	1 May 2004

Table 10.3 (continued)

States	Association Agreements	Application	Commission opinion	Start of negotiations	End of negotiations	Signing of Accession Treaty	Accession
Turkey	12 September 1963; additional Protocol from 23 November 1970	June 1987	20 December 1989	Candidate status December 1999; projected start 3 October 2005	N/A	N/A	N/A

Notes: * Stabilization and Association Agreement
** Planned for 17 March 2005, but delayed by the European Council decision from 16 March 2005 (http://news.amnesty.org/index/ENGEUR640012005; reference 13.05.2005)

Sources:
General: Accession Treaty Series no. 32 (2004). http://www.europa.eu.int/comm/enlargement (references 13.05.2005); Conclusions of Copenhagen European Council (December 2002); Nugent (2004: 276–7); Baun (2000: xi).
Country specific: Bulgaria: http://novinite.com/view_news.php?id=47075 (reference 13.05.2005), Croatia: http://www.europa.eu.int/comm/external_relations/see/croatia/index.htm (reference 13.05.2005), http://europa.eu.int/comm/external_relations/see/news/2004/ip 04_507.htm (reference 13.05.2005), Romania: http://www.roinfocentre.be/media_news_207.asp (reference 13.05.2005).

A first observation that can be made on the basis of this table is that enlargement has become a multiple step process. The breaking of the enlargement process into stages is an important innovation relevant to our model. In past enlargements, there would be relatively fewer stages. The typical enlargement cycle would consist of the issuing of a Commission Opinion on the readiness of the candidate, the opening of negotiations, the closing of negotiations and accession. By contrast, the last enlargement process has been organized as a multiple step process structured around intermediary points at every one of which accession can still be stopped. At the same time, passing each of these stages does not increase the promise of acceptance. This could be illustrated with the case of Turkey, which received candidate status in 1999, but negotiations had not started until 2005. Croatia, similarly, had been promised to start negotiations in 2005, but had not actually started by summer 2005 as the conditions set by the EU had not been fulfilled. All of the multiple sub-stages of the enlargement process have conditions attached to them. A country aims first to be accepted as a candidate by the EU, then to start negotiations and so on. This ensures the candidate stays on the path of reform and increases the uncertainty of applicants regarding the end and the date of accession.

The first hypothesis, which we formulated above, concerns the period between the announcement of the date of accession and the actual accession. Since the announcement of this date affects conditionality, we expected that the EU will keep this period as short as possible. Despite repeated calls and demands for a final date, the CEE applicants received a date more or less at the end of their negotiations, in December 2002 and could accede in May 2004. For Bulgaria and Romania, the decision to join the Union on 1 January 2007 was taken in December 2004 and the Treaty of Accession was signed in April 2005. The period between announcing accession and the actual entry of a candidate is thus about two years. The ever riskier process of ratification of the treaties of accession by 15 member states (in the case of the first eight) and by 25 (in the case of Bulgaria and Romania) does not allow for a much shorter period between signing of the accession treaty and actual accession.

The announcing of these dates has implications for the effectiveness of conditionality and the way in which both the EU and the candidate continue with their reform strategy. Knowing that the end is in sight reduces the effectiveness of conditionality. This brings us to the second hypothesis we developed. Once accession is announced, we expect that the EU will no longer rely on conditionality as a tool of inducing domestic reform. In addition, the candidate will slow down its domestic reforms in as far as these are driven by EU enlargement conditionality. This expectation is reinforced by the fact that between the announcement of a date of accession and accession no further negotiations take place. The negotiations on the various chapters of the *acquis* are formally closed, and the Commission only monitors the progress of the candidate during this period. The infinite repeated game of the accession negotiations is converted into basically a one-shot game in which conditionality, as indicated, is ineffective. Let's focus first on the EU-side of this hypothesis related to the proposed conditions.

The characteristics of the conditions the EU sets, the reform demands, the degree of intensity and salience of conditions vary from year to year and from country to country. EU enlargement conditionality is not based on a single or several related conditions (for example economic reform, liberalization, human rights), but is multi-faceted and diverse, in fact consisting of multiple sub-conditionalities. These are organized around the EU's Copenhagen criteria and later additions such as the Madrid administrative capacity criterion (Dimitrova, 2002). Remarkably, not all of these conditions matter equally for accession. The European Commission, the main EU body dealing with enlargement negotiations, developed the practice of singling out, in their yearly evaluation reports, several reform conditions which are of the greatest significance for a country's progress. Thus we have a hierarchy of salience of conditions. Furthermore, though in much previous writing on this topic it has been assumed that pressure from the EU is a constant across candidates (for example Dimitrova, 2002), this is not really the case. Some candidates have been pressed more than others and on a wider range of issues. Thus the intensity of conditionality varies from country to country. This is shown in Table 10.4, which summarizes key conditions set by the Commission by enlargement years.

First we made an inventory of the total number of conditions used by the Commission in the regular reports. We counted 34 different conditions in total covering most areas of the *acquis communautaire* and the enlargement *acquis*, that is the criteria set out especially in this enlargement.[13] A condition is regarded as sufficiently dealt with by a candidate if it is not mentioned again in one of the subsequent years. Second, we counted the number of conditions for each candidate separately for each year and calculated the ratio between this number and the actual number of conditions. Based on this, the table presents the proportion of conditions highlighted for a given candidate in a given year compared to all conditions used by the Commission. Following our hypothesis, we expected that, in the case of the EU-8, the use of conditionality would drop in 2003, the moment the date of accession was in sight.

The Commission's final reports on the progress of Bulgaria and Romania in May and September 2006 suggested both countries had

Table 10.4 The intensity of EU conditionality

Candidate:	1997	1998	1999	2000	2001	2002	2003	Mean 1997–2003	2004
Slovenia	0.35	0.26	0.18	0.12	0.09	0.09	0.03	0.16	
Hungary	0.29	0.26	0.21	0.18	0.09	0.09	0.06	0.17	
Estonia	0.26	0.24	0.24	0.15	0.12	0.09	0.09	0.17	
Czech Republic	0.32	0.21	0.21	0.18	0.18	0.15	0.09	0.19	
Lithuania	0.38	0.32	0.26	0.21	0.15	0.12	0.06	0.21	
Poland	0.35	0.32	0.32	0.29	0.26	0.18	0.15	0.27	
Slovakia	0.47	0.44	0.35	0.26	0.21	0.15	0.09	0.28	
Latvia	0.47	0.44	0.41	0.38	0.32	0.24	0.12	0.34	
Bulgaria	0.41	0.41	0.35	0.29	0.26	0.26	0.21	0.31	0.09
Romania	0.47	0.41	0.41	0.35	0.32	0.26	0.15	0.34	0.06
Average EU-8	**0.36**	**0.31**	**0.27**	**0.22**	**0.18**	**0.14**	**0.09**	**0.22**	
Average CEEC's	**0.38**	**0.33**	**0.29**	**0.24**	**0.20**	**0.16**	**0.11**	**0.24**	**0.02**

Source: own compilation based on the European Commission's Regular Reports at http://www.eu.int/comm/enlargement/docs/index.htm (consulted at 25 May 2005).

addressed the majority of the conditions set for them and thus were ready to accede. Nevertheless, in both reports, the Commission suggested 'rigorous accompanying measures' (safeguards), as a way to protect the EU's interests should the two countries fail to make progress in areas where reforms needed further action such as corruption or reform of the judiciary. This was seen by some commentators as an indication that the two countries' politicians had limited their efforts once they were assured of an accession date in either 2006 or 2007.

The data in Table 10.4 indicates that on average and for each year an applicant needed to satisfy about 24 percent of the conditions set out during the accession process. The highest number of different conditions is found in the initial stages of the enlargement process (before the start of the negotiations on the various chapters of the *acquis*). The moment the negotiations start, the candidates are faced with 38 percent of all conditions. This percentage drops to 9 percent for both the EU-8 in 2003 and 2 percent for Bulgaria and Romania in 2004, the year in which the date of accession is known. This decrease is in line with our expectation that the EU no longer relies on conditionality when accession comes into sight. An alternative explanation for this drop in conditionality would be that the Commission cannot credibly recommend the admission of new members to the European Council and the European Parliament if it increases the number of conditions at the very end of the proposed negotiations period. However, this different explanation of the drop in conditions, as presented in Table 10.4, also implies that conditionality becomes ineffective the moment a decision on the accession date is about to be made.

The other expectation following from same hypothesis refers to the behavior of the candidate, which is expected to slow down its reform in view of accession. This slowing down is a result of the reduced effectiveness of conditionality. In other words, conditionality has, in a certain way, reached its expiration date.

Finding evidence for this hypothesis is more complicated. First, few studies exist linking specific conditions with a candidate's performance. Previous research by Dimitrova (2002) on administrative reform suggests that states considered as forerunners based on Commission rankings as well as public statements tended to do less in their administrative reform than states which were more uncertain in their prospects of accession. The Czech Republic, for example, made little move to comply with the EU's condition on introducing civil service legislation, since it was highly unlikely that the Union would leave this country out of the enlargement process (Dimitrova, 2005: 87). This resistance to reform is also reflected in the ranking of this country in the EU's scoreboards of transposition after it became a member state. These rankings can be found in Table 10.5.

Focusing on the internal market, the scoreboard of the European Commission (2004) provides information on how the new member states perform with regard to the transposition of internal market directives directly after their accession. It shows the number of directives the new member states did not yet notify and did not yet fully transpose. A limitation of this data is that these numbers were provided by the new member states themselves.

Based on the two available indicators, a compliance index has been constructed. This index suggests that especially the Czech Republic, Slovakia and Latvia are lagging behind in implementing the internal market *acquis*. The Czech Republic's performance can be explained by the low intensity of EU conditionality combined with the slow pace of administrative reform noted above. The Slovak and Latvian cases, however, are cases of high conditionality pressure. Moreover, the negotiations with Slovakia, Latvia and Lithuania started in February 2000 (see Table 10.3), which was two years later than the other new member states. Conditionality may have worked for two years, but with the announcement of membership in December 2002, their reforms and implementation of the *acquis* may have slowed down. The exception is Lithuania,

Table 10.5 Compliance to the internal market acquis*: notification and transposition of EC directives in the EU-8*

	Directives not yet notified		Directives not fully transposed		Compliance index
Lithuania	12	0.8%	18	1.2%	***1.83***
Slovenia	87	5.7%	27	1.8%	***1.11***
Poland	60	3.9%	257	16.8%	0.49
Estonia	127	8.3%	124	8.1%	0.38
Hungary	168	11.0%	38	2.6%	0.33
Latvia	290	19.0%	70	4.6%	***−0.90***
Slovakia	193	12.6%	426	27.9%	***−1.37***
Czech Republic	360	23.6%	163	10.7%	***−1.89***
Average EU-8	***162***	***10.6%***	***140***	***9.2%***	

Note: The compliance index is the non-weighted mean of the standardized values for each of the columns in the table, rescaled so that a negative value reflects low compliance.

Source: European Commission (2004); The information in the table reflects the situation on 31 May 2004.

which suggests the importance of domestic factors. Thus a complication interpreting the ranking in Table 10.5 is that the performance of the new member states is only partly affected by conditionality. Other factors, such as administrative capacity and domestic incentives to push for change, also play a role. More specifically, the administrative capacity to handle conditionality and to implement domestic changes is an important mediating factor. A next step would be to open the black box of the state and identify the domestic variables such as reform of the EU coordination system or centralization of the core executive (Zubek, 2005) that play a role in compliance.

CONCLUSIONS

This chapter has brought the effectiveness of EU conditionality in the last and future enlargement rounds into the spotlight. Building on an increasing number of studies emphasizing the importance of conditionality in the preparation of candidate states for the complex demands of the EU's multi-level system of governance and external market, we have asked the question, is conditionality always as effective or does it have an expiration date? To answer this, the chapter presented the enlargement negotiations as a bargaining process over EU membership. The game theoretical analysis above showed that there are incentives for cheating in this bargaining process. The government of the candidate country, on the one hand, faced with the costs of reforms and potentially declining popularity, might be tempted, in order to decrease domestic costs, to postpone reforms or comply only symbolically with the conditions set out by the EU. Once such a deviation from the agreement is detected, the Union may decide to postpone further negotiations and stop the enlargement process. The EU, on the other hand, may prefer to have a stable and democratic neighbouring country, but may not be inclined to grant it full membership. It may therefore stimulate the candidate to introduce various reforms without granting it the 'reward' of EU membership. A decision on entry could, in principle, be delayed or even postponed for many years. In this context, the risk of breaking off the negotiations is high, while the prospect of EU membership or substantial domestic reform is low.

In order to secure enlargement, the EU could commit itself by setting the date of accession of the candidate. However, this action will completely erode the effectiveness of conditionality, since the candidate will no longer push for domestic reforms.

The empirical part of this chapter showed that, in line with our expectations, the EU does not commit with a 'hard' date for accession until the process of negotiations is over and the accession treaty is signed. The period between signing and accession is determined by ratification considerations, but is kept short as conditionality cannot be expected to work in this period and compliance with EU rules can be ensured once a state is in and the possibility of European Court of Justice (ECJ) sanctions exists. Furthermore, the EU's awareness of the ineffectiveness of conditionality, once accession is announced, is illustrated with the substantial reduction in conditions when accession comes into sight. The expected impact on the candidate's behavior, by slowing down some of its reform, is more difficult to establish, since it also depends on other, domestic factors, including administrative capacity. The case of the Czech Republic stands out since a low intensity of the EU conditionality combined with a slow pace of administrative reform has led to a rather low compliance with the internal market *acquis*.

In contrast to recent studies on conditionality such as the volume edited by Schimmelfennig and Sedelmeier (2005a, b), this chapter focuses exclusively on conditionality and not on the domestic arena and shows that regardless of domestic circumstances, the effects of conditionality vary in time, depending on how close a state may be to accession. We have also shown that EU conditionality varies in intensity even though most existing case studies have assumed to be constant.[14] These findings have implications for future enlargements (for example with Turkey) in which we can expect an even more drawn out process with more stages and less willingness from the EU to commit to a date. The scope of conditions which is very broad should also be considered – while they aim to induce reforms in a wide area of policies and institutions, their very number may lead to a decrease in credibility. In this respect singling out several conditions seems a more successful strategy. Last but not least, as our analysis has shown, in order to reap the benefits of enlargement, both the EU and applicants must be patient and operate with a long term horizon – a condition not currently present in the political landscape in Europe.

NOTES

1. A lively debate between experts and practitioners on the uses of conditionality has been taking place under the auspices of the World Bank (see the Development Policy Forum: Conditionality revisited, at http://web.worldbank.org/WBSITE/EXTERNAL/PROJECTS/0,contentMDK:20292755~pagePK:41367~piPK:51533~theSitePK:40941,00.html). The IMF has also undertaken a review of its conditionality practices in early 2000–01. This chapter deals only with EU conditionality, which we see as sufficiently distinct to merit special attention, although some of our hypotheses should hold also for conditionality as practices by international organizations.
2. Another important question is whether the EU has, over the last ten years, introduced sufficient internal reforms to maintain or improve the efficiency of its decision-making process. See König and Brauninger (2000, 2004) and Steunenberg (2001, 2002) for a further discussion of these problems.
3. These were: (a) the stability of institutions guaranteeing democracy, the rule of law, human rights and respect for and protection of minorities; (b) the existence of a functioning market economy, capable of coping with competitive pressures and market forces within the Union; and (c) the ability to take on the obligations of membership, including adherence to its aims of political, economic and monetary union (Copenhagen European Council, Conclusions of the Presidency).
4. The Brussels European Council in December 2004 decided that Turkey had made sufficient progress in fulfilling the political criteria from Copenhagen that, provided some crucial pieces of legislation came into force, it could start negotiations on 3 October 2005.
5. In any event, the right hand side of the equation has to be smaller than 1 as the discount factor, w, varies between 0 and 1. This is ensured if $b > c > d$, which equals our assumption about the payoff structure of the game.
6. One variation of this game is to indicate that players do not know for sure when the game is going to end. They do know that the game is of a finite type and thus will end after some period. This modification, which only affects the likelihood of ending the game, does not change the outcome. Since players do know that the game ends after some known number of rounds, it will lead to defection in each period of the game. Whether the game may possibly end at the next round, before the last round is reached, does not change the basic game-theoretical logic (see Myerson, 1991: 309–10; Hovi, 1998: 92).
7. The safeguard clauses are included in the Treaty of Accession.
8. As in the case of the Accession treaties with Bulgaria and Romania signed in April 2005.
9. Cited in the Dutch national newspaper *NRC Handelsblad*, 13 May 2005.
10. For example, if a nationalist leader gains ground in the electoral struggle by appealing to the electorate with promises of stopping accession and the reforms demanded by the EU.

11. In this chapter we focus on hypotheses related to the applicant country, as, for the moment, we assume that enlargement involves sufficient benefits to the EU and its current member states. It is also possible to further analyse the gains to the EU and formulate hypotheses underlining the magnitude of these benefits.
12. Following their 'demand' driven approach, Mattli and Plümper (2002) assume that the choice of applying for EU membership is solely determined by the applicant country. Using this assumption they analyse the political-economic features of countries that applied with those that did not (yet) apply. This includes countries such as Ukraine, Moldova and Russia. The question remains whether this comparison makes sense from the perspective of the EU, given its restrictive approach to enlargement.
13. We also clustered these conditions into 22 main categories and performed the same analysis, as some of the conditions overlap. Although the number of conditions per country now differs, we found the same patterns as reported in the text.
14. For a study that presents evidence of variation, see Schwellnus, 2005.

REFERENCES

Baun, M. (2000), *A Wider Europe: The Process and Politics of European Union Enlargement*, Lanham, MD: Rowman and Littlefield.

Binmore, K. (1992), *Fun and Games: A Text on Game Theory*, Lexington, MA: Heath and Company.

Dimitrova, A. (2002), 'Governance by enlargement? The case of the administrative capacity requirement in the EU's Eastern enlargement', *West European Politics*, **25**, 171–90.

Dimitrova, A. L. (2004), 'Enlargement driven change and post communist transformations: A new perspective', in A. L. Dimitrova (ed.), *Driven to Change: The European Union's Enlargement Viewed from the East*, Manchester: Manchester University Press, pp. 1–17.

Dimitrova, A. L. (2005), 'Europeanization and civil service reform in Central and Eastern Europe', in F. Schimmelfennig and U. Sedelmeier (eds), *The Europeanization of Central and Eastern Europe*, Ithaca, NY and London: Cornell University Press, pp. 71–91.

Dimitrova, A. L. and G. Pridham (2004), 'International actors and democracy promotion in CEE: the integration model and its limits', *Democratization*, December, **11** (5), 91–112.

European Commission (2004), *Internal Market Scoreboard No. 13*, Brussels: Internal Market DG (July).

European Commission (2005), *Second Implementation Report of the Internal Market Strategy 2003–2006*, COM(2005)final, Brussels.

Grabbe, H. (1999), 'A partnership for accession? The implications for conditionality for the Central and Eastern European applicants', RSC working paper RSC 99/12, Florence: European University Institute.

Grabbe, H. (2001), 'How does Europeanization affect CEE governance? Conditionality, diffusion and diversity', *Journal of European Public Policy*, **8**, 1013–31.

Grabbe, H. (2003), 'Europeanisation goes east: power and uncertainty in the EU accession process', in K. Featherstone and C. Radaelli (eds), *The Politics of Europeanisation*, Oxford: Oxford University Press, pp. 303–31.

Hovi, J. (1998), *Games, Threats and Treaties: Understanding Commitments in International Relations*, London and Washington, DC: Pinter.

König, T. and T. Bräuninger (2000), 'Governing the enlarged European Union: accession scenarios and institutional reform', *Central European Political Science Review*, **1**, 42–62.

König, T. and T. Bräuninger (2004), 'Accession and reform of the European Union: a game-theoretical analysis of Eastern enlargement and the constitutional reform', *European Union Politics*, **5**, 419–39.

Maniokas, K. (2004), 'The methed of the European Union's enlargement to the east: a critical appraisal', in A. Dimitrova (ed.), *Driven to Change. The European Union's Enlargement Viewed from the East*, Manchester: Manchester University Press, pp. 17–37.

Mattli, W. and T. Plümper (2002), 'The demand-side politics of EU enlargement: democracy and the application for EU membership', *Journal of European Public Policy*, **9**, 550–74.

Moravcsik, A. and M. A. Vachudova (2003), 'National interests, state power and EU enlargement', *East European Politics and Societies*, **17**, 42–57.

Myerson, R. B. (1991), *Game Theory: Analysis of Conflict*, Cambridge, MA: Harvard University Press.

Nugent, N. (2004), *European Union Enlargement*, Houndmills: Palgrave Macmillan.

Osborne, M. J. and A. Rubinstein (1994), *A Course in Game Theory*, Cambridge, MA: MIT Press.

Plümper, T., C. Schneider and V. Troeger (2003), 'Regulatory conditionality and membership accession in the EU: evidence from a Heckman selection model', mimeo: University of Konstanz.

Powell, R. (1991), 'Absolute and relative gains in international relations theory', *American Political Science Review*, **85**, 1303–20.

Schimmelfennig, F., S. Engert and H. Knobel (2003), 'Costs, commitment and compliance: the impact of EU democratic conditionality in Latvia, Slovakia and Turkey', *Journal of Common Market Studies*, **41**, 495–518.

Schimmelfennig, F. and U. Sedelmeier (2004), 'Governance by conditionality: EU rule transfer to the candidate countries of Central and Eastern Europe', *Journal of European Public Policy*, **11**, 661–79.

Schimmelfennig, F. and U. Sedelmeier (2005a), 'Conceptualizing the Europeanization of Central and Eastern Europe', in F. Schimmelfennig and U. Sedelmeier (eds), *The Europeanization of Central and Eastern Europe*, Ithaca, NY and London: Cornell University Press, pp. 1–29.

Schimmelfennig, F. and U. Sedelmeier (2005b), 'Conclusions: the impact of the EU on the accession countries', in F. Schimmelfennig and U. Sedelmeier (eds), *The Europeanization of Central and Eastern Europe*, Ithaca, NY and London: Cornell University Press, pp. 210–29.

Schmitter, P. C. (1995), 'The international context of contemporary democratisation', in G. Pridham (ed.), *Transitions to Democracy: Comparative Perspectives from Southern Europe, Latin America and Eastern Europe*, Aldershot, UK and Brookfield, VT: Dartmouth.

Schwellnus, G. (2005), 'The adoption of nondiscrimination and minority protection rules in Romania, Hungary, and Poland', in F. Schemmelfenning and U. Sedelmeier (eds), *The Europeanization of Central and Eastern Europe*, Ithaca, NY and London: Cornell University Press, pp. 51–70.

Smith, K. E. (2003), *European Union Foreign Policy in a Changing World*, Cambridge: Polity Press.

Steunenberg, B. (2001), 'Enlargement and institutional reform in the European Union: separate or connected issues?' *Constitutional Political Economy*, **12**, 349–68.

Steunenberg, B. (2002), 'Enlargement and reform in the European Union', in B. Steunenberg (ed.), *Widening the European Union: The Politics of Institutional Change and Reform*, London: Routledge, pp. 3–20.

Shubik, M. (1970), 'Game theory, behavior, and the paradox of the prisoner's dilemma: three solutions', *International Journal of Game Theory*, **14**, 181–93.

Vachudova, M. A. (2001), 'The leverage of international institutions on democratizing states: the European Union and Eastern Europe', RSCAS working paper no. 2001/33, European University Institute, Florence.

Vachudová, M. A. (2005), *Europe Undivided: Democracy, Leverage and Integration After Communism*, Oxford, New York: Oxford University Press.

World Bank (2005), *Review of World Bank Conditionality: Issues Note*, Washington, DC: Operations Policy and Country Services, accessed at http://siteresources.worldbank.org/PROJECTS/Resources/REVIEWOFBANKCONDITIONALITYJan3105.pdf.

Zubek, R. (2005), 'Complying with transposition commitments in Poland: collective dilemmas, core executive and legislative outcomes', *West European Politics*, **28** (3), 592–619.

Conclusion: Hobbes and the political economy of power

Donald Wittman

INTRODUCTION

Is the choice in Iraq between anarchy and a ruthless dictatorship or is there a middle way? And if there is a middle way in Iraq or elsewhere, what conditions foster such an outcome? The fundamental political problem is that the power to prevent anarchy is also the power to impose one's will, which I will refer to as the Hobbesian dilemma. Yet we do observe relatively benign dictatorships (as in Singapore) and a relative respect for property and civil rights in the democracies of North America and Western Europe. Here, I discuss why the choice need not be limited to brutish anarchy and a self-aggrandizing Leviathan. I also derive the conditions that encourage the middle solution. At the same time, I explain why dictatorships are inclined to make bad economic policies.

For a person trained in public choice theory, the puzzle is why governments are not always repressive military regimes and dictatorships. Public choice emphasizes the self-interest of bureaucrats, politicians and special interest groups (typically within a democratic setting). But the net result in these models is a relatively modest increase in government expenditure (relative to what the median voter might desire) in favor of the special interests. Here, we consider a much more profound possibility that arises when certain segments of society, particularly the military, have the power to coerce. One would expect that those with military and political power would further their own self-interest at the expense of the rest of the population. Functioning democracies and benign autocracies appear to be contrary to the whole public choice paradigm. This chapter tries to explain why the dire predictions of a raw application of public choice need not be the case in practice.

Before proceeding further, it is important to show that democratic elections do not by themselves resolve the issues raised. As Iraq so clearly demonstrates, a democratic election is not sufficient if the losers think they can achieve their ends with force. In many Latin American countries, the army has taken over when the military was dissatisfied with the democratic process. Other countries with democratically elected leaders have been unable to solve problems of predation, corruption and lawlessness. Furthermore, an elected majority can run roughshod over the minority even if there is a constitution that says otherwise. As a final example, elected presidents can become authoritarian leaders, especially at moments when they believe they cannot win the next election (Africa provides many examples).

Unfortunately, clear and unambiguous answers to the beginning questions are not easy. There are only about 150 countries. Even including time series data does not raise the degrees of freedom significantly as there is a high correlation within each country from one year to the next. Furthermore, the direction of causation is not always clear and there are many exceptions to any generalities that can be made. The most that can be said is that there are various factors that influence the outcome.[1] I will now consider each of these factors in turn.

HOMO ECONOMICUS VERSUS HOMO SAPIENS

Hobbes uses the metaphor of humans as being wolves or selfish predators. This is Homo Economicus in the extreme. But man is a social animal rather than a sociopath and therefore the median human has some positive regard for others. It is this positive regard that may temper excessive exploitation by those who are in power of those who are not.[2]

Of course, humans vary in their capacity for empathy. If rulers were an unbiased sample of the population, then rulers would be a bell-shaped curve of types on the ruthless–benevolent dimension. However, it is quite likely that rulers are not an unbiased sample. For example, in any situation where the road to power is through violence such as civil war, the most ruthless, paranoid and cunning individual may win. It therefore should not be surprising that when these men gain power, they remain ruthless, paranoid and cunning (Pol Pot, Mao and Lenin are some examples). Yet George Washington did not become a dictator, perhaps because the war was fought against an external enemy not an internal one (many of the loyalists fled to Canada).

In a democracy where the list of candidates running for office is not severely restricted, the politician must appeal to a majority of people. If voters can on average detect sincerity, then a majority of voters would on average not vote for a candidate that would go against the wishes of the majority. So this is a possible explanation for why there is a difference between democracy and autocracy and why the more ruthless typically do not take power in democracies. The most ruthless (toward their own citizens, but not necessarily against others) usually, but not always, lose elections.

To the extent that democracy relies on the median voter, the median voter need only have a modicum of altruism to generate government policies that respect civil rights and that do not exploit 49 percent of the population. This is easiest to illustrate mathematically in terms of policies to redistribute wealth from the rich to the poor. Consider the following thought experiment. You might hesitate to give $1000 to a charity that helped the poor because you do not weight the welfare of others as much as you weight your own welfare. However, suppose that there is a proposition on the ballot that taxes the richest 60 percent $1000 each and gives the poorest 20 percent $3000 each. You would probably be more willing to vote for this proposition (even if you were being taxed) than undertaking the individual charitable act because your loss would be minor compared to the overall gain to all the poor people (see Wittman, 2003, for an extended discussion). Similarly, one might be willing to forgo some small personal gain in wealth if there were an increase in civil rights and/or wealth for everyone. And if it were your own civil rights, you would be even more interested in protecting them.

But as noted in the opening remarks, democracy is only a partial answer. The question then becomes why the military accepts the democratic choice instead of installing someone who reflects the preferences of the military leaders. We will come back to this issue in a later section.

RETURNS TO PREDATION

In the previous section, the answer to why some political systems are not highly predatory was that not all humans are predatory and therefore more benign governments are possible (especially when the means to power have been achieved peacefully). Of course, even under the best of circumstances, one cannot rely on the altruism of rulers. In this section, we provide a different answer. Predatory rulers may choose to curb their predation because their long-run returns are higher this way.

A country's wealth may be based on its minerals, forests, farmland and fisheries, or human capital. Human capital seems extremely hard to exploit. It is hard to control either how much another person thinks or the nature of the person's creativity. It is more efficient to tax the income from human capital than to try to control it, but even here the taxation is limited as excessive taxation will lead to reduced investment in human capital, in the first place. While revolutions often involve destruction of those with human capital to prevent counter revolutions or to fulfill ideological ends (as was the case with the Khmer Rouge), a stable political system must be more careful in this regard because such disregard for human capital will mean less wealth to exploit for the country's leaders. It is, therefore, not surprising that those countries that have the highest human capital are also those countries with the least oppressive regimes and that in those countries with oppressive regimes, the people with the most political capital are treated the best. However, Mao's cultural revolution is a counter-example as intellectuals were treated very badly.[3]

At the opposite end of the continuum is mineral wealth. Although some human capital is needed for the exploitation of minerals, most of the income from mineral wealth is a rent that does not depend on productivity. So the expropriation of mineral wealth has far fewer negative consequences for productivity than the attempt to appropriate human capital. Other things being equal, the rewards from political power are much higher when the economy is based on rents (as is the case for oil extraction) than when it is based on human capital. This means that competitors for power will be willing to face greater costs in trying to obtain control. In turn, the present leaders of the country will want to undertake more repressive measures to maintain control. Not surprisingly, those countries with the greatest oil and mineral wealth as a percentage of GDP are typically run by autocratic rulers who disregard civil liberties in order to prevent the seizure of wealth by others (see Paldam, this volume). And when they are not successful in this regard, the country is likely to face a long and brutal civil war. Canada, however, is an interesting exception.

Farmland is an in-between case. The Soviet experience is an enlightening example. Stalin tried to tax the peasants by forcing them to sell wheat to the state at below market prices, thereby easing the strain on the proletariat and allowing for increased industrial production. But his tax was so excessive that the peasants cut back on their sales of wheat and instead raised pigs. Facing a crisis of too little bread for the urban workers, Stalin collectivized the farms, which ultimately reduced productivity enormously and led to the famine of 1932–3 (a famine far worse than pre-revolutionary famines). So in this example, the attempt to exploit the peasants ultimately backfired.

In US history, slave labor was associated with cotton and sugar cane, not apple and vegetable production, suggesting that that exploitation depends on the technology, not on the personality of the people owning the farmland.

Olson (1993) and McGuire and Olson (1998) developed the theory of the stationary bandit (autocrat). The essence of their argument is that the bandit will provide public good investment if this increases the bandit's ability to extract wealth in the future. Furthermore, the stationary bandit will maximize the bandit's present value by tempering the exploitation of wealth, lest individuals reduce their effort. As I have just argued, the need to temper exploitation is increased when human capital is primary and reduced when rents are collected. Using the language of game theory, cooperation is reduced when the game is zero-sum rather than positive-sum.

Given the above argument, it is not surprising that, with the exception of oil based economies, all countries with above $5000 per capita income in 1985 dollars are stable democracies and score high on the Gastell index (see Paldam, this volume, and Przeworski, 2006).[4] However, it appears that Robert Mugabe, Kim Jong Il, and a host of other autocrats have not read McGuire and Olson. We will deal at length with this point in the following section.

MAINTAINING POWER: WHY DO AUTOCRATS SO OFTEN UNDERTAKE INEFFICIENT POLICIES?

As the collectivization example suggests, autocrats often undertake inefficient policies that persist over long periods of time. So further explanation is needed.

It could be that the leaders are stupid when it comes to economic matters and there is no one willing to challenge them (see Wintrobe, 1998). Economists generally eschew such answers, but economists usually concern themselves with competitive markets, not the market for authoritarian control. In competitive political markets (that is, democracies) leaders that undertake grossly inefficient policies are easily removed from office. In autocracies, coercion allows a leader to stay in power despite catastrophic economic policies (see Bueno de Mesquita *et al.*, 2001; Wintrobe, 2002). And so we have observed Mao's 'great leap forward', Stalin's promotion of Lysenko's mistaken views of inherited traits (stupidity is not limited to economic concepts), and the like.

Still economists crave more rational explanations. The most likely answer is that property rights and economic growth may reduce the ability of the autocrat to remain in power by increasing the power of others. As a consequence, the autocrat may restrict growth (as in North Korea or in Mexico where the PRI stayed in power for 70 years despite low economic growth).

At present, we have only a limited understanding of why growth would reduce the ability of the autocrat to remain in power. Greater productivity makes for increased welfare of the citizens, which should in general decrease their desire to overthrow the government. Bad economic conditions do not improve the likelihood of the incumbent being re-elected in democracies. Here are some stabs at finding a rational explanation for autocrats favoring low levels of economic growth.

Authoritarians fear organizations not directly under their control because organizations allow citizens to coordinate their activities, including plotting against the authoritarian. Authoritarians therefore tend to place great restrictions on citizens' ability to organize. For example, censorship reduces the ability of the opposition to coordinate and overthrow the incumbent power (see Kuran, 1997). Even a coup (which involves relatively few people) is difficult in an authoritarian regime. It is hard for plotters to find co-conspirators when one is not sure where others stand, there is considerable spying, and the cost of a failed coup is death. More widespread revolts require greater coordination and spread of information, something that is difficult when the government controls the media and will not report such incidents until it is sure that the conspiracy has been squelched. So restrictions on civil rights can maintain the leader in power if the restrictions themselves do not give sufficiently greater impetus to the opposition.

In the Soviet Union, limited telephone service prevented political organization, but at the same time reduced economic coordination. More generally, control over all aspects of life, including the economy, may increase the authoritarian's tenure by preventing organized resistance. But central control of all organizations undermines the competitive process and reduces economic growth. In an authoritarian regime with deep roots into the economy, everything is political, and initiatives from the bottom are much harder to implement than initiatives from the top. Suppose that someone develops a new method of distributing goods, as Wal-Mart has done. In the United States, Wal-Mart had to overcome some bureaucratic hurdles, but it is nothing like what would have happened in the Soviet Union, even if the idea had been generated by some cooperative enterprise. The decision to allow such a distribution method would have to be analysed in terms of how it might upset the power structure, thereby making what should be a small decision into a much more complex and global one. In order for the initiative to pass, too many parties would be involved. With such high transaction costs, change and initiative are stifled and economic growth reduced.[5] In a nutshell, the authoritarian model is hierarchical while the model of economic success is both more anarchic and horizontal (cooperative exchange).[6]

A somewhat related argument is that a flourishing economic sector would change the coin of the realm from coercion to money. Those with money might be able to bribe underlings of the political sector, thereby undermining the power of the autocrat. However, autocrats tend to use their power to garner economic wealth. So it is not clear why they use inefficient economic policies, such as owning government monopolies, to gain wealth rather than through bribes and the collection of taxes. Perhaps the best answer is that there is a tradeoff: a growing economy implies a greater surplus to the authoritarian, but also increases the political risk of being overthrown.[7] Authoritarians tend to like stability in the domestic sphere because that means that they will remain in power.[8] Because economic growth is unpredictable in its consequences, the authoritarian leader may prefer to control a less prosperous economy.

Another version of the same argument is that those who gain power through coercion may tend to solve economic problems by coercion, as well. After all this is the tool that worked for them in either getting or maintaining power. This seems to explain the behavior of Stalin, who criminalized work place violations, used forced labor, and collectivized agriculture rather than using monetary incentives (for the Soviet experience, see Gregory and Harrison, 2005; for the role of coercion more generally, see Wintrobe, 1998).

Here is a third possible explanation. If the citizens of North Korea knew how bad things were compared to the rest of the world (and South Korea, in particular), then they would revolt. Keeping the North Koreans in the dark would be next to impossible in an open economy. So, Kim Jong Il is willing to forgo the economic growth that goes with an open economy to prevent being overthrown. There are two problems with this answer. One, it assumes that the people in North Korea have not been able to figure out that they are poor and oppressed. It also assumes that this policy maintains Jong Il in power more than if he opened up his economy as the Chinese have done.

A fourth explanation assumes that the autocrat's time in power is very limited and thus the autocrat steals while in power rather than building for the future. That is, the autocrat is not a stationary bandit, but a temporary one.[9] This probably explains the behavior of many autocrats in Africa, where the tenure is often short. However Bueno de Mesquita *et al.* (2003) have shown that on average dictators last in power longer than democrats (Castro is an obvious example). As a possible counter to Bueno de Mesquita and his co-authors the lives of former dictators tend to be short while the lives of former heads of democracies tend to be long and financially rewarding (President Clinton has made millions writing his autobiography and giving lectures). So perhaps dictators have a shorter time horizon after all.

Finally, autocrats may be indifferent to economic growth as long as they and their coterie are doing well. The welfare of others is not important for their political survival. And even in very poor countries autocrats can live very well.

Because there are so many examples of autocrats pursuing low growth policies for so long (the Soviet Union for decades, China for centuries, and countless other countries), one searches for a rational explanation. In this section, I have provided a political answer – growth may shorten the autocrat's tenure in office. Nonetheless, this account does not explain the contrary result – that a number of autocracies have pursued high growth policies. Singapore and present-day China are obvious examples.[10] Indeed, the People's Action Party has remained in power in Singapore because of the high growth policies. The interesting question is how the Communist Party in China can stay in control despite the decentralization of economic power and whether it will be able to remain in power. Finally, democracies are not immune from bad economic policies – India's socialistic model crippled growth for the first 50 years of its independence.

A REVERSE ARROW OF CAUSALITY

In the previous section, we asked why autocrats might choose low growth economies. In this section, we reverse the arrow of causation and ask why backward economies might 'choose' autocrats, and more generally, we ask what circumstances increase the demand for them.

Centralization of power, but not necessarily autocratic centralization of power, may be a response to political, military and economic circumstances. Poor countries may require extensive investment in social overhead investment, which requires relatively large transfers of wealth. A significant degree of centralized power may be required to enforce such large transfers. Another version of this argument has been made by Dudley (1991). When information storage is costly and transmission is relatively cheap, as in the Soviet Union, then centralized power is optimal. However, when storage becomes cheap relative to transmission, then decentralization becomes more likely.

Hobbes argued that Leviathan was needed to solve the problem of anarchy, but a more social science explanation might be that the greater the potential for anarchy, the more control the central power needs to impose, so maybe Tito and Saddam Hussein were necessary solutions to highly fractured societies. But India has not chosen this path.

There are technological and 'ecological' reasons for the centralization of military power. External military threats often lead to an internal consolidation of military power to create an effective counter force. As McNeill (1984) pointed out, scale economies in military technology are the key to whether military power is centralized. If the ruler suffers as many casualties in putting down a revolt as do the rebels, then his power is likely to be weak or temporary. With tanks and jet aircraft as the dominant technology, the Shiites had little chance against Saddam Hussein. However, with Stingers and rocket-propelled grenades, the Afghans were able to drive out the Soviets.

So far, we have provided explanations for greater centralization of power, not for greater exploitation. However, the greater the centralization of power, the greater the potential for exploitation because there are fewer constraints on power. The words of Lord Acton resonate: power corrupts and absolute power corrupts absolutely. We will pursue this idea to greater length in the following section.

ANARCHIC EQUILIBRIUM

While intellectually it is easier to understand a situation where there is a monopoly of power, in the real world power is likely to be more diffuse. The observed outcome is likely to be the equilibrium of the various military, political and economic forces. To best gain insight, consider the international system. Despite the argument by some that the US exerts hegemonic (monopoly) power, this is certainly not the case as witnessed by the inability of the US to control events in Iraq or influence that tiny island called Cuba, just 90 miles from Key West, Florida. In the real world, every country would like to have more influence on the international stage, but even the most powerful countries are limited at the margin by the countervailing power of other countries. And while the international system is not without war, peace is, on average, the prevailing outcome among dyads (even geographically contiguous dyads).

In a similar vein, domestic politics might more fruitfully be viewed not as a monopoly of power held by one group (or hegamon) but as an equilibrium of various forces. Thus the ability to impose one's will is limited because the power of any one group is limited. In many countries, the poor do not have the military and/or political power to expropriate the rich, nor do the rich have the ability to remain in power without sharing some of their wealth with the poor (see Acemoglu and Robinson, 2006, and Przeworski, 2006, for extended arguments). So predation may be limited because in equilibrium the power to predate is limited. We will come back to this issue when we focus on military power.

CULTURE

Culture may temper predation by those in power. Consider slavery. Today, it is unlikely that any US president would want to enslave African-Americans even if slavery enabled those in power to increase their control and become wealthier. Yet Washington and Jefferson had slaves.

Economists do not like to use culture as an independent variable. Przeworski (2006) has argued that culture is just another word for equilibrium and that it has no extra explanatory power. Yet different people have faith in different institutions (democracy, theocracy, royalty) and the proportion of people who believe in these vary from country to country. That is, some people value these institutions in and of themselves, rather than as instruments towards their own welfare (in political science, this is known as legitimacy).[11] In both pre- and post-World War II France, the support for a royalist as opposed to a democratic government was relatively high compared to the US. No doubt those who supported a royalist government would on average gain more from a royalist government than they would from democracy. But this is not the whole explanation. Some people who would benefit in a narrow economic way from a royalist system still might prefer a democratic or theocratic system (in this way, culture interacts with the social animal argument). Suppose that tomorrow the Catholic population in the United States were instantly replaced by the present occupants of Saudi Arabia, Yemen and some other religious intolerant countries (or that yesterday the royalists from France replaced Canadian voters). It is not clear that the bill of rights or even the present democratic system would survive despite the separation of powers and other supposed safeguards.

COMPETITION DURING WAR

Economists often see competition as a means for improving welfare. Groups compete for control. Typically no one group can assert complete control. We considered this possibility in the section on anarchy – the more power is dispersed, the less any particular power center can exert its control and exploit others. What happens when there is an actual war? In such cases, there may again be competition among the groups for partisans in the fight. At least in theory, competition may improve the welfare of those being competed for. Yet, when it comes to actual warfare and coercion, the logic seems undermined by the facts. Those who live in contested areas are often victims of both sides. Why does the competition for the 'swing voter' make things worse for those in the middle when there is a civil war? The answer seems to be that elimination seems more productive than co-option.

We will get back to the issue of competition in the next section.

THE MILITARY

Since Locke's *Second Treatise of Civil Government* (1690) and Montesquieu's *Spirit of the Law* (1748), writers have made much of the separation of powers of government into the executive, legislative and judicial branches. No doubt, at the margin, this separation reduces the power of any one branch to foster its own ends as Madison famously argued in the *Federalist Papers*. Yet, I have always found this line of analysis rather superficial. First, there is nothing to prevent a coalition across the branches of like-minded individuals. More important, neither the judiciary nor the legislature (nor sometimes the executive) has control over the military, where the power to coerce ultimately resides. So, once again, we are back to the Hobbesian conundrum, but in its deepest manifestation. Why don't the military and the police exercise their power to promote their own ends, be it economic or political (as one suspects is happening in Iraq)? As noted in our introductory remarks, even in democratic systems, we need to ask why those with the power to coerce do not do so. As we will see, to a large extent the answers have been provided in the previous sections.

Perhaps the most important reason for the military not exerting its will is that the military may not be monolithic, particularly so, when the country is democratic. Although the military is almost always unified when facing an external enemy, it is less commonly so with regard to domestic politics.

In the early history of the US, the existence of state militias prevented the centralization of military power in the hands of the federal government, but it still does not explain why the state militia did not exploit citizens of the state. The first answer is that there was competition between the states – a race to the top. Greater exploitation of the citizens of one state would lead to migration to a state with less exploitation (see Brennan and Buchanan, 1980; Wittman, 2000; Spolaore, 2006, for a discussion of beneficial competition). This was relatively easy as there were few linguistic, cultural or physical barriers. The 13 colonies were a group of contiguous states, not 13 islands separated by vast distances. There was also a hinterland where people might escape predation by the state. It would have made little sense in terms of a cost-benefit analysis to have erected physical barriers to prevent emigration as was done in the Communist countries nearly two centuries later (see Friedman, 1977). A second reason is that power was diffused quite evenly among the citizens. Most male citizens owned a rifle. The more powerful weapons such as canon were not very mobile. So there was little centralization of military power. Of course, the same is not true today. So we must consider more subtle explanations when considering more recent times. It seems that there are two stable equilibria: (a) diffuse and (b) monolithic.

In most democratic countries, the army and police force are not monolithic because the individuals that populate them are not recruited from any one segment of society. Many countries have a universal draft and often their officer corps either more or less reflect the pattern of interests in the society as a whole or else would not obtain the allegiance of their lower ranked soldiers in the event of an attempted military takeover.[12] Indeed it has been argued that the rise of democracy in Europe is intimately connected to the use of mass armies, initiated by Napolean.

Of course, this just moves the question, one step back – why doesn't the military become monolithic. The answer appears to be that no one group is willing to give up its power to another group. This occurs within the military and outside of it. The executive is not willing to give up power to the military that it does not have to; similarly, within the military, no groups are willing to have their members excluded from further recruitment. Therefore diffuse military power is kept diffuse by not allowing the military to restrict its recruitment to certain ethnic groups or to those with particular ideological stances.[13] Indeed, in some countries (Kuwait for example) people in the military do not have the right to vote, thereby restricting their ability to make policy.

A useful contrast is Iraq where the power to coerce was monolithically under the control of Saddam Hussein.[14] The Republican Guard was mostly Sunni, and most of the Sunni were recruited from certain tribes and locations loyal to Hussein (that is Tikrit). The regular army had ill-trained and ill-equipped Shiites as cannon fodder, but the leaders were Sunni. Finally, the Fedayeen Saddam (a group of armed paramilitary enforcers) were perhaps the most loyal and most tribally affiliated with Saddam.[15] If Saddam had remained in power, it is extremely unlikely that the make-up of the military would have shifted its ethnic base in any meaningful way. Post-Saddam, the private militias have essentially captured control over the military apparatus, making it difficult to change the military into a force for national unity.

Many of the arguments used in the previous sections apply in this section, as well. In a stable democratic system, the people recruited to be military leaders are not wolves (sociopaths), but people who, in one way or another, value the democratic system.[16] So if there are some who would like to overthrow the democratically elected government, others might very well resist even if they might gain personally from such a coup. And, ignoring the preferences for democracy, the diffuse interests of the military make it unlikely that a majority of the military would gain from a coup, making a successful coup unlikely; and if success were likely, the means could probably be achieved more readily and at less cost through the ballot. To use the language of economics, a Pareto improving trade among a large and diffuse group is more easily done within the context of a legislature than within a hierarchical system such as the military.

ANARCHY

Countries live in a state of anarchy, but they are not constantly at war. Tribes may also be in a state of anarchy with each other, and they too need not be in a constant state of war.[17] Although recent history shows a more dismal outcome, Afghanistan was relatively peaceful in the 1960s and early 1970s despite the fact that the country was more a collection of tribes than a government. So centralized power is not the only answer to anarchy. Another alternative is 'tribal anarchy'.[18] The problem is that anarchy is typically not a stable equilibrium (see Hirshleifer, 1995), especially so, when there are economies of scale in military power. So centralization of military power seems inevitable when there are economies of scale, but, as we have argued, diffuse preferences of the military may make it less monolithic and less predatory.

CONCLUDING REMARKS

Economists like to provide simple models to explain events. But when we try to explain the more than occasional absence of extreme exploitation by those who ostensibly have the power to coerce, and at the same time try to explain why others employ extreme forms of coercion, we must fall back on several explanations. Limited ability to exploit (either because one has limited power to coerce or because coercion itself does not produce much benefit to those with power) is a consistent theme throughout this chapter. Another theme is that preferences (culturally influenced or screened for in obtaining power) may induce greater or lesser exploitation, depending on the screening device and the nature of the culture. More empirical studies are needed to determine the importance of these arguments in explaining whether Leviathan is just a paper tiger, and if not whether Leviathan takes advantage of its coercive power to promote its own selfish ends.

ACKNOWLEDGEMENTS

I would like to thank Bryan Caplan, Leonard Dudley, Mario Ferrero, Daniel Friedman, Manfred Holler, Ryan Oprea and Barry Weingast for very helpful comments.

NOTES

1. Note that we looking for social science answers, not philosophical answers. For the latter, see Buchanan (2000) who provides a public choice perspective.
2. See Eusepi and Cepparulo (this volume) for further discussion.
3. On the other side of the ledger, the average level of education in democratic India is less than authoritarian China. At the other end of the economic spectrum is Singapore,

where there are limited civil rights. However, it cannot be characterized as a police state.

4. Of course some countries with low per capita income are stable democracies. India is a prominent example.
5. Those brought up in East Germany seem to lack the initiative of their West German counterparts.
6. This argument can be used to explain the slow growth of China in previous centuries despite its early invention of pottery, printing and gunpowder – everything down to the smallest detail was regulated by the state (see Landes, 2006). However, Diamond (1999) provides a different argument – that China did not face competitive pressure from other countries as was the case for the various countries of Europe. While European competition also meant many more wars, it did have the byproduct of spurred innovation (particularly in warfare) because those that did not innovate would be overcome by other countries. See also Wittman (2000). But perhaps, in backward societies, centralization increases growth. See pp. 258–9 on reverse causation.
7. During the Korean War, China relied on private enterprise for industrial products and war supplies. Afterward, Mao expropriated the capitalists, saying: 'During the past one and half years, the capitalists made a huge fortune in the Korean War and advanced their political status. Now, they are in high spirits and are viciously attacking us. It is high time for us to fight back by using various means and excuses. If we do not make them infamous in the society, more and more people will be sympathetic with them and side with them.' With such a motivation, the state launched a so-called Five Anti Campaign (anti-bribery, anti-tax-evasion, anti-cheating in quality, anti-stealing state assets and anti-stealing state economic intelligence), whose ultimate purpose was to reduce the political and economic influence of the capitalists. See Chong-En *et al.* (1998).
8. Dictators may be more adventuresome in the international arena if they want to increase their domain of power.
9. Whenever power is secure, those with power will have longer time horizons. This includes 'special interests', who gain from growth as there is more to exploit.
10. Other examples include Hitler and Pinochet. Hitler was responsible for an extremely high growth rate and reduction of unemployment during the time span 1933–1939. Perhaps one could say that dictators produce high variance outcomes.
11. Culture may also serve as a coordinating device regarding who will get what. Note that some cultures may promote exploitation and the individual's inclination towards vengeance while other cultures may tone down the impetus to exploit others in the society. See Binmore (1994) for a discussion of moral norms as coordinating devices.
12. Falaschetti and Miller (2001) explain why diffuse power is necessary.
13. There are exceptions. In the US, communists have not served; and in Israel, Orthodox Jews are not subject to the draft. In almost all countries, females are typically not a significant part of the military. Of course, the military is not an unbiased sample of the population. According to http://www.armytimes.com/story.php?f=1-292925-2513919.php only about 17 percent of the US military, as opposed to about 50 percent of the general population, view themselves as Democrats.
14. Another insightful example is Cuba, where Fidel Castro's brother Raul is head of both the police and the army.
15. The division of military power into parts made it more difficult for any one group to overthrow Saddam. All authoritarians worry about how to organize the military and police so that they are unable to coordinate against them. This takes a non-negligible portion of the social surplus.
16. In those countries that alternate between democracy and military dictatorship, the military often inculcates values that they view as being superior to democracy.
17. But violence is still endemic to this world. By examining skeletons, anthropologists estimate a surprisingly high proportion of males die violent deaths.
18. Of course, this does not reduce the Hobbesian dilemma; it only reduces it to a smaller scale as tribal chiefs can extort the members of their tribe. For a spirited defense of anarchy, see De Jasay (1997).

REFERENCES

Acemoglu, D. and J. A. Robinson (2006), 'Paths of economic and political development', in B. Weingast and D. Wittman (eds), *The Oxford Handbook of Political Economy*, Oxford: Oxford University Press.

Binmore, K. (1994), *Game Theory and the Social Contract, Volume 1: Playing Fair*, Cambridge, MA: MIT Press.

Brennan, G. and J. M. Buchanan (1980), *The Power to Tax: Analytical Foundations of a Fiscal Constitution*, Cambridge: Cambridge University Press.

Buchanan, J. M. (2000), *The Limits of Liberty: Between Anarchy and Leviathan* (*Collected Works of James M. Buchnan, Vol. 7*), Indianapolis, IN: Liberty Fund.

Bueno de Mesquita, B., J. Morrow, R. M. Siverson and A. Smith (2003), *The Logic of Political Survival*, Cambridge, MA: MIT Press.

Chong-En, B., D. D. Li, Y. Qian and Y. Wang (1998), 'State predation and contract enforcement: information decentralization as a commitment device', Stanford University Department of Political Science working paper.

De Jasay, A. (1997), *Against Politics: On Government, Anarchy and Order*, London: Routledge.

Diamond, J. (1999), *Guns, Steel and Germs*, New York: W. W. Norton.

Dudley, L. (1991), *The Word and the Sword: How Techniques of Information and Violence Have Shaped Our World*, Oxford: Blackwell.

Falaschetti, D. and G. Miller (2001), 'Constraining Leviathan: moral hazard and credible commitments in constitutional design', *Journal of Theoretical Politics*, **13,** 389–411.

Friedman, D. (1977), 'A theory of the size and shape of nations', *Journal of Political Economy*, **85**, 59–77.

Gregory, P. and M. Harrison (2005), Allocation under dictatorship: research in Stalin's archives, *Journal of Economic Literature*, **18**, 721–61.

Hirshleifer, J. (1995), 'Anarchy and its breakdown', *Journal of Political Economy*, **103,** 27–52.

Hobbes, T. (1651), *Leviathan*, reprinted 1962, London: Collier Macmillan.

Kuran, T. (1997), *Private Truths, Public Lies: The Social Consequences of Preference Falsification*, Cambridge, MA: Harvard University Press.

Landes, D. (2006), 'Why Europe and the West? Why not China?', *Journal of Economic Perspectives*, **20**, 3–22.

Locke, J. (1690), *Two Treatises of Government*, reprinted 2003, I. Shapiro (ed.), New Haven, CT: Yale University Press.

McGuire, M. C. and M. Olson (1998), 'The economics of autocracy and majority rule: the invisible hand and the use of force', *Journal of Economic Literature*, **34**, 72–96.

McNeill, W. (1984), *The Pursuit of Power, Technology, Armed Force and Society Since AD 1000*, Chicago, IL: University of Chicago Press.

Montesquieu (1748), *The Spirit of the Law*, reprinted 1989, Cambridge: Cambridge University Press.

Olson, M. (1993), 'Dictatorship, democracy, and development', *The American Political Science Review*, **87**, 567–76.

Przeworski, A. (2006), 'Self enforcing democracy', in *The Oxford Handbook of Political Economy*, B. Weingast and D. Wittman (eds), Oxford: Oxford University Press.

Spoloare, E. (2006), 'National borders and the size of nations', in *The Oxford Handbook of Political Economy*, B. Weingast and D. Wittman (eds), Oxford: Oxford University Press.

Wintrobe, R. (1998), *The Political Economy of Dictatorship*, New York: Cambridge University Press.

Wintrobe, R. (2002), 'The contest for power: human rights and economic efficiency', University of Western Ontario working paper.

Wittman, D. (2000), 'The size and wealth of nations', *Journal of Conflict Resolution*, **44** (6), 868–84.

Wittman, D. (2003), 'When does altruism overcome the intransitivity of income distribution?', in *Rational Foundations of Democratic Politics*, Albert Breton *et. al.* (eds), Cambridge: Cambridge University Press.

Index